Centralization or Fragmentation?

*Europe Facing the Challenges
of Deepening, Diversity,
and Democracy*

ANDREW MORAVCSIK
Editor

A Council on Foreign Relations Book

The Council on Foreign Relations, a nonprofit, nonpartisan national membership organization founded in 1921, is dedicated to promoting understanding of international affairs through the free and civil exchange of ideas. The Council's members are dedicated to the belief that America's peace and prosperity are firmly linked to that of the world. From this flows the mission of the Council: to foster America's understanding of its fellow members of the international community, near and far, their peoples, cultures, histories, hopes, quarrels, and ambitions; and thus to serve, protect, and advance America's own global interests through study and debate, private and public.

THE COUNCIL TAKES NO INSTITUTIONAL POSITION ON POLICY ISSUES AND HAS NO AFFILIATION WITH THE U.S. GOVERNMENT. ALL STATEMENTS OF FACT AND EXPRESSIONS OF OPINION CONTAINED IN ALL ITS PUBLICATIONS ARE THE SOLE RESPONSIBILITY OF THE AUTHOR OR AUTHORS.

Council on Foreign Relations Books are distributed by Brookings Institution Press (1-800-275-1447). For further information on Council publications, please write the Council on Foreign Relations, 58 East 68th Street, New York, NY 10021, or call the Director of Communications at 212-434-9400. Or visit our website, www.foreignrelations.org.

Library of Congress Cataloging-in-Publication Data

Centralization or fragmentation?: Europe facing the challenges of deepening, diversity, and democracy/edited by Andrew Moravcsik.
     p. cm.
Includes bibliographical references.
ISBN 0-87609-224-5 (pbk.)
  1. European Union. 1. Moravcsik, Andrew.
  JN30.C45 1998
  341.242'2—ddc21

                                                                    98-9064
9 8 7 6 5 4 3 2 1   CIP

The paper used in this publication meets the minimum requirements of the American National Standard for Information Sciences—Permanence of Paper for Printed Library Materials, ANSI Z39.48-1984

Typeset in Palatino

Composition by AlphaWebTech
Mechanicsville, Maryland

Printed by Automated Graphic Systems
White Plains, Maryland

Foreword

Since its members signed the Maastricht treaty in late 1991, the European Union (EU) has advanced toward achieving the treaty's goals. Border controls between many countries have disappeared. Accession negotiations with a number of central, eastern, and southern European countries are proceeding. And, perhaps most importantly, a majority of EU members will adopt a single European currency, the euro, on January 1, 1999.

Yet all is not well in Europe. Each of these developments has created new political tensions among members, while the scourge of unemployment has continued to plague European economies and societies. As Europe moves into the 21st century, countries will have to adapt both to regional changes that the Maastricht treaty set in motion and to the competitive forces of a global economy.

This volume, edited by Andrew Moravcsik, addresses the major challenges the European Union will confront in the coming years. Will it succeed in fostering greater cooperation among members and achieving "ever closer union"? Will the less-developed applicants for EU membership from the east and south fit easily within the existing superstructure? Will the Union succeed in becoming more democratic and less bureaucratic? The authors of this volume examine the nuts and bolts of European Union machinery including economic, monetary, social, and foreign policy and present a compelling argument that "ever closer union" will only be possible with greater balance and flexibility among supranational, national, and subnational actors.

Gary C. Hufbauer
Maurice R. Greenberg Chair, Director of Studies
Council on Foreign Relations

Acknowledgments

In addition to those who commented on individual articles, we would like to thank Alberta Sbragia for early assistance, Fareed Zakaria, Barry Eichengreen, and Charles Kupchan for collegial support, and the Council's W. Averell Harriman Study Group on Transatlantic Relations for advice and comment.

Contents

Chapter 1

Europe's Integration at Century's End

Andrew Moravcsik

In the wake of World War II, few observers imagined that European nations—let alone two hereditary enemies like France and Germany—would cooperate in one of the most extraordinary international institutions of the twentieth century. For two generations, the European Union (EU, formerly the European Community or EC) has symbolized the cooperative commitment to postwar European economic growth and geopolitical stability. In doing so, moreover, it has fundamentally altered the way Europeans—and, increasingly, observers across the globe—think about national sovereignty and identity.

The EU is today the most highly developed and broadly effective voluntary intergovernmental organization in human history. It is more than a single, integrated market and trading block among fifteen countries and over 300 million people, which would itself be a monumental achievement; it is a unique quasi-constitutional polity. The EU is as well the dominant source of European economic and social regulation, whether in the area of trade liberalization, monetary stabilization, environmental and consumer policies, legal re-

The paper benefited from conversations with Nigel Evans, Erik Jones, Philip Gordon, Charles Kupchan, Paul Pierson, Alberta Sbragia, Helen Wallace, Joseph Weiler, and the W. Averell Harriman Study Group on Transatlantic Relations of the Council on Foreign Relations in New York.

1

quirements for gender equality, high-technology research and development programs, immigration and asylum policy, or "high" foreign policy. In 1988 Jacques Delors, president of the European Commission, predicted that 80 percent of all of Europe's social and economic legislation would soon be made in Brussels, the seat of the EU, rather than in national capitals. When the European Commission, an independent body in antitrust matters, challenged aspects of the recent merger between Boeing and McDonnell-Douglas, a series of direct telephone calls from U.S. president Bill Clinton to a number of prime ministers and presidents of major European governments was unable to alter the decision. The U.S. president was told that the policy is made by an autonomous body in Brussels and cannot be overridden by national chief executives.

The recent acceleration of European integration dates back to the signing of the Single European Act (SEA) in 1986 and the Treaty on European Union (the Maastricht Treaty) five years later. These two agreements, along with ancillary arrangements concerning the EC budget and enlargement—including the Treaty of Amsterdam, signed in June 1997 and soon to be ratified—have committed European governments to a series of challenging long-range goals. Among these are the creation of a single integrated market without internal borders (the "Europe 1992" project); common regulatory agencies operating in many areas, like the environment; a transition to a single European currency (Economic and Monetary Union or EMU); a more unified foreign and (perhaps also) defense policy; the democratization of the EU's supranational institutions; and the EU's geographical enlargement to include, over time, up to fifteen new states in eastern and southern Europe.[1]

The adaptation of EU institutions to the realization of the ambitious goals of monetary union, enlargement, and cooperation in foreign and defense policy will set the EU's agenda for the coming decade, which will probably witness at least four extended rounds of interstate negotiations. The first set of negotiations, likely to occupy European governments for the next two years, will consider the details of the transition to EMU and a single currency. A second set of negotiations during this period must authorize a new EU budget, since the current one is due to expire in 1999. A third set, probably

---

1. Cafruny and Rosenthal (1993); Keohane and Hoffman (1991); Sbragia (1992).

to be held around the year 2000, will again take up issues discussed at the recently concluded Intergovernmental Conference (IGC 96), which concluded with the Treaty of Amsterdam. Given the overriding focus on EMU, national leaders opted for a modest agreement, with significant changes limited to those concerning the legal status of immigration and police cooperation (the "third pillar") and an expansion of the influence of the European Parliament. Left for future decision were improvements in the efficiency and legitimacy of EU institutions necessitated by enlargement and deeper cooperation in foreign policy, as well as areas of internal security such as immigration, asylum, and policing. A fourth and final set of negotiations, scheduled to begin sometime after the year 2000, will consider enlargement itself. The focus will be on applications for EU membership from up to five eastern and southern European countries, surely including Poland, Hungary, and the Czech Republic. Arrangements for the entry of the "first wave" of new countries are likely to be completed around the year 2005. Throughout this period, moreover, the incremental expansion of EU legislation is sure to deepen cooperation in environmental and social policy as well as other regulatory areas.[2]

The realization of these ambitious plans will create significant political, economic, and social strains within Europe, as well as new challenges for the United States. Unprecedented constraints on national sovereignty, requirements for costly policy convergence, demands for transnational redistribution, fundamental disagreements on the nature of collective decisionmaking, and heated debates over domestic ratification of various agreements are almost certain.

These developments are already visible. Since the signing of the Maastricht Treaty in 1991, European integration has become much more controversial. Fierce debates over ratification erupted in Britain, France, Denmark, and Germany. For the first time in a generation, European elites and publics outside the extreme Right and Left expressed fundamental doubts about the desirability of major steps toward European integration. Not since the era of General Charles de Gaulle have European politicians so openly discussed fundamental issues of democratic accountability and national sovereignty. The polarization of public and elite opinion appears to be

2. Club de Florence (1996).

eroding the broad consensus that supported integration for the past three decades. At that time, a majority of West Europeans held the reflexive conviction that the EU promotes regional prosperity, peace, and stability at relatively little cost to national sovereignty.

This critical juncture marks an appropriate moment to reassess both the immediate and the long-term future of European integration. The chapters in this volume focus on four key policy areas, while this introductory chapter draws broader, longer-term institutional implications. In the substantive chapters, Erik Jones considers monetary policy; Giandomenico Majone, regulatory and single-market policy; Paul Pierson, social welfare policy; and Philip Gordon, foreign and defense policy.

Each author has three aims. The first is to provide a background overview of current European policies and programs in the wake of the SEA, the Maastricht Treaty, and the disappointing outcome to IGC 96. The second is to describe the national positions, bargaining dynamics, and potential outcomes of upcoming negotiations, including the transition to EMU, budgetary changes, and eastern enlargement. Taken together, these chapters summarize the most important developments in the EU coming during the next half decade.

The third aim, one touched on in all the chapters but treated in greater detail in this chapter, is to evaluate the long-term prospects and likely outcome of cooperation over the coming decades—the future trajectory of European state formation. Given the fundamental nature of the challenges facing the EU, this is an appropriate time to reconsider deeper questions that have remained dormant since the mid-1960s. What will be the likely scope and form of the ultimate European polity? What is the probable equilibrium mixture of national, regional, and global governance in the longer run?

This introductory chapter summarizes the findings of the four substantive chapters and develops a common underlying argument concerning the institutional trajectory of the EU. Given the challenges of "deepening, diversity, and democracy," I argue, European integration can continue to centralize policymaking in Brussels only by simultaneously permitting unprecedented flexibility, fragmentation, and differentiation. The belief that the EU must remain legally unified, with all countries accepting the common obligations (a shared *acquis communautaire*, Europeans term it), and that the deepening of substantive cooperation necessarily implies greater administrative centralization and legal coherence, based in Brussels, had long remained unquestioned among those who favor European integration. Now, however, it is no longer feasible; moreover, it may well not even be desirable. Member governments are no longer as willing as they once were to accept all EU obligations, to permit other governments equal participation in all decisions, or to grant the same benefits. Integration is instead becoming more flexible and fragmented. Deeper cooperation is increasingly achieved through exemptions and special arrangements, long transition periods, the exclusion of recalcitrant member governments through criteria for participation in particular policies, opt-outs by recalcitrant countries, special arrangements to facilitate abstention, and ad hoc side payments to poorer countries to secure their assent.

This trend, like that toward greater public questioning of integration, is already clearly visible. Over the past decade, cooperation on monetary issues, social welfare, border controls, foreign policy, and research and development has been achieved only by permitting the fragmentation of the EU into, as Europeans term it, a "multispeed," "variable geometry," or "à la carte" organization. Today governments speak openly, in a way that would have been unthinkable just five years ago, of creating an exclusive "core" of EU governments with separate rules, policies, and institutions. As recently as five years ago, the only prominent European political figure calling for this sort of flexibility was the "Euroskeptical" former British prime minister, Margaret Thatcher, who proclaimed: "We should aim at a multi-track Europe in which *ad hoc* groups of different states—such as the Schengen Group—forge various levels of cooperation. . . . Such a structure . . . would accommodate the diversity of post-Communist Europe."[3] Today the demand for flexibility has become the rallying cry for a core group of the most federalist governments, including France and Germany.

Current debates concern not whether, but the terms under which, governments may opt out of specific policies. In the future, it is widely understood that foreign and defense policy cooperation will be impossible without provisions for exceptions, opt-outs, and ve-

3. Thatcher (1995, p. 490).

toes. The single market cannot and will not be applied uniformly across the EU. Even the common agricultural policy (CAP), the bedrock of the *acquis communautaire* of the original Six, is likely to be extended eastward only with long transition periods. Some already speak of unprecedented twenty-five-year transitions.

Management of the resulting tension between the need for centralization and the reality of fragmentation will dictate the institutional development of the EU over the coming decades. Underlying this tension is a trade-off. On the one hand, the centralization of decisionmaking in Brussels—common policymaking, greater majority voting, and delegation to supranational institutions—is a necessary device to ensure more credible commitments on the part of member states at least in certain areas. On the other hand, the ongoing erosion of sovereignty, greater diversity of preferences, and the rising demand for popular participation create pressure for flexibility. The result of this tension—one found in federal systems throughout the world—is an uneasy compromise in which centralization and fragmentation occur simultaneously. The trajectory of this dialectical evolution is, however, strikingly different from those of the national polities with which we are familiar. Over the long term, the EU appears not to be moving toward the United States of Europe some of its founding fathers imagined nor toward a breakup into fully sovereign countries or regions. Instead, the outcome is likely to be an unprecedented balance among supranational, subnational, and national governments. This shift away from a federalist, centralizing ideal toward a goal of balance between national and federal authority is one of the most striking shifts in the discourse of European integration over the past five years.

The remainder of this chapter is organized as follows. The first section reviews the history of European integration up to the SEA and the Maastricht Treaty. The second section reviews three major challenges facing the EU. I term them "deepening, diversity, and democracy," each of which heightens the tension between centralization and flexibility. The third section reviews alternatives for managing this tension and overcoming the resultant financial, institutional, and democratic overload. A concluding section summarizes and briefly sketches the long-term implications for the process of EU state formation.

The Origins of European Integration:
From Messina to Maastricht

European integration as we know it today began in 1950 with a proposal for an organization designed to coordinate the coal and steel industries of six countries (Belgium, the Federal Republic of Germany, France, Italy, Luxembourg, and the Netherlands). This organization became the European Coal and Steel Community (ECSC). The ECSC was followed in 1957 by the Treaty of Rome establishing the European Community; since 1993 it has been called the European Union.[4] Initial commitments in the Treaty of Rome centered on the creation of a common market, which eliminated tariffs and many quotas, instituted a common tariff vis-à-vis third countries, and established a preferential system of agricultural trade with common prices.

The EU has tended to move forward when the interests of the major member governments converge. Three primary concerns motivated European governments to negotiate the Treaty of Rome. The first was partisan advantage. Centrist, particularly Christian Democratic, political parties, supported European integration in the 1950s. These parties, some initially skeptical of integration, came to support it in part because the "European movement" offered a pro-Western, internationalist alternative to communist and neofascist ideologies. This was an important motivation for European federalists in France, Italy, and a divided Germany. By contrast, a wide range of political parties in countries like Great Britain and Denmark, countries without any tradition of communist or fascist politics, remain skeptical, even hostile, to "European" ideology.

A second motivation for integration was geopolitical stabilization. Integration, argued ECSC founders Robert Schuman and Jean Monnet, was a means to solve the "German problem" by tying Germany firmly to its western neighbors, thereby stabilizing the entire region geopolitically. Although this became less of a concern after the entry of West Germany into NATO in 1955, German chancellor Konrad Adenauer, much like Helmut Kohl thirty years later, saw

---

4. For a detailed analysis of motivations, bargaining, and institutional choices, from which the narrative below is taken, see Moravcsik (1998).

integration as a means to normalize Germany's relations with the West and increase support for goals such as Western defense in the 1950s and 1960s, détente in the 1970s, and German reunification in the 1980s.

The third and ultimately most important motivation for integration was economic.[5] Europe was then and remains now an area of relatively high economic interdependence, with levels of trade many times larger than those of non-European industrial countries like the United States or Japan. The particular form of trade that dominates intra-European transactions, moreover, namely intra-industry trade in manufactured goods, was and remains particularly favorable to liberalization. Unlike trade in primary goods, intra-industry trade tends to limit the economic dislocation associated with large sectoral net winners and losers.[6] The major economic trend in postwar trade was a large intra-industry trade boom among all developed countries, whether or not the countries in question participated in regional integration schemes. With levels of imports and exports between Europe as a whole and the outside world roughly equivalent to those of North America or Japan, Western Europe constituted a natural area in which to integrate markets and stabilize factoral flows.[7] By 1970 industrial tariffs had been removed and an agricultural policy established.

In the decade and a half that followed, the EC continued to widen geographically and deepen substantively. Britain, Ireland, and Denmark joined in 1973, followed by Greece in 1979, Spain and Portugal in 1985, and Sweden, Finland, and Austria in 1993. Environmental, antitrust (termed "competition policy" in Europe), social, and regional policies developed as well. The most significant substantive commitments made in this period were in monetary policy, as Erik

5. Milward (1992).
6. Milner (1988). More broadly trade liberalization in Europe, like the multilateral process taking place among all industrialized countries, was a response to the massive redirection of trade and investment from North to South to North to North channels after World War II. For a more comprehensive argument, see Moravcsik (1998, chapters 1 and 2).
7. Pelkmans (1984). Within this consensus, individual countries pursued particular interests. Germany, with its competitive exporters, sought trade liberalization in manufactured products, while France and Italy sought a protected European market for industrial and agricultural products, the latter largely at the expense of third-country producers, notably those in the United States.

Jones describes in chapter 2 of this volume. Monetary cooperation during the 1970s and 1980s—first under a loose arrangement nicknamed the "snake" and after 1979 under the European Monetary System (EMS)—sought to moderate wide fluctuations in European currency values and to reduce the costs of imposing needed domestic macroeconomic discipline.[8]

What were the underlying motivations for monetary integration? Many argue that European monetary cooperation has been driven primarily by geopolitical concerns over rising German power and influence in Europe, as well as West Germany's concern to increase its flexibility in dealing with the East. However, close examination of the relevant decisionmaking, as Jones hints, reveals that the primary motivations were economic, with geopolitical concerns accorded only secondary importance.[9] France has long sought to reduce the political and economic costs of macroeconomic stabilization; when its governments firmly committed themselves to such stabilization, as did Valéry Giscard d'Estaing in 1977 and François Mitterrand in 1983, effective cooperation became possible. In West Germany, Schmidt and, to a lesser extent, Kohl saw the EMS primarily as a means of limiting the real appreciation of the deutsche mark (DM), an outcome favored by Germany's export-dependent industrial sector, and as a way to loosen the constraints on domestic macroeconomic policy imposed by the Bundesbank, an outcome favored by most German governments. Geopolitical concerns about German influence, efforts to support *Ostpolitik*, and "European" ideology motivated national leaders, even in Germany, only on the margins. Hence Germany has staunchly refused to endanger its domestic commitment to a balance of external competitiveness and low domestic inflation, no matter what the ideological and geopolitical imperatives.

Largely due to this German reticence, the institutional commitments underlying both the snake and the EMS were weaker than their founders had hoped. Arrangements for financial credits and intervention to support depreciating currencies, which would have made adherence to the system less costly to weak-currency countries, were never created, primarily due to Bundesbank opposition.

8. Gros and Thygesen (1992).
9. Moravcsik (1998, chapters 5 and 7).

10   Andrew Moravcsik

As Jones observes, monetary cooperation was also fundamentally constrained by cross-national divergence in macroeconomic policy preferences and performance. During periods of macroeconomic convergence, in particular during the late 1970s and mid- to late 1980s, the system worked well, but during periods of divergence, such as the early and mid-1970s, the early 1980s, and the early 1990s, it came under stress. Divergence was often triggered by a weak dollar, which tended to drive the DM upward and the French franc and Italian lira downward, splitting apart the system. Under such circumstances, the system functioned in an asymmetrical manner. In other words, the cost of adjustment was borne almost entirely by weak-currency countries, which were able to maintain fixed exchange rates only by accepting currency overvaluation and high interest rates, while Germany gained competitive and stable exchange rates with little or no sacrifice of domestic macroeconomic autonomy.[10]

The Institutional Legacy

Perhaps the most striking legacy of the first three decades of European integration was the EU's unique institutional structure. This structure goes beyond the secretariat and rules for unanimous decisionmaking found in most international organizations. Sovereignty is instead "pooled" through arrangements for "qualified majority voting" (QMV) among member governments and "delegated" in certain cases to supranational officials, who enjoy greater autonomy in the EU than elsewhere.[11]

Why have individual governments sacrificed their sovereignty? Some European institutions—for example, the European Parliament—exist primarily because certain governments, such as Germany and Italy, espouse a federalist ideology or because others, such as the Benelux countries, seek a counterweight to the dominance of the larger countries. More often, however, European governments have supported institutional pooling and delegation if

10. This is a general quality of most fixed exchange rate regimes. See Kirshner (1995, p. 9); Kindleberger (1970, p. 198).
11. Keohane and Hoffmann (1991).

and only if it was necessary to increase the credibility of future commitments to cooperation made by themselves and their partners. Majority voting has been used to lock in agreement in order to implement proposals in areas, such as single-market liberalization, judged to be of common concern.

European governments accepted such commitments regardless of their ideological predilections. Thus German governments favored QMV, voting to secure French cooperation on a common policy toward the General Agreement on Tariffs and Trade (GATT) and autonomous central institutions in order to ensure that a European Central Bank remains independent, while French governments favored centralization of policymaking so as to secure German cooperation on agricultural policy. Even leaders ideologically opposed to strong supranational institutions, such as General de Gaulle in the 1960s, pursued this strategy, as does the Gaullist descendant Jacques Chirac today. Chirac favors centralization of monetary policy to impose greater collective control over Germany's Bundesbank.[12]

In the 1950s, many scholars and European activists predicted that economic cooperation would necessarily lead to the centralization and internationalization of political decisionmaking in a federal system based in Brussels. Since then, however, political integration has in fact proceeded unevenly, leading to centralization primarily in those areas—notably the single market and monetary policy—where the need for a credible commitment or coordination outweighs the risks of surrendering sovereignty. The result is a curious hybrid of federal and intergovernmental elements. The EU's quasi-constitutional structure combines elements traditionally found only in domestic governance, such as a supreme court and a parliament; elements of classic international institutions like the United Nations and GATT, such as a dominant role for national diplomatic representatives, in areas such as foreign and defense policy, social policy, and immigration; and unique elements, such as the powerful Commission with significant formal legislative power.

EU decisionmaking procedures fall into three broad categories, depending on whether the actions under consideration involve

12. For detailed evidence, see Moravcsik (1998).

12   Andrew Moravcsik

changes to the Treaty of Rome itself, new legislation within the treaty framework, or enforcement of existing rules.

Changes to the treaty itself—roughly equivalent to revisions of a European constitution—continue to take place by unanimous votes of member governments, meeting in classical intergovernmental forums, sometimes termed Intergovernmental Conferences or IGCs. Recent IGCs produced the Single European Act, the Maastricht Treaty, and, most recently, the Treaty of Amsterdam. Similar procedures govern the accession of new members. The second category of decisions, those concerning everyday EU legislation, are roughly equivalent to conventional national lawmaking. Everyday EU legislation passes through a unique institutional process in which authority is divided among three institutions, each with a distinctive role.[13]

The most influential of these institutions is the Council of Ministers, a forum similar to that found in most international organizations, where diplomatic representatives from each member government vote on EU legislation. On the most sensitive issues, votes must still be unanimous, but most other issues are now decided by qualified majority voting. This is done through a weighted voting system in which 70 to 80 percent of the votes are needed to pass legislation, with the votes of large countries counting five times as much as that of tiny Luxembourg.

Of secondary but nonetheless considerable importance in everyday legislation is the Commission, an executive bureaucracy based in Brussels and headed by commissioners nominated by, but not formally responsible to, national governments. The Commission employs a staff (translators and clerical staff excluded) of somewhere between 3,000 and 4,000 officials. It is important in the legislative process for most economic issues because it enjoys the unique right to propose legislation to the Council of Ministers. Without a Commission proposal, the Council cannot legislate; such proposals can be amended only by unanimous vote of the member states.[14]

Of tertiary but increasing importance in the legislative process is the European Parliament (EP), a body of more than 600 parliamentarians directly elected by citizens of member states and divided in-

13. Nugent (1991).
14. This power is of particular importance when the Council of Ministers votes by qualified majority, since a greater number of more ambitious outcomes are possible. Tsebelis (1994).

formally into transnational groupings of Socialists, Christian Democrats, and other parties. In the EU system, in contrast to national systems, the Council of Ministers remains the true legislative body, but the EP has a right, only rarely exercised, to veto or propose amendments to certain pieces of legislation. Sometimes, within the so-called co-decision procedure introduced at Maastricht and expanded in the Treaty of Amsterdam, such efforts end in face-to-face negotiations between the Council and Parliament.

The third category of EU decisionmaking involves the implementation and enforcement of legislation and treaty provisions. Implementation is often delegated to the individual member states, but the Commission sometimes has specific powers, similar to those of independent regulatory agencies in the United States, to interpret and enforce regulations or to represent the EU abroad. The Commission, for example, sets daily agricultural prices, conducts World Trade Organization (WTO) tariff negotiations, vets mergers, and decides competition (antitrust) complaints against firms and states for anticompetitive practices (the Boeing case being a recent example) or for receiving illegal state subsidies.

Enforcement is bolstered by the European Court of Justice (ECJ), a unique body of fifteen judges who rule on the applicability of EU laws. Individuals or states almost never bring cases directly to the ECJ and to the Commission relatively rarely; cases are generally referred to it by national courts. Over the years, the EU has succeeded in asserting for the Treaty of Rome constitutional status in Europe. In most cases, European law preempts national laws and is often applied directly by national authorities—a quiet process of legal centralization not unlike the early development of the Supreme Court in U.S. history. After many decades, the supremacy of ECJ decisions over national law is now almost universally accepted within member states.[15]

The Relaunching of Integration: The Single European Act and the Maastricht Treaty

As late as 1985, despite intermittent monetary cooperation and hundreds of European regulations already on the books, the EC was

15. Burley and Mattli (1993, pp. 41–77).

widely viewed as a moribund customs union mired in disputes over issues like the harmonization of truck taillights and the subsidization of sugar producers. While the number of rules and regulations was increasing, particularly in the environmental area, deeper cooperation in trade or monetary policy appeared to be a forgotten dream of postwar European idealists. Combined with declining competitiveness in high-technology industries, increasing U.S. and Japanese competition, low growth, and rising unemployment, this led in the early 1980s to a general sense of "Eurosclerosis" or "Europessimism."

Such perceptions were reversed with the signing of the Single European Act (SEA) in 1986, which soon became famous worldwide as the basis for the Europe 1992 program.[16] Spurred by national concerns over competitiveness, pressure from multinational firms, and the political leadership of a new Commission president, former French finance minister Jacques Delors, the SEA aimed to create a unified "single European market" by eliminating nontariff trade barriers (NTBs). These NTBs were not from "at the border" measures, like tariffs and quotas, but "behind the border" measures, such as financial intervention and divergent national regulations. The SEA combined nearly 300 proposals into a single package to be completed by the end of 1992. Proposals included regulation of the environment, banking and insurance, social security, industrial standardization, food processing regulation, industrial subsidies, government procurement, consumer protection, and many other sensitive issues often closely related to public purposes or special interests. Roughly at the same time, a number of EC governments signed the Schengen Agreement, which committed them to eliminate border checks.[17]

The SEA and the Europe 1992 plan revitalized European integration. The vision of a single market without borders galvanized business and public opinion; the speed with which legislation passed accelerated; and a timely surge in the business cycle spurred transborder investment, exports, and growth.[18] Between 1986 and

16. For a comprehensive review of its sources, see Sandholtz and Zysman (1989); Cameron (1992); Moravcsik (1991).
17. On the dynamics of EU regulatory harmonization, see Nicolaïdis (1993).
18. The significance of EC legislation increased, although, interestingly, the total number of legislative acts passed per year did not. Wessels (1996).

1990, President of the Commission Jacques Delors emerged as a world figure, treated almost like a head of government, while European integration became a focus of regional and worldwide journalistic attention.

The origins of the current move toward a single currency, the most salient issue in the EU today, date back to 1987–88, when French president François Mitterrand and the government of Prime Minister Jacques Chirac, unsatisfied with the asymmetry and weakness of the EMS, proposed a move to economic and monetary union. This had been a goal of all French governments since the late 1960s, except for a brief hiatus in the early 1980s.[19] At a December 1991 summit meeting at Maastricht in the Netherlands, European chief executives reached unanimous agreement on the Treaty on European Union, generally referred to as the "Maastricht Treaty." They agreed to move ahead with EMU in 1997 if a sufficient number of countries qualified by meeting standards of low inflation and deficits, stable currencies, and declining government debt, or otherwise in 1999 if any met such conditions.

Soon thereafter—now expected to be just after the millennium—a European Central Bank (ECB) would take over a joint monetary policy, and qualifying national currencies would be converted into a single European currency. It was later agreed to name the currency the "euro." In order to qualify, governments had to meet four "convergence criteria," which reflected in large part the anti-inflationary preferences of the German government: low inflation, budget deficits, and debt; as well as no exchange rate movements vis-à-vis the EMS basket of currencies. The British government, under pressure from "Euroskeptic" Conservatives opposed to the then prime minister, John Major, was granted a special opt-out clause, which permitted it to reconsider at the last moment whether to join. The Danish Parliament and the German Constitutional Court later imposed similar requirements unilaterally.

Pressure for EMU cannot simply be explained as a necessary policy response to greater trade and capital interdependence or as the result of policy convergence toward low inflation, although obviously these factors were necessary conditions for its emergence. As

19. For a good overview of various factors that may have played a role in the movement toward the EU, see Sandholtz (1993).

Jones describes in his chapter, increased economic interdependence has undermined macroeconomic autonomy in many countries, but pressure for EMU reflects a deliberate attempt by countries like France to relax external constraints on their domestic monetary policies—a policy pursued consistently for over two decades. EMU, it is argued, would increase the credibility of French monetary policy, thus providing a reliable check on the power of unions and restraining government spending, and simultaneously impose foreign control over the Bundesbank, whose policy preferences tend to be more anti-inflationary than those of the French government. The result, it is hoped, would be a lower level of macroeconomic constraint (that is, lower interest rates and more room for fiscal policy) than is conveyed by current participation in the EMS.

Given the Bundesbank's prestige and autonomy, as well as public concern about inflation in Germany, Chancellor Helmut Kohl's government remained more skeptical; nonetheless, it consistently supported EMU on two conditions, which had formed the consistent basis of German policy since 1965. First, the European currency had to be as stable (noninflationary) as the DM, an arrangement that was seen as ensuring the continued competitiveness of German exporters. Germany not only insisted on the autonomy of the European Central Bank but imposed convergence criteria, strict standards of low inflation and fiscal probity that all potential members must meet. Second, simultaneous progress should be made toward deeper EC foreign policy cooperation and greater powers for the EP, moves important to ensure parliamentary and public support.

In promoting EMU with strict conditions, leaders like Kohl and his then foreign minister, Hans-Dietrich Genscher, sought at once to promote the economic interests of German firms, to increase their personal electoral prominence by advancing a vision of Europe popular in Germany, and to signal Germany's commitment to Europe during the process of German reunification. The latter is generally treated as the primary motivation for Germany's support of EMU, but it should not be exaggerated. The Kohl government was clearly committed to EMU years before November 1989, when the Berlin Wall fell; remained so well after 1990, when German unification was completed; and could easily have reneged.[20]

20. Moravcsik (1998, chapter 6).

France and Germany could not act alone. Some critics in weak-currency countries like Spain, Italy, and Greece remained skeptical; then British prime minister Margaret Thatcher opposed outright any surrender of monetary sovereignty. Yet business and public opinion support for Europe across a number of countries was strong enough to overcome these concerns. As had occurred during the SEA negotiations, the threat of exclusion from negotiated arrangements kept recalcitrant countries like Britain in the game. Financial interests in the City of London, the banking center of Europe, for example, were particularly concerned about the consequences of other governments moving ahead without Britain; government officials took the same view. German reunification gave governments an extra, although only secondary, reason to pursue EMU, namely a desire to tie Germany into western Europe during what was expected to be a tumultuous period with strong temptations for unilateralism or neutralism. The Franco-German resolve to move forward with EMU predated the fall of the Berlin Wall by quite some time and would continue even after unification was completed in August 1990.

The technical and political arguments for EMU reflected the optimism about European monetary cooperation prevailing in the late 1980s.[21] This optimism resulted not simply from the apparent success of the single-market program but from the stability of the EMS, which experienced no exchange rate realignments between 1987 and 1992. At the time the Maastricht Treaty was signed, it appeared that nearly all EU members might well participate in EMU.

Such optimism, as Jones recounts, proved transient. The decline of the dollar and German reunification led to a tightening of domestic monetary policy and upward pressure on the DM; by 1992–93, the EMS had, for all practical purposes, collapsed. An increasingly acrimonious period of tension marked by massive intervention to stabilize weak currencies culminated in two exchange rate crises, during which the French government sought first to force Germany to provide unconditional support for the French franc and then tried to force Germany out of the EMS. The Bundesbank, for its part, sought a French devaluation. In the end, Britain and Italy left the system, Spain devalued, and the constraints on remaining curren-

21. McNamara (1997).

cies, including France's, were reduced to an essentially symbolic level. (France remained within exchange rate bands of plus or minus 15 percent, imposing almost no short-term limit on policy.) The experiences of 1992–93 left European policymakers convinced that under conditions of high capital mobility and still-divergent economic priorities, exchange rate stability was impossible without tighter institutional constraints and more symmetrical obligations—that is, without EMU.

The Maastricht Treaty also moved forward in areas of political integration, although not as far as Germany and other more federalist-minded governments had originally advocated. The treaty authorized a small expansion of the powers of the European Parliament; established EC cooperation on issues of immigration and policing; increased the symbolic prominence of cooperation on foreign policy and discussions about defense, the so-called common foreign and security policy (CFSP); expanded the use of majority voting in environmental policy; and established a European social policy from which Britain, in an unprecedented move, opted out entirely. Reflecting the disappointment of some countries, notably Germany, at the slow progress on nonmonetary issues, the treaty called for another IGC to be convened in 1996 to discuss further reform.[22] Shortly thereafter another round of financial transfers was dispensed to ensure the support of poorer member governments, many of which saw little hope of meeting the convergence criteria by 1999.

European leaders expected ratification of the Maastricht Treaty, largely by national parliaments, to be unproblematic. Little more than marginal resistance in Britain, where Tory Euroskeptics held key votes in Parliament, was predicted. When, however, the treaty was submitted to a public referendum in Denmark in 1992—a country with a strong tradition of direct participation in politics, a strong social welfare state, and a skepticism toward European ideology—it was narrowly rejected. Criticisms of the undemocratic procedures in the EC (the so-called democratic deficit), as well as perceived threats to social protection, played a prominent role. Women, gov-

22. The Treaty also changed the name of the institution from the European Communities to the European Union—the latter including the new CFSP and immigration/policing policies, as well as the core economic functions, still termed the "European Communities."

ernment employees, the uneducated, rural residents, Social Democrats, and recipients of social security payments, as well as those on
the radical Right and Left, opposed the treaty in disproportionately
large numbers.

The Danish vote would have been a footnote in the history of
European integration had not French president François Mitterrand
decided to take a political gamble. Presiding over a deeply unpopular Socialist government, he sought to strengthen domestic support
by mobilizing traditional French approval for Europe through a referendum on the treaty. Given polls showing 70 percent support for
European integration and traditional Gaullist opposition to integration, he expected the issue to be more divisive for his right-wing opponents than for the ruling coalition. The tactic was nonetheless opposed by nearly all his advisers. The advisers were prescient, for the
result was instead a public debate that mesmerized the French nation for months, splitting both the Left and the Right. For the first
time in a generation, many leading French politicians publicly questioned the fundamental partisan, economic, and geopolitical justifi-
cations for European integration.[23] Although the treaty was eventually ratified—the French referendum produced a *petit oui* of less
than 51 percent of the vote, and the Danes narrowly ratified a
slightly diluted treaty in a second referendum. A trans-European
discussion had taken place in which organized opposition to
Europe emerged for the first time in decades. The democratic deficit
had become a watchword, and the EU was connected in the minds
of publics, rightly or wrongly, with opposition to social welfare and
full employment.[24]

The Challenges of Deepening, Diversity, and Democracy

In the wake of the Maastricht referendums, many predicted that
new domestic and international constraints would impede the
course of European integration. The Intergovernmental Conference
(IGC), launched in mid-1996 and concluded in June 1997 with the
signing of the Treaty of Amsterdam, provides evidence of the diffi-

23. Meunier-Aitsahalia and Ross (1993).
24. See chapter 4.

culty of reaching decisions among fifteen member governments, each now facing heightened public scrutiny as well as a diminished external threat from the East. National leaders shied away from potentially controversial decisions in preparation for enlargement, such as reweighting votes in the Council or reapportioning Commissioners, enhancing independent defense and foreign policymaking capacities, expanding significantly the use of QMV, or setting up a definitive mechanism that permits a small core of countries to move ahead on their own within the EU. Instead, they made minor changes, increasing judicial oversight over immigration and police cooperation, expanding the European Parliament's role in the legislative process at the expense of the Commission, and including Britain, now under the Labour government of Tony Blair, in the social policy.

Yet it would be a mistake to treat the modest outcome of the recent IGC as a harbinger of long-term decline. To be sure, convinced federalists often propound the so-called bicycle theory of integration—more properly a metaphor—whereby if the integration process ceases to move forward, it is likely to collapse.[25] Yet this adage has been proven false in the past. The reasons why national leaders shied away from major decisions at Amsterdam were short term, not long term. First, with the final decision to move forward to a single currency scheduled for 1998, it was widely feared that a prolonged public debate over an ambitious Amsterdam Treaty might impede the transition to EMU. Second, with enlargement negotiations unlikely to be completed for nearly a decade, there is much time to reconsider institutional reforms. Some insiders expect not just one but two more IGCs to amend the treaty before enlargement is completed. Politicians, always loath to make difficult decisions before absolutely necessary, preferred to wait.

In less prominent ways, European governments continue to move forward. With institutional adaptation to EMU, enlargement, budgetary challenges, and foreign policy, the EU agenda has never been so crowded. Although there are deep disagreements involving the timing and the institutional form of these transitions, there is widespread agreement that at least some countries will move ahead in all areas. Choices on these issues are fundamental and will help

25. Ross (1995).

decide what sort of polity Europe will eventually become. In making these decisions, European governments must overcome three concrete challenges, which I term "deepening, diversity, and democracy." These terms refer, respectively, to more intensive interstate cooperation on particular issues, greater diversity of membership, and greater public involvement in EU policymaking. Each of these challenges makes it more difficult, and perhaps also less appropriate, to seek the uniform, centralizing institutions of the past. Governments must strike a new balance between *centralization* and *flexibility*—a controversial trade-off in all federal systems.

The Challenge of Deepening

"Deepening" is the name commonly given to the intensification of EU cooperation in specific substantive areas. New proposals for deeper cooperation—further regulatory liberalization to improve the single market, social policy harmonization, monetary union, coordination of defense and foreign policy—are creating pressure for both the centralization of policymaking in Brussels, on the one hand, and greater fragmentation or decentralization of policy, on the other.

COMPLETING THE SINGLE MARKET. The decade since the signing of the SEA has seen the passage of more than 300 pieces of legislation, most of them concerning the elimination of regulatory nontariff trade barriers (NTBs). These include the partial liberalization of banking, telecommunications, and transport services, the elimination of numerous regulatory restrictions on processed food, the harmonization of environmental and social regulations, the reduction of quotas and nontariff barriers in major sectors like automobile production, and the passage of various industrial standards. In addition Commission oversight on state subsidies and government procurement has been strengthened, while the Schengen Agreement of 1985, which the Treaty of Amsterdam recently incorporated into the EU with numerous exceptions, has suppressed customs formalities among a subset of EU members.

There is widespread agreement that the single market remains the core of the EU. Support for the internal market is the one principle that all countries, from antifederalist Britain to federalist Italy, from wealthy Luxembourg to struggling Greece, strongly and consistently support, scattered opposition to particular measures notwithstanding. The business world tends to be favorable to the single market, as does public opinion, despite fears in some countries about the resulting pressures to lower social welfare protection. This consensus is so broad that other policies, notably monetary union or environmental harmonization, are often defended as means of reinforcing the single market. There is little dissatisfaction with the ever deepening institutionalization of policymaking. The currently extensive use of QMV in this area is only challenged on the margins—for example, in matters concerning indirect taxation or state subsidies—while even Euroskeptical Britain favors a stronger role for the European Court of Justice in enforcing EU single-market rules.

The EU's primary focus on market liberalization and regulatory harmonization gives rise to a unique institutional division of labor between the EU and its member states. As Giandomenico Majone argues in chapter 3, the EU can be thought of as a "regulatory state," that is, a form of governance in which the government rules by regulation and judicial interpretation, not by taxing and spending. The EU has little fiscal authority, with a tax base limited to approximately 1.25 percent of Europe's gross national product (GNP), between one-thirtieth and one-fiftieth that of the member states. Thus the EU has come to play a role somewhat analogous to that played in the United States by independent regulatory agencies backed by an active judiciary and a semi-autonomous executive—without the power of Congress to tax and spend. In the United States scholars term this complex an "independent fourth branch of government."[26]

In Majone's view, the comparative advantage of the EU regulatory state lies in its relative transparency and neutrality, which insulate it from special interest pressures. Only those groups with very strong and largely parallel interests across all member governments—such as multinational firms or wheat farmers—can "capture" EU policymaking. The result, according to Majone, is a more efficient, technocratic mode of decisionmaking better able to take account of the public interest, understood as the interests of diffuse

26. Majone (1993).

constituencies like consumers and constituents—as well as more competitive businesses. This is recognized across the Atlantic: the U.S. government and American multinational firms generally favor EU efforts to liberalize and harmonize regulations.

These advantages have been realized without, as many feared, ushering in a race to the bottom in which competitive pressures progressively erode national regulatory standards. There are two reasons for this. The first is the relatively high standard of living throughout Europe, which means publics demand and governments provide relatively high regulatory protection. The EU facilitates this process by transmitting information and policy ideas to poorer countries as they reach the stage of development where higher regulatory protection is demanded. The second is that firms in countries with lower regulatory standards sometimes accept higher regulations where they are required to secure entrance into the domestic markets of richer countries. EU standards are thus relatively high. This tendency is encouraged by a specific clause in the Single European Act (article 100A4) that permits governments to opt out of EU harmonization if they seek higher standards of public protection, a safeguard seldom invoked but always available.[27]

Although the single market remains the area of EU policymaking with the greatest uniformity and the least flexibility, it remains far from perfect. There are, even here, strong pressures for fragmentation. Proposed legislation has long been blocked in some particularly sensitive areas, such as the harmonization of indirect taxation and various forms of ground transport regulation. EU legislation seems to have had relatively little effect in areas such as deregulation of air transport and retail banking, where governments and "national champion" firms have found other ways to protect market shares. Strong EU action against state subsidies to industry or discriminatory government procurement requires Commission and often Council approval, which is often obstructed by interested parties. Discriminatory regulations designed to protect producers, as in

27. Vogel (1995). Articles 100A4 and 36 of the Treaty permit governments to exempt themselves from harmonization if they provide high regulatory protection for their citizens. The line between regulatory protection and trade protection is often a fine one, particularly since "bootlegger-Baptist" coalitions containing both types of protectionists may form.

the case of small breweries in Denmark, Germany, and elsewhere, have sometimes been replaced with stringent environmental regulations on packaging, which continue to inhibit trade but are legal under the Treaty of Rome.[28] Implementation of EU directives remains largely within the administrative discretion of member governments, although under oversight by the ECJ, and there is considerable concern about the uneven results. Article 100A4 permits opt-outs. Perhaps most striking, a nascent "flexibility" clause was included in the Treaty of Amsterdam, which permits a majority of countries, with Commission approval, to cooperate within the EU without including all other member states. Although this clause is currently difficult to invoke, it is surely a harbinger of future trends, as a subgroup within the EU moves forward to EMU.

SOCIAL POLICY. In contrast to the highly developed social welfare states of Western Europe, the emerging European regulatory state is only marginally involved in social welfare policy. As Paul Pierson notes in chapter 4, the Maastricht Treaty's Social Protocol, the farthest reach of EU social policy, creates effective regulation only in areas of welfare policy with few direct financial consequences. These include provisions to inform workers of company policies and the centralization of company unions or matters that are relatively uncontroversial, such as minimal health and safety rules. Few of these policies, moreover, can be decided by majority vote. The most critical areas of social and labor regulation—collective bargaining, domestic social welfare provision, worker benefits, and the right to worker co-decision—remain entirely outside direct EU regulation. In the half decade since Maastricht, only two pieces of social policy legislation have been passed.[29]

Even this minimal social policy, very close to a lowest common denominator of what already exists among nearly all governments, is controversial. It was too much for the British Conservative government, which initially opted out at Maastricht, leaving social policy as an anomalous area conducted under EU law but with fourteen rather than fifteen participating governments. Some social

28. Golub (1995).
29. Lange (1993). Skepticism of social policy is backed by a majority of conservative governments in the member states, despite majority Social Democratic control of the European Commission and Parliament.

regulations, such as a directive to impose a 48-hour week, have been passed as health and safety or internal market measures and have generated considerable opposition within Britain. On entering office in 1997, however, the Labour government of Tony Blair immediately announced it would accept the social policy and did so at the recent IGC.

The main reason why the EU lacks a developed social policy, Pierson argues in his chapter, is quite simply the lack of convergence among national interests. Large differences in productivity and per capita GNP across European countries, not to mention variation in specific forms of social welfare provision, make it difficult and probably undesirable from both an economic and a political perspective to harmonize European wages or social welfare benefits. Current pressure comes largely from countries with higher social protection whose rules would remain unaffected by common European rules but which seek to bind those with lower social protection to the same standards. While unions in high-wage countries like Germany would benefit if wages and social spending were raised in poorer countries, the result would surely be to usher in an economic recession in Portugal, Spain, Ireland, Greece, and even Britain.

Thus if there is cooperation, Pierson argues, it is more likely to *limit* social benefits than to expand them. Most European governments today view a reduction of welfare expenditures as basically desirable but politically difficult. Although national social welfare states are nowhere near collapse, a consensus in most countries recognizes that privatization of pensions, budgetary austerity, and greater labor flexibility are necessary so as to maintain the essence of social welfare systems over the decades to come. This consensus extends not just to businesses concerned about competitiveness but also to citizens opposed to tax increases, governments concerned about fiscal stability in the face of an aging population, and even many social democrats seeking a solution to high unemployment. The EU provides a convenient scapegoat for such reforms. Many supporters of fiscal consolidation, particularly in countries like Italy and Belgium that have large government deficits or decentralized politics, favor market integration and the EU as means of legitimating constraints on consumption and government spending.[30]

30. Moravcsik (1994).

The indirect effects of the single market on social welfare provision are similarly negative.[31] Many argue that the EU regulatory state, not least its provisions for EMU, weighs in against redistributive policies favored by social democrats and toward retrenchment favored by conservatives. Unanimity voting makes it difficult to pass significant EU social provisions. The market-oriented nature of the treaty renders it nearly impossible for the European Court to impute a European right to social welfare, as it has imputed extensions of the right to free movement.[32] The liberalization of trade and capital flows creates pressure for lower wages and benefits, as firms threaten to move to lower-cost jurisdictions inside the EU. Rules also restrict some types of subsidies to firms and poorer regions. Still, Pierson concludes, demographic and fiscal constraints play a more important role than interdependence in limiting social welfare provisions.

On balance social policy marks the limit of economic integration. It is an area of regulation in which there are few common interests among member governments and where the focus of policymaking is thus likely to remain fundamentally at the national level. Forces favoring fragmentation will continue to dominate pressures for centralization in the foreseeable future.

ECONOMIC AND MONETARY UNION. Most observers, including those in the financial markets, now expect some subset of EU members to move ahead to EMU between 1999, when exchange rates are to be "irrevocably" fixed, and 2002, when a single currency is to be introduced. A successful transition for the eleven countries that now seem likely to move ahead continues to depend, however, on labor peace and governmental resolve in both France and Germany. Even assuming the political will of elites remains firm, the transition to EMU will not be without difficulty, nor is its final form yet clear.

31. The EU may also have indirect effects on social policy, Pierson argues. Some are positive. Pierson observes that previous economic and social policy decisions may sometimes create pressure for the expansion of social policy, a process of "spillover" that has influenced policies on gender equality and migrants' rights. Yet such indirect social welfare policies are restricted to a few areas like gender equality and the rights of migrants. They are thus unlikely to substitute for direct legislation.

32. Scharpf (1994b).

The issues raised by the transition to EMU demonstrate how centralization of EU policymaking increasingly engenders conflicts of interest among member countries that can be managed only through a process of simultaneous centralization and fragmentation. Further monetary integration is impossible without greater centralization, since only an autonomous ECB offers the credible commitment to low inflation demanded by Germany. A single currency without a central bank makes little sense. Having surrendered substantial policy autonomy by renouncing devaluation and, in the wake of the Single European Act, forgoing the imposition of capital controls, governments now seek to reduce the risks of foreign devaluation. Yet monetary union, as we have seen, also requires substantial macroeconomic convergence. Each government will seek to lock other governments into a set of macroeconomic standards preferable to it, but such standards cannot be appropriate for all fifteen governments. The result is simultaneous pressure for centralization of monetary activity, on the one hand, and for the exclusion of those governments unable or unwilling to converge to the macroeconomic standards, on the other. There is thus little chance that all EU governments will move ahead together in 1999.

From an economic perspective, the feasibility and desirability of a common monetary policy depend on its consequences—more specifically, on the extent to which a single policy can function without creating greater economic dislocation in the form of excess unemployment or inflation. There is general agreement that an EMU including all EU countries would be impractical, not only because current inflation rates diverge but also because divergence in macroeconomic policies as well as differences in wage, spending, and inflation behavior would render centralized macroeconomic management inappropriate. In economic terminology, the entire EU does not constitute an "optimum currency area."

Most economists maintain that only a small number of core countries (roughly France, Germany, the Netherlands, Luxembourg, and Denmark) currently have sufficiently similar patterns of macroeconomic response—business cycles, inflation, government spending, wage demands—to benefit unambiguously from a single currency. (The existence of such asymmetric responses posed a less acute problem under previous exchange rate arrangements like the

EMS, in which exchange rate adjustments could absorb divergences.)[33] Ultimately the designation of an optimum currency area is a judgment not simply about current economic realities but about political will and institutional rigidity. The weakest currency countries, such as Greece, remain unwilling or unable to adjust their domestic economic institutions to the standards of the core, but some other countries, notably France and the Netherlands, have successfully done so.

The emergence of a common set of norms is hindered by the fact that the evolving design of EMU does not, at least on the surface, reflect a balanced compromise, let alone a consensus, among the views and institutional traditions of various EU member countries. Instead, it is patterned largely on German priorities, notably a strong commitment to low inflation enforced by an autonomous central bank. Germany has insisted not only that the European Central Bank (ECB) be more independent than any national central bank but that strict convergence criteria be included for participation in EMU, criteria that will in turn impose both substantial cuts in government spending and higher interest rates. These conditions were set down over strong (if cautiously expressed) opposition by the French and Italian governments. The German position reflects in part historical concerns about inflation, in part legitimate fears that profligate countries, now constrained by national markets, will take advantage of European-wide capital markets in the new European currency regime to finance continued deficits, thus raising interest rates for others while also modestly increasing the risk of sovereign default.

Since the signing of the Maastricht Treaty, the German government has both advanced and retreated. Fearing that its neighbors will meet the convergence criteria but then revert to previous policies under the EU, Germany has demanded that its partners accept a "stability pact." Currently under negotiation, the stability pact would impose a strict limit on government deficits at 3 percent of gross domestic product (GDP), enforced by fines on offending countries (termed "deposits") totaling many tenths of a percent of

33. Even where national economies diverge, factor mobility may offset differences. Where workers are willing and able to respond to shocks by moving from depressed to expanding areas, or if governments offset differences through transfer payments, economic divergence will impose lower costs.

GNP—a remarkable sum, even if exceptions would be made in the case of severe recession. The stability pact reflects not a technocratic consensus among European governments that budget deficits and inflation must be reduced—it was opposed by France and Italy—but Germany's particular concerns. As in the case of convergence criteria, weak-currency governments favored more explicit political control over the ECB and looser restrictions on deficits. At the same time, the German government quietly accepted an unweighted one-country, one-vote arrangement at Maastricht and appears willing to contemplate the participation of Belgium and Italy, which would weight the ECB toward countries with traditionally higher inflation rates.

If the EU moves forward, it must follow one of two paths: the "soft" euro or the "hard" euro scenario. In the "soft" euro scenario, which looks increasingly likely, countries like Italy and Spain would be members from the start and their votes would likely lead to a common currency substantially weaker vis-à-vis the dollar and yen than the current DM. Many in France and Italy clearly have gambled, apparently successfully, that the Kohl government will interpret the convergence criteria loosely at the last minute (a possibility created by some vague wording in the treaty) to permit more weak-currency governments to enter, or compromise the stability pact (as suggested by the result of the Dublin EU summit in December 1996). Such a policy should not be seen as a betrayal of the "German" interest—it is a policy that would be quietly supported by pro-Europeans and by export-oriented business in Germany, who have long seen monetary cooperation primarily as an instrument to dampen DM appreciation, keep exports competitive, and expand the limits on macroeconomic stimulation. The government, still facing a difficult fiscal situation, might favor it as well for political reasons. Nevertheless, opposition from the Bundesbank, backed by public opinion, might still imperil ratification.[34] In the end, the German position is likely to have hidden flexibility, to be exploited by Kohl himself during the final moments of the bargaining, as has happened many times before. In this "soft" euro scenario, there would be strong incentives for other governments, notably the British, to enter in order to dampen appreciation of the pound, which is

34. Moravcsik (1998, chapters 4, 6).

likely to receive much of the capital fleeing the euro. Developments over the past year make it overwhelmingly likely that at least eleven governments will move forward this spring.

The alternative scenario has been the "hard" euro one, based on the exclusion of some, probably most, EU member governments. Those that cannot meet strict convergence criteria, will not accept stability conditions, or cannot maintain exchange rate parity with the DM will be left outside.[35] In this scenario, the first wave of EMU countries would be reduced to a core including Germany, France, the Netherlands, Luxembourg, Denmark, and Belgium. Even under this scenario, however, membership may expand over time. In this scenario, EMU bloc will maintain macroeconomic policies roughly comparable to Germany's today. The euro is likely to be a strong currency, relative to the dollar and the yen. The success of this arrangement will depend on the capacity of government spending and labor markets to adapt to stringent constraints.

Whether the "soft" euro or the "hard" euro scenario unfolds depends on domestic politics in France and, above all, Germany. If business and government triumph over the Bundesbank, partisan opposition and public opinion, the "soft" euro option is likely to emerge; if the latter forces prevail, the "hard" euro is the more likely outcome. The French government may be able to influence this domestic German process on the margins by threatening nonparticipation under certain circumstances. Yet such a threat, even by a Socialist government, may lack credibility. Alternatively, the "hard" euro may emerge even with a large number of members if the ECB strongly asserts its independence. Some expect it to do this in order to build up its anti-inflationary credibility.

Jones argues in chapter two that a relatively "hard" euro EMU is indeed likely to emerge, but in its current form it is neither economically nor politically sound for Europe.[36] Economically, as with the proposed balanced budget amendment in the United States, the excessive deficit procedure might disable automatic stabilizers in the

35. To be sure, the convergence criteria and the fear of being relegated to a second tier of European states have been effectively employed by Italy and Spain as a justification for the imposition of austerity recommended by many economists, but this has taken place under a more flexible regime.

36. See the editorial and discussion in the generally pro–EMU *Economist*, December 14, 1996, pp. 18, 23–25.

economy. Governments may be forced to cut spending during downward swings in the business cycle, thus promoting recessions—a tendency exacerbated by the stability pact. Such a one-sided obsession with disinflation is now widely credited as a cause of the Great Depression of the 1930s. Economic analyses confirm, moreover, that while higher inflation does not generally produce higher long-term growth, it does not reduce growth either, suggesting that each government might be better off seeking a more moderate domestic policy without enduring the high costs of convergence.[37]

The EMU, Jones suggests, may also be politically unstable for two reasons. First, current proposals require that the ECB dictate national monetary policies beginning in 1999, while the Council of Ministers, an international body without collective democratic accountability, will have the discretion to impose massive fines. If such procedures are viewed as undemocratic, they may undermine the public legitimacy of both EMU and European integration more generally. Second, the response of organized labor to the new constraints may be destabilizing.[38] The ECB system may be prone to *greater* wage inflation than the status quo. The creation of a single currency may increase transparency, permitting unions to coordinate better their activities across borders and thereby strengthen them. Moreover, the lack of centralized EC-wide unions may render the ECB weaker than expected. Strong central banks, it is often argued, cost effectively constrain wage increases only in countries like Germany and Sweden with centralized wage-bargaining systems. Such systems enforce uniform wage discipline across the economy, often led by the inflation-conscious tradable goods sector. In a more decentralized Europe, representatives of decentralized unions at the national, sectoral, or plant level will be tempted to free ride, seeking generous settlements for their own members at the expense of others. To restrain such behavior, stricter macroeconomic discipline must be imposed than is currently required.

The fate of excluded countries raises a final concern. The institutional relationship between members and nonmembers of EMU is the area in which the tension between centralization and fragmenta-

37. Gros (1996).
38. Hall (1994).

tion is perhaps clearest. Strict convergence criteria make it more difficult for outsiders to enter EMU, yet EMU members have an incentive to pressure weak-currency outsiders not to exploit the strong-currency commitment of members through depreciation. Just as Germany once favored the EMS as a way to keep its currency competitive, now all EMU members have an incentive to limit currency depreciation by other EU members. This has already sparked open conflict; for example, when France recently demanded, albeit unsuccessfully, that penalties be imposed on Italy and Britain following devaluations of the lira and the pound. Such conflict between insiders and outsiders is a natural consequence of a fragmented EMU.[39]

Hence EMU is another representative case of the existing tension between centralization and fragmentation. The EMU will be possible only with a restricted number of participating governments, continuing tension over macroeconomic policy, and greater distance between countries inside and outside the arrangement. Some American economists unschooled in world politics have recently predicted that the interstate tensions within EMU are likely to be so great as to trigger war among EU member states with different domestic institutions and macroeconomic priorities.[40] To anyone even casually familiar with the results of quantitative and qualitative studies of the origins of war—notably the consistent finding that democracies do wage war on one another and that institutionalized cooperation to promote economic interdependence, including the EU, has only a very minor impact on the incidence of war—this prognosis is clearly absurd.[41] Considerable economic dislocation and interstate bickering may nonetheless result.

INTERNAL AND EXTERNAL SECURITY. Since the early 1970s, European governments have informally coordinated a considerable portion of their foreign policies. Foreign ministry officials regularly consult one another on major issues. The European Council and Parliament issue policy statements on a wide range of topics. Informal alignment of policies toward the United Nations and other international organizations is common. Due to the sensitivity of governments to any loss of sovereignty over "high politics," however, most of this

39. Alesina and Grilli (1992).
40. Feldstein (1997).
41. O'Neal and others (1996); Doyle (1986); Moravcsik (1996).

cooperation is conducted without formal voting procedures or participation by EU institutions like the Court or Commission. Instead, foreign policy is often discussed through a loose intergovernmental process founded in the early 1970s, when it was called European Political Cooperation (EPC), and was recently expanded in the Maastricht Treaty, when it was renamed the Common Foreign and Security Policy (CFSP).

The result is less consistent coordination than in the area of foreign trade policy, where the existence of a common external tariff compels the fifteen to negotiate as a bloc both in bilateral tariff discussions with the United States and in multilateral negotiations in the WTO.[42] Negotiated when evidence of the severity of the Yugoslav crisis was becoming quite clear, the Maastricht Treaty marked only a symbolic step toward tighter EU foreign policy cooperation. The CFSP process outlined therein provides for regular staff meetings, exchanges of diplomatic information, a minimal secretariat, and a formal mechanism for policy coordination by unanimous vote. In a cumbersome double-voting system more symbolic than real, governments can authorize by unanimous vote the use of QMV in implementing preapproved policies. The treaty also authorizes cooperation on defense issues in collaboration with the Western European Union (WEU), a minimally institutionalized and previously moribund defense organization created in the 1950s, although it provides no formal institutional mechanism for doing so.

Yet in the almost five years that have elapsed since Maastricht, as Philip Gordon demonstrates in chapter 5, foreign policy cooperation has no major successes to its credit. The most fundamental reason is not, as many believe, the principled opposition of certain governments to the erosion of national sovereignty in the field of foreign affairs, although this surely exists, but instead the lack of common concerns and interests. Despite constant protests to the contrary from disappointed European officials, a retrospective look at the crises in Bosnia and various conflicts within the former Soviet Union reveals no cases in which even unlimited QMV would have led to a more active European policy.[43] In short, foreign policy coop-

42. This implies that member governments must cooperate if they are to impose trade sanctions, although the failure of to do so effectively in either the Falklands or South Africa cases suggests that in practice it tends to be difficult to gain assent from all fifteen members. See citations in Moravcsik (1995, pp. 157–89).
43. Lori Fisler Damrosch, 1993.

eration remains weak because of the relative unimportance, viewed from the national interests of EU governments, of the collective choices facing Europe. Thus the sad truth is that while Bosnia was a humanitarian tragedy, it was not viewed as a threat to the vital interests of any EU member state.

Still, a majority of governments, led by those with more limited foreign policy autonomy and strong federalist aspirations (for example, Germany, Italy, Spain, and the Benelux countries), pressed in the IGC 96 for deeper EU foreign policy and defense cooperation, including a permanent secretariat, a formal role for the Commission, and majority voting. A coalition of countries with a prestigious heritage of unilateral foreign policy initiatives (France and Britain), or a tradition of neutralism (Denmark, Ireland, and Sweden), or particularist foreign policy concerns (Greece) opposed such efforts. (The French position, as always, remained ambivalent.) All governments favor continued informal cooperation, perhaps with a secretariat, on humanitarian and peacekeeping matters, but there is no consensus on pooling or the delegation of sovereignty. No further breakthrough is expected unless governments agree to greater flexibility and fragmentation in the form of an arrangement whereby a subset of governments can act in the name of the EU while others remain uninvolved. A first step was taken at Amsterdam, where a provision for "constructive abstention" permits a subset of governments to move ahead on foreign policy issues using EU funds without participation by others—a modest step toward greater flexibility.[44]

In defense policy, and despite the rhetoric of politicians, there has been no serious move to replace NATO as the dominant military organization in Europe. Quite the opposite: the recent Amsterdam Treaty restricts the EC and the WEU to so-called Petersberg tasks of peacemaking, humanitarian resscues, and peacekeeping. NATO was strengthened as the preeminent security institution in Europe.[45] Even the most radical position in the recent IGC, supported by a mi-

44. These alignments resemble those over NATO expansion, where Germany favors widening decisionmaking to include Russia, while Britain and France remain skeptical.

45. European Policy Centre (1997, p. 2). The Petersberg Tasks, so named in the WEU Petersberg Declaration of June 1992, include humanitarian and rescue missions, peacekeeping, and crisis management or peacemaking.

nority of countries including France, did not foresee the elimination of NATO but instead the creation of a parallel European military organization with some capacity for independent action. Within the EC, it is likely that governments will agree to permit subsets of governments to move forward on their own with the approval and perhaps modest financial support of nonparticipating members. The ultimate limits on such autonomous policies, as Gordon makes clear in his chapter, are economic. Unilateral sanctions are unlikely to be effective without U.S. participation, while the Europeans are unlikely to invest in the military and foreign policy apparatus necessary to act completely independently of the United States in defense policy. Anything more than modest coordination of small operations would require a substantial increase in European defense spending and thus appears financially unrealistic without the active support of the United States through NATO. This implies that the United States will retain a de facto veto over major operations, modest peacekeeping aside, for the foreseeable future.

Greater incentive for cooperation exists in discussions of internal security—that is, asylum, immigration, and police policies, which constitute the so-called third pillar of Maastricht. Cooperation in these areas is driven in large part by the Schengen Agreement to abolish internal customs formalities, in which most, but not all, EU members participate. The removal of internal border controls creates a strong incentive to establish more effective cooperation on external controls and policing. This is also of particular interest to those governments with relatively open asylum and immigration policies or greater vulnerability to transnational crime, notably Germany, with long borders with eastern Europe, but also to some southern European countries, open to the Mediterranean. Britain, by contrast, with only twenty-four points of entry (ports, airports, and the Chunnel) and no national identity card, or Denmark, bordering on Scandinavia, or even France, more insulated than Italy or Spain, remain more satisfied with domestic controls. Although the election of a Labour government led Britain to abandon its social policy opt-out, it did not reverse British opposition to border controls. Both Britain and Ireland, while willing to cooperate on policing, rejected cooperation on border controls.

Yet governments, like that of Germany, with greater concerns about immigration issues have a countervailing incentive not to surrender too much control over policies that could impose high costs on them. This was impressed on Kohl by the German regions, which blocked any concessions in the Treaty of Amsterdam. Hence while the treaty moved asylum and border policies to the "first pillar," permitting greater involvement by the Commission, Parliament, and Court, it also retained unanimity voting. The result was so modest that some speculated afterwards that "it might . . . have been better to leave the Schengen Agreement outside the Union Treaty."[46] Yet in the end, just enough symbolic improvement was made on policies concerning crime, drugs, and immigration to depict the IGC as a "success."[47]

In sum, here, as in internal-market, monetary, and foreign policy, no recent step toward deepening and institutional centralization has been possible without simultaneous fragmentation, including the explicit exclusion and voluntary opting-out of governments.

Diversity: Widening and the Problems of Enlargement

While member governments debate the deepening of the EU in regulatory, social, monetary, and foreign policy, they are also considering "widening"—that is, geographical expansion of the EU to include the new democracies of central, southern and eastern Europe. If all the countries discussed as potential members—including Poland, Hungary, the Czech Republic, Slovakia, Slovenia, Romania, and Bulgaria; the Baltic states of Lithuania, Latvia, and Estonia; as well as Mediterranean countries such as Malta, Cyprus, and even Turkey—were to join, the EU would nearly double in size to twenty-eight members. In fact, only three of the four "Visegrad" countries (the Czech Republic, Hungary, and Poland) are almost certain to enter in the "first wave" of enlargement around 2005. In its recent "Agenda 2000" report, the Commission recommended—after overcoming severe internal disagreements—Slovenia and Estonia as well. This limited expansion poses a far more modest challenge.

46. European Policy Centre (1997, p. 3).
47. See, for example, the way leading European newspapers portrayed the Dublin EU summit of December 1996.

Widening creates pressures for fragmentation due to the greater number and diversity of member governments whose policies must be coordinated. Not only are there significant disagreements over the speed and scope of enlargement, but there is general agreement that the entire body of existing common policies (the *acquis communautaire*), particularly those involving financial outlays, cannot be extended to new members without substantial reform. Some members also feel that efficient decisionmaking with more than fifteen members requires significant institutional reform, including greater use of majority voting.

The main problems do not stem from the East. To be sure, in the first years of the transition considerable doubts arose whether the Visegrad countries were ready to impose the highly developed regulatory structure, industrial modernization, and monetary rigor required to integrate with Germany or France; the Commission's recent report still maintains there is much left to be done. Yet the record of the past five years suggests a guarded optimism that a modest enlargement over the next decade is economically sustainable. Some postcommunist governments took advantage of the need to rewrite domestic laws to adopt EU standards, thereby preventing the consolidation of economic interests potentially opposed to harmonization.[48] The trade of central and east European countries has shifted toward the West and away from exports of traditional products (steel, chemicals, and food).[49]

Intra-industry trade patterns not unlike those among current members are emerging in a number of sectors; this pattern of trade is likely to cause only modest dislocation in the West. Where cross-sectoral trade patterns persist, as in the textile industry, much of it is driven by foreign direct investment (FDI) by Western firms. For the West, the net employment effects of trade adjustment appear to be small and are offset by efficiency gains, sometimes internalized to the same sectors, such as textiles and clothing.[50] Since FDI has flowed into the region at a slower rate than expected, the flood of low-wage exports some feared is not likely to develop; the position of former socialist states within the European trading system is

48. Keohane, Nye, and Hoffmann (1993) describe this process as "anticipatory adaptation."
49. Gros and Gonciarz, (n.d.); European Commission (1994, p. 6).
50. Dittus and Anderson (1995).

close to what economic fundamentals predict is stable. Hardest hit by the shift are likely to be Spain, Portugal, and Greece, which compete in some of the same relatively labor-intensive sectors. Finally, the importance of NTBs already appears to be declining on both sides, although administered protection and quotas remain significant barriers to EU markets.

Yet enlargement is likely to sharpen conflict within the EU because of its distributional implications. Accession requires unanimous support from existing members, among whom there remain substantial conflicts of interest over the implications of enlargement for trade and aid. Central and east European enlargement has consistently been favored by Germany, Austria, and the Scandinavian countries, all of which trade and invest heavily in the region and, as front-line states, would suffer disproportionately from potential geopolitical or domestic political disorders. These governments argue that EU expansion will stabilize fledgling democracies in the region as well as integrate them into Western economic markets. Something similar is said to have occurred following the Iberian accession in the 1980s.[51] For an entirely different reason—enlargement is one way to dilute unpleasant pressure for monetary union and social policy—Britain also supports enlargement.

France, Italy, Spain, Portugal, and Greece, all of which would benefit relatively little from expanded exports or geopolitical stabilization, remain more skeptical. These countries fear increased competition in price-sensitive manufactures, such as chemicals, steel, textiles, and leather goods, as well as a sharper struggle for scarce EU subsidies, which are spent primarily on "structural" funding in poorer regions and on agricultural supports. The level of underlying opposition should not be underestimated. France's initial goal, cloaked by Mitterrand's 1990 proposal for a European Confederation, was even more extreme: to relegate east European countries to an apparently permanent second tier.[52] Such opposition helps explain why, despite the creation of the European Bank for Reconstruction and Development, aid to former socialist countries remained largely bilateral, indeed mostly German, and why a generous EU or Western "Marshall Plan," much favored by some

---

51. Moravcsik (1995).
52. Haggard and Moravcsik (1993).

commentators, never emerged.[53] Even Germany remains skeptical of broader enlargement.[54]

Yet it is difficult for European governments to oppose enlargement publicly. The difficulty lies not simply in the diplomatic embarrassment of overtly excluding fledgling democracies. After all, trade agreements and enlargement could be—and may yet be—staved off through obstructionist negotiating tactics, long transition periods, and the multiplication of exceptions. The decisive factor has instead been Germany's informal but firm insistence that rapid enlargement to a few east European countries be considered a quid pro quo for EMU. Thus at the Copenhagen Summit of June 1993, EU governments accepted enlargement in principle—although no specific date was set and opportunities for future delay and obstruction remain. In the interim relatively generous "Europe Agreements" have been signed with the most immediate neighbors, marking a significant move toward free trade in manufactured products. French officials have been quoted as hinting that enlargement may prove more "difficult" if EMU does not go through as planned.[55]

The expansion of EU regional, structural, and agricultural subsidies raises more serious issues. With a relative per capita income of only 30 to 40 percent of the European average, considerably lower than previous accession candidates, and a relatively high percentage of the population in agriculture, extension of the current common agricultural policy (CAP) unchanged to even the most developed countries of east central Europe, such as Poland, Hungary, and the Czech Republic, would require very large additional transfers from existing members to new ones. It is generally accepted, however, that the next consideration of the EU budget, due in 1999, will not raise net EU taxation from its current rate of just under 1.3 percent of GDP; even mainstream German politicians are now saying that Germany may seek to reduce its net contribution. In IGC 96, the Commission seized on this problem as an opportunity to propose CAP reform whereby price supports would to be cut and subsidies transformed into direct payments. Yet the Commission has

53. Kramer (1993, p. 222); Haggard and Moravcsik (1993).
54. Interview with national officials, May 1997.
55. Interviews with French officials, 1996. "Reflection Group," available on-line at http://europa.eu.int.

pursued this goal for four decades, since *before* the CAP was created, only to be blocked repeatedly by farmers. CAP reform is unlikely to occur swiftly. Instead, there is discussion of very long transition periods—totaling up to twenty-five years—for fully integrating the farms of the new members into the CAP.

A final concern, more prosaic but more immediate, is the efficiency of decisionmaking in an EU comprising twenty to thirty members. This issue forms the centerpiece of federalist contributions to IGC 96. It is widely argued that without greater use of majoritarian institutions in the Council of Ministers and European Parliament, as well as a reform of the structure of the Commission, European decisionmaking will grind to a halt. The precise grounds for this fear are rarely made explicit. In fact, this concern does not seem to have altered the position of national governments on such issues; those who favored majoritarian institutions in the past continue to do so. If, as now seems probable, enlargement over the next decade is limited to a handful of countries, current institutions can surely be maintained.

It is therefore not surprising that national leaders decided to forgo large institutional changes in the most recent IGC. Even the relatively minor matters of readjusting voting weights of large and small countries in the Council and reapportioning seats on the Commission were postponed for a number of years.[56] Larger governments have been concerned about the steady decline in their relative influence in the Council of Ministers, where weighted voting favors smaller countries. For their part, smaller governments are concerned that a rationalization of the Commission—necessary to maintain efficiency as the EU expands in size—will leave some countries without a commissioner. An opportunity for a quid pro quo therefore presents itself, with larger countries gaining more voting power in the Council in exchange for ceding what has traditionally been a second commissioner. There is no reason to undertake a politically risky move, however, until enlargement is imminent.

A final dimension of potential conflict—perhaps the most important in the longer term—concerns differences in political culture.

56. See the contributions of the Commission, Intergovernmental Committee, and the Interim Report to the IGC. Available on-line at http://europa.eu.int.

Citizens in some eastern European countries may feel a symbolic attachment to the ideal of Europe, as appears to have been the case in Spain and Portugal. Nonetheless, as the membership of the EU expands and moves further away from the original Six, it will tend to include an increasing proportion of new and prospective countries for which the notion of a European identity lacks strong popular support. This is due to the absence of either a Christian Democratic heritage or a connection between integration and peace as well as in some cases an active tradition of neutrality. The instinctively skeptical attitude toward integration that we find in Britain, Ireland, Greece, Denmark, Portugal, and Sweden, as well as in prospective new members like Cyprus, reflects this trend.[57] And although serious consideration of Turkish accession has been postponed and the subject of Russian accession has not yet been considered seriously, many observers believe that both lie outside the border of any ideologically coherent conception of Europe. Both would in any case be suspect because of the precarious position of their democratic institutions, the preservation of which remains a de facto precondition for EU membership. Yet these problems are many years off. There is little support for moving beyond a total of twenty members in the near future.

In sum, enlargement and greater diversity are likely to place greater strains on the integrity of existing policies. Reapportionment of votes in the Council and Commission, already controversial, is a relatively tractable issue. Reform is likely before enlargement. More difficult questions of financial transfers and political culture may alter the fundamental bargains on which integration has hitherto been based.

*Democracy: Prospects for and Problems of
Greater Accountability*

The surprisingly vehement public debate over the Maastricht Treaty in both Denmark and France, as we have seen, raised the issue of a "democratic deficit" in Europe. To many, the EU is too re-

---

57. Not to mention those countries that rejected membership, such as Norway and Switzerland.

moved from popular control and oversight to be legitimate. To many as well, the EU appears to be governed by a distant group of unaccountable technocrats in Brussels and autonomous judges in Luxembourg intent on constructing a European superstate. Such supranational officials appear to be backed by national ministries concerned with technical matters and national politicians who collude to exploit their constitutional powers in foreign policy–related issues so as to increase their domestic autonomy.[58]

Pressure for greater democratic participation and transparency stems not only from the publicity surrounding Maastricht but also from two other factors. First, over the past five years the EU has expanded to include countries such as Sweden that have a strong tradition of direct popular involvement and transparency in government. Second, the fact that the deepening of integration now includes social, monetary, foreign, and regulatory policy has raised demands for greater popular participation. Not only are such policies more salient, but national leaders have exacerbated the general public's suspicion and discontent by deliberately scapegoating EU institutions—as Jones and Pierson suggest in their contributions to this volume—blaming the EU for unpopular policies of fiscal austerity, monetary discipline, and the reduction of subsidies.

There is widespread concern that the present situation is unstable and may undermine the legitimacy of integration. Without democratization, some argue, it may become impossible to ratify any new initiatives and perhaps even the final implementation of EMU in certain EU countries. Voters may press for obstruction or selective withdrawal. Already one unexpected result was a wholesale expansion of the European Parliament's co-decision powers in the Treaty of Amsterdam to twenty-three new areas. Yet fears have already been expressed that this result will further undermine the speed and coherence of the EU legislative process.[59]

Institutional Responses: Managing Deepening, Diversity, and Democracy

Deepening, diversity, and democratization will likely create political strains unlike anything seen since the tumultuous 1960s. A

58. Moravcsik (1994).
59. European Policy Centre (1997, p. 3).

universal international consensus on new policies will become increasingly elusive, conflict over financial redistribution will intensify, and legitimacy will become more difficult to obtain. Despite rhetorical flourishes to the contrary, European leaders are quickly coming to the realization that these challenges can be met only by introducing greater flexibility into EU institutions.

As recently as the opening of the current IGC, less than a year ago, this was still unclear to many. In preparation for the negotiations, the Commission floated ambitious plans to reform agricultural spending, streamline decisionmaking, and increase Commission and Court influence over foreign and immigration policymaking—all with the aim of maintaining the centralizing impulse of integration. Yet a preparatory committee of national government representatives swiftly rejected almost all such proposals, suggesting instead minimalist reforms.[60] The final results were even more minimalist, and in the few areas where progress was made it tended to institutionalize the practice of opting out. This outcome reflects not only caution by governments seeking to avoid a repetition of the difficult Maastricht referendums, thereby upsetting movement to monetary union, but also a greater respect for fundamental underlying disagreements among member governments concerning the future of the EU. As we have seen, this trend takes the EU in a direction long favored by Euroskeptics like Margaret Thatcher.

Yet the modest results of the IGC do not resolve problems but only postpone them. The challenges of deepening, diversity, and democratization, in the form of budgetary reform, enlargement, monetary union, and continued national debates over integration can be delayed for a brief period of time, but they cannot be avoided. Their resolution will define the future of European integration. In each case, the likely result is an institutional compromise that combines greater centralization with greater flexibility. Three institutional means of managing this dilemma are examined next: reform of decisionmaking procedures, reform of EU spending policies, and reform of institutions for popular participation.

60. Report of the "Reflection Group" is available on-line at http://europa.eu.int.

Managing Institutional Overload: Creating Consensus

The combination of new issues, new members, and new demands for democratization, as we have seen, will place great strain on EU decisionmaking institutions. New initiatives in foreign policy issues and domestic affairs require unanimity; as the number of members grows, the probability that at least one government will oppose any given measure increases. When expanded to twenty-five governments or more, as foreseen over the coming decades, the current system is likely to lead to gridlock and stagnation. Gridlock would not be entirely unwelcome to the current British government, which opposes nearly all proposals for deeper cooperation, except in the single-market area, but most other governments are concerned that if the EU does not reform itself, it will become ineffective. This is likely to be exacerbated by democratization, whether in the form of increased powers either for the European Parliament or for national parliaments; both will create an extra hurdle for the passage of any meaningful legislation. The result, I argue below, is likely to be even greater flexibility.

Two alternatives to the continuation of decisionmaking by unanimity have been proposed, one introducing greater centralization, the other greater flexibility. The centralizing solution, supported by the Commission and some federalist member governments, would strengthen QMV and the role of the Commission. Majority voting is, in essence, a constitutional tool used by those who favor deeper integration in a given area to compel a minority of opponents on any particular issue to agree. Majoritarianism increases decisionmaking output, but only by depriving each government of some of its sovereign power—that is, by increasing the probability that it will find itself in the minority and have an undesirable policy imposed on it.[61]

Such loss of sovereignty is tolerable where all governments agree on a common policy goal, such as the construction of the single market, to achieve which they are prepared from time to time to make sacrifices on specific issues. Problems occur, however, when the parties face disagreement over fundamental objectives. Typically, a

61. In the IGC, the Commission initially suggested a reduction in the votes required to pass legislation, but this received no support. Available on-line at http://europa.eu.int.

majority of EU governments in IGC 96 currently claim to favor expansion of majority voting to new issues but cannot agree on which
ones. In matters relating to defense policy, social spending, and
taxation, nearly all European governments currently resist efforts to
impose uniform policies. In foreign and domestic affairs, as we have
seen, governments with a tradition of independent action, particularly France, Britain, Sweden, and Denmark, strongly oppose majority voting. Even the expansion of majority voting to additional
environmental and social issues remains controversial. In the IGC,
majority voting is unlikely to be introduced on more than certain
asylum and immigration issues; yet even this modest step meets
with British skepticism. No government is prepared to renounce
unanimity regarding changes to the treaty itself.

An alternative solution to the gridlock problem is greater flexibility—that is, more exceptions to EU rules. In particular, flexible or
multitrack arrangements address the gridlock problem by permitting a few governments to move ahead of all the others. Although
multitrack solutions permit governments to tailor solutions more
closely to their diverse preferences, they do so by undermining the
uniformity of EU rules.

In fact, the EU has traditionally been far more flexible than might
appear on the surface. The common market and agricultural policy
conceal much diversity. Exceptional quotas have persisted for generations within the customs union. Agricultural prices were uniform only for a few years after 1968 before governments, led by Germany, unilaterally offset exchange rate shifts with unilateral price
changes and border taxes; governments have also long maintained
their own parallel regional and agricultural subsidy programs.
Fifteen-year transition periods for some agricultural products were
imposed when the CAP was extended to Spain and Portugal. R&D
programs were possible only through a maximally decentralized,
ad hoc arrangement known as *juste retour*, where each country decides how much to commit, if anything, to each project, and financing is entirely tied to participation.[62] Regulatory harmonization under the SEA was possible only after richer countries were permitted

62. Such policies are governed by "juste retour," in which each country gains the
same financial benefits it puts in. Potentially stronger provisions in article 130M
have never been applied. Sandholtz (1992).

to exempt higher regulatory standards from EU harmonization. At Maastricht, the British opted out of social policy entirely but permitted the other fourteen members to move ahead within EU institutions—an unprecedented arrangement that required the recalculation of voting rules and rethinking of legal precedents. Monetary cooperation under the EMS and now EMU has always been possible only with the participation of fewer than all member countries. The Schengen Agreement eliminating border controls has not been expanded to all members; its incorporation into the treaty led to explicit British and Irish opt-outs. Since Maastricht, the British, Danish, German, and Austrian governments claimed the right to make a final sovereign decision on EMU, despite previous commitments.[63]

The central institutional issue now facing the EU is the exact form that flexible or multitrack decisions should be permitted to take; that is, the institutional conditions under which governments can opt out. There are currently two competing positions on proper multitrack arrangements: those governments that find themselves perpetual outliers, such as that of Britain, favor maximum flexibility, the so-called à la carte approach; more centrist governments favor greater centralization, the so-called hard-core approach.

Britain, which alone favors the maintenance of unanimity in all areas, has called for an à la carte Europe, whereby—existing single-market obligations aside—each government may unilaterally select those policies in which it desires to participate. From the perspective of Britain and other recalcitrant governments, à la carte arrangements offer the best of all worlds: where it is disadvantageous to be excluded, as in many market liberalization measures, Britain could opt in; where it is advantageous to be excluded, Britain could opt out. Britain, Spain, and Greece make no secret of their view that low national environmental and social regulations, or currency devaluation, can provide important and legitimate comparative advantage. Richer, more highly regulated and more pro-European governments consider the à la carte approach unfair and exploitative. In their view, it sanctions "social dumping," competitive devaluation, and other forms of international free riding. Recognition of the right of EU member states to opt out of obligations, moreover,

---

63. Weiler (1995b).

would mean that governments would have much less incentive to compromise.[64]

France and Germany accordingly reject the à la carte approach in favor of a hard-core arrangement. In such an arrangement, a minimal set of policies—again the single market—would be binding on all governments, but a central core of member countries could move ahead on other policies. In some proposals, any government seeking to participate in one of the core policies would be obliged to accept them all. This proposal is attractive to more federalist-minded countries, since it permits them to move ahead on their own but maintains pressure on laggards to accept the same obligations. Some potential EMU members believe, moreover, that future coordination of fiscal and regulatory policy among members may be necessary to stabilize EMU and seek an institutional structure that would facilitate such coordination without risking a veto from nonmembers.

At Amsterdam, the governments moved forward cautiously to promulgate a general principle permitting flexibility. Any such arrangement must include at least a majority, be consistent with other obligations, not harm (and be open to) nonparticipants, and be instituted pursuant to a Commission proposal. The precise scope of these provisions remains to be seen. The number of participants in various issues is likely to vary, as has already occurred in the area of social policy.

The most likely outcome of all this maneuvering is even greater increases in the already confusing set of ad hoc institutional arrangements. Hence the current system of CAP subsidies is unlikely to be extended in its entirety to new entrants. Even Germany and the Netherlands, which are among the most federalist of member governments, insist on the exclusion of some governments from EMU pending compliance with the convergence criteria. Few believe that deeper cooperation on foreign or domestic policy is possible without veto and opt-out rights, at least over particularly sensitive decisions. In the IGC, a core of countries is pressing to incorporate the Schengen Agreement eliminating border controls and establishing common immigration standards into the treaty. Yet some EU governments are likely to opt out, while non-EU mem-

---

64. Wessels (1995, pp. 401–03).

bers like Norway and Iceland, members of the Scandinavian Pass-
port Union, may become de facto participants. On foreign policy
questions, governments are likely to maintain the right to exempt
themselves from decisions. Treaty revision must continue to be un-
dertaken by unanimity.[65] Varying numbers of participants and a
proliferation of opt-outs constitute a lawyer's nightmare but may be
the most effective means of maintaining efficient EU policymaking.

Over time multitrack solutions may lead either to stagnation, if
increasing numbers of governments find exclusion advantageous,
or to increased pressure for further integration, if exclusion imposes
large costs on outsiders.[66] Where integration imposes relatively high
costs on excluded parties, as in exclusion from a rapidly growing
free-trade zone through tariff barriers or high product standards,
exclusion is likely to lead in time to pressures for integration, as has
occurred with single-market issues and may occur with monetary
union. Where, by contrast, governments find exclusion advantageous, as when it permits them to free ride on their counterparts in a
free-trade area by maintaining lower regulatory and social standards, flexibility is likely to undermine pressures for cooperation.

Managing Financial Overload: Conflict over
Redistributive Transfers

Most of the major innovations in EU history have been expedited
by financial inducements. Financial transfers have traditionally
been used to secure the agreement of countries with relatively low
per capita incomes or particular problems. In the 1950s, the Treaty
of Rome provided financing for current and former French colonies.
During the 1960s, the EC was held together by negotiation of the
CAP, which organized large financial transfers from Germany to
France, as well as to Italy and the Netherlands. In the 1970s, British
doubts concerning EC finances, as well as the formation of the EMS,

65. From this uncoordinated process of issue-by-issue negotiations, an informal
hard core may emerge, yet the existence of fundamental differences between France
and Germany on institutional issues makes this unlikely. To be sure, both agree on
the expansion of QMV to regulatory issues, but France sides with Britain in opposing
its use in interior and foreign affairs, as well as any expansion of powers of the EP.
66. Pisani-Ferry (1996); Oye (1992).

led to an expansion of regional financing directed particularly at Britain. Over the past decade, the Single European Act and the Maastricht Treaty created large structural funds that flowed to poorer regions of Europe. The structural funds, while only 1 to 2 percent of German government expenditures, total 5 to 10 percent of GDP in poorer countries like Portugal.

The extension of existing agricultural and regional policies to eastern European countries, even just the Visegrad countries, would, as we have noted, greatly increase the financial liabilities of current members. Neither the continuation of the status quo nor wholesale reform is a likely development. We have seen that there is little likelihood that current members will increase their contributions. An alternative, sought by the Commission for decades, would be the rationalization of existing institutions by cutting agricultural subsidies and redirecting regional subsidies to poorer areas— thereby freeing funds for new entrants. Although the slow decline in EU farm population and current budgetary pressures throughout Europe are facilitating such efforts—the recent Uruguay Round settlement marked one such effort, cutting some price subsidies by 20 percent—governments oppose any sudden reform. Hence any transfers to eastern Europe will require either a large increase in funding by current rich countries or large cuts in benefits to poorer ones; neither step is politically feasible today.

Instead, the result is likely to be greater flexibility. In such a case, new central and east European entrants will be offered a less generous subsidy arrangement than that prevailing in Western Europe, perhaps connected to a long-term transition arrangement. As we have seen, proposals for transitions of up to twenty-five years have been floated informally. This will not block the entry of Visegrad countries, for their bargaining power is likely to be minimal in any enlargement negotiations and to force them to accept membership without a large net subsidy, as was the case with nearly all previous candidates.[67] Over the longer term, however, demands for net transfers to the East are likely to be attached to the first major policy initiatives following their entry—which will probably occur well over

67. Examples include Italy in 1957, Britain since the early 1970s, and Greece in 1979. Large subsidies to late entries like Britain, Spain, and Portugal were negotiated *after* they had entered, usually in response to obstruction of EC bargains on other issues.

a decade from now. The fear of such obstruction helps explain why
EU governments are seeking to push the process of deepening, including EMU and reweighting of votes, as far as possible before
moving on to widening.

Managing Democratic Overload: Ensuring Popular Legitimacy

We have seen that increasing demands for democratic accountability in the EU have raised fears that a legitimacy crisis will erupt,
obstructing future cooperation. Plans to increase the powers of either the European Parliament or national parliaments have prolifer-
ated. In fact, governments are likely to reach ad hoc accommoda-
tions with those who seek greater participation in EU politics,
maintaining both the predominance of national executives in EU
policymaking and the current unevenness of parliamentary and
public control across national governments. To understand why
this is so, it is useful to examine more closely the two major arguments advanced by supporters of democratization.[68]

First, advocates of democratization argue that current arrangements are unstable and likely to provoke a backlash from national
publics angered by the lack of democratic accountability. Such an
assessment may be accurate in the longer term, but some may dispute its relevance today, when the reverse appears to be the case.
Governments have continued to move forward, if slightly more
cautiously and with more attention to flexibility, on a range of issues, many of which are highly unpopular among European voters.
Although there is little evidence that European voters could be induced to support integration through democratization, there is considerable evidence that they oppose integration today. Hence in the
short term, democratization is almost certain to undermine integration, which helps explain why, despite protestations to the contrary,
even governments that favor some transfer of powers to the EP
have advanced relatively modest proposals. And few if any governments support increases in the power of *national* parliaments.

Second, supporters of democratization assert that the democratic
deficit introduces an unwelcome bias into EU policymaking. This

---

68. I leave purely normative arguments aside.

argument, already discussed above in the section on social policy, is particularly widespread among European social democrats. Many maintain that EU institutions—the jurisprudence of the European Court, the structure of the Treaty of Rome, the failure to extend majority voting to most social policy measures—favor the market liberalization beloved by business, while obstructing a sound social policy.[69] Some argue that this bias lies behind blue-collar discontent with the EC, which was most recently reflected in the results of the Austrian elections to the European Parliament. The far-right anti-European Freedom party gained almost 28 percent of the vote, less than 2 percent below the ruling Socialist party. Government officials, it is argued, are unwilling to change a current arrangement that increases their domestic autonomy.[70]

Yet, as noted above, considerable skepticism toward such arguments is justified. EU institutions do not so much favor business per se as they strengthen national executives and ministers by insulating them from short-term, more particularistic bureaucratic and interest group pressures. National leaders, insofar as they can work in concert, do exploit constitutional foreign policy powers to conduct what would normally be domestic policies without parliamentary oversight. This allows them to seek broader, longer-term goals—an institutional characteristic just as critical for European economic cooperation as the power of the American presidency (traditionally bolstered by congressional "fast-track" authority) is to U.S. trade policy. Such means are often necessary to implement policies with major domestic distributional effects, such as trade liberalization, monetary integration, and regulatory harmonization, particularly when such policies create concentrated losers and diffuse winners.[71] No government in Europe actually supports an *expansion* of the welfare state.

Whether the result is less or more representative of diffuse interests than more democratic policy processes is not certain, but there are good reasons to believe it is often *more* representative. There is a broad consensus in European countries hamstrung by labor union inflexibility, high government deficits, uncompetitive wage costs,

69. Scharpf (1994a).
70. Franklin and others (1996).
71. Destler (1991).

and regulatory incoherence that current policies are unsustainable in the long run and, therefore, some movement toward market-oriented policies is required. Today many European governments, notably that of Italy, seek to exploit EU rules to restrict government spending and impose monetary stability.[72] Even if European governments did agree on the desirability of democratization, there is little agreement on how to go about it. The German and Italian governments officially support increases in the powers of the European Parliament. Others, led by the Swedish and Danish governments, officially favor an increase in the oversight exercised by national parliaments on activities of the Council of Ministers, a position to which the British and French are said to be sympathetic, perhaps in the interest of preventing any increase in EP power. Now mobilized, national parliamentarians in a number of countries are likely to block any large grant of power to the EP, whereas participation by fifteen or more national parliaments would slow an already cumbersome legislative process.

These trade-offs between participation and efficiency of decision-making, and perhaps even more ironically, between participation and representation, help explain why beneath the rhetoric, most European politicians, Commission officials, and informed observers remain highly skeptical of democratization. Led by small enthusiastic constituencies based in countries like Germany, Italy, and Belgium, democratization will continue to be an important issue, but opposition from national leaders, parliaments, and even the general public is unlikely to permit more than incremental change, particularly in the powers of the European Parliament, anytime soon.[73] Thus the Treaty of Amsterdam, in which a set of national representatives generally unwilling to give serious consideration to more than a minor expansion of EP co-decision rights suddenly agreed to a last-minute expansion of co-decision, came as a surprise. One possible explanation is that an expansion of the powers of the European Parliament (which comes largely at the expense of the Commission, rather than national governments and, in particular, national executives) is the favored solution of national leaders to the legitimacy

72. Giovannini (1995); Wooley (1992).
73. Weiler (1995a).

crisis of the EC. Empowering national parliaments would be more costly.

The alliance of those governments that oppose any change and those who oppose centralization of power in the EP will work to maintain the diversity of current national arrangements.[74] The overall result is likely to be an expansion of the powers of the Council of Ministers, as favored by France and Britain, and of the Parliament, as favored by Germany, Italy and others, at the expense of the Commission.

The Future of European Integration Viewed from across the Atlantic

During the 1990s, as we have seen, European integration has entered a difficult period in which, for the first time in a generation, fundamental goals are being debated publicly. These debates center on the proper institutional balance between centralization and flexibility. Centralization—in the form of greater majority voting, Commission powers, expansion to new issues, and enlargement to include new members—is necessary to increase the credibility of national commitments to policy coordination deemed to be in the common interest. Flexibility—in the form of exceptions, exclusion, and local control—is required to manage rising costs of policy adjustment imposed by deepening, diversity, and democratization. Hence the proliferation of proposals for "variable geometry" and uneven reform of spending policies. The current trend in European integration is for centralization and fragmentation to occur simultaneously as new tasks are subject to EU policy coordination.

In the analysis above, we have seen that similar tensions can be traced through internal-market, social, monetary, and foreign policies, although each area has a distinctive trajectory. Forces for cen-

74. In most countries, the trend is likely to be toward a marginally closer oversight role for national parliaments. In countries with traditions of parliamentary activism and a skepticism of Europe, notably Denmark and Sweden, oversight may be particularly tight; in countries with a strong executive, notably France, oversight may be looser. Nowhere, however, is parliamentary control likely to be as great as in purely national matters, not least because within the EU any national parliament may be overruled by a legally binding majority vote at the supranational level.

54   Andrew Moravcsik

tralization dominate internal market policy, which remains the core of the *acquis communautaire*, although substantial areas of regulation remain unharmonized. At the other extreme, forces for flexibility dominate social policy, which will remain in national hands for the foreseeable future. Between the two extremes lie monetary and foreign policy, which seek to incorporate both imperatives. In both areas, intensive demands for policy coordination are balanced by radical proposals and policies of fragmentation in the form of exclusion and exemptions.

Extrapolating this trend toward heightened tension suggests a future model of state formation at the European level quite different from existing nation-states. Today almost no major European politician espouses publicly the goal of creating a United States of Europe, as was often heard in the 1940s and 1950s, although some surely continue to hold this ideal in private. Public criticism of dubious but formerly widely accepted verities—such as the role of European integration in preventing war in Europe—has become widespread.[75] In its place is emerging a system of multilevel governance in which forces of centralization and fragmentation achieve varying balances across different issue areas.[76] One element of this system, which has received much attention in the scholarly literature, is the increased transnational activity of private and supranational actors. More fundamental to our concerns here is the shifting balance between centralization and flexibility within EU institutions.

This emerging balance of centralization and flexibility distinguishes the EU from historical cases of nation-state formation in that it is designed largely to coordinate and harmonize the activities of preexisting and powerful states. In contrast to nation-states in their period of modern development, the EU is not the primary source of external security, national identity, dynastic glory, social benefits, or even internal security—nor is there any particular reason to believe it should be.[77] Instead, it is a secondary instrument for curbing the excesses of existing nation-states, particularly in the economic realm. From the beginning, it has existed in symbiosis with active, expanding functions of nation-states—a relationship

75. For a skeptical view of the link between integration and war, see Moravcsik (1996).
76. Scharpf (1994b).
77. Spruyt (1994).

quite unlike that of national governments to their constituent enti-
ties during the process of state formation.[78]

Thus the resulting trajectory over time is quite different from that
found in the history of most existing nation-states. Most of the latter
tended to reinforce their monopoly over public functions as they
developed, whereas the EU has seen a process more like that in con-
sociational democracies like Belgium and Switzerland, in which
centralization and fragmentation coexist and are linked by bargaining among elites. There is little evidence that the EU is systematically replacing national allegiances, social practices, and cultural
habits. Instead, it is creating another layer of political identification
that limits national prerogatives without claiming to supplant the
nation-state across the board. As compared with nineteenth- and
twentieth-century states, this identification is based mainly on civic
and commercial concerns such as shared democratic principles and
commercial advantage, and far less on shared institutions of cultural identity, educational advancement, military organization, or
economic redistribution. Moreover, the constituent polities of the
EU are immeasurably more powerful vis-à-vis the central state than
their domestic counterparts: declining feudal and corporatist rem-
nants or the atomized individuals and groups of modern society.
There is no counterpart in the modern history of European state formation to the constituent member states of the EU, which have orders of magnitude more financial and human resources at their disposal than the central authorities in Brussels. Moreover, as the
number of member countries multiplies, their democratic concerns
intensify, the difficulties of deeper policy coordination increase, and
both the benefits and the costs of further European integration rise,
further exacerbating tensions. The result is a dynamic of simultaneous centralization and fragmentation quite different from that experienced by nation-states.

This ambivalence is certain to confuse and trouble outside observers, not least Americans. From across the Atlantic, the multileveled, nonhierarchical, open-ended nature of EU policymaking appears to signal the failure of a European project aimed at crafting a
federal polity in the image of America—a goal readily intelligible
and ideologically congenial to Americans. Those Americans given

78. Weiler (1996).

to a less sentimental, more practical assessment tend to view EU institutions through the prism of NATO—an institution hierarchically dominated by a handful of countries and, at least until recently, dedicated to one clear purpose to which all member governments were strongly committed. Measured by either standard—progress toward a United States of Europe or consolidation of a focused international institution like NATO—the multileveled, nonhierarchical, open-ended nature of policymaking within a more flexible EU appears, particularly to outside observers, to be opaque, irresolute, and ineffective.

Yet neither standard is appropriate. Both fundamentally misunderstand the nature of European integration, thereby rendering it all too easy for outside observers to conclude that the process of European integration is faltering. As we have seen, precisely the opposite is true. The modest outcome of IGC 96, increasing conflict over fundamental visions of Europe, greater flexibility of EU institutions, and dilution of the federalist vision of a United States of Europe are not forerunners of failure but signals of success. They are the growing pains of an institution that has succeeded in establishing itself as the primary center of policymaking across a wide range of issues. Pressures for fragmentation, we have seen, are the obverse of success in deepening existing policies and widening to include neighboring countries. To interpret the resulting political difficulties as irresolution is to misunderstand the European project fundamentally, just as to misinterpret battles between Washington and the states or between the president and Congress as signaling the absence of polity is to misunderstand the American system of government. The EU is not a single-purpose pact among nations; it is a political system within which fundamental political issues are debated and resolved. Thus intense demands for deepening, widening, and democratization have elicited equally intense demands for fragmentation, flexibility, and differentiation. The fact that such debates take place is a sign not of Europe's failure, but of its triumph.

Interpreting developments in the EU accurately is not important simply for those who interact with Europe. There is good reason to believe that this type of more flexible, open, and ambiguous international institution can be a model for many multilateral organizations in a new, democratizing post–cold war world. Consider, for example, the role of NATO in organizing post–World War II European cooperation in foreign and defense policy. For American observers, this is often seen as a model. During the cold war, European foreign and defense policy arrangements placed absolute priority on maintaining unity and credibility vis-à-vis a perceived Soviet threat. The result was a commitment to NATO decisionmaking that was hierarchical, rigid, and ideological and that commanded universal adherence among members—all qualities perceived as essential to its all-important function of credible deterrence. Since even a hint of a failure to follow the rules could undermine the faith in deterrence for all, a strong presumption existed against unilateralism. No international organization or domestic group was permitted to challenge the unique role of NATO. When it appeared during the early 1970s, for example, that the Communist party might come to power in Italy, Henry Kissinger considered covert intervention to prevent it.

With the passing of the cold war, the central politico-military challenge to U.S. and European foreign policymakers—preventing nuclear, chemical, and biological proliferation aside—is no longer the maintenance of an unambiguously credible deterrent against an adversary superpower but the facilitation of sporadic humanitarian and stabilizing intervention in conflicts, such as that in Bosnia, that no country sees as a major threat to vital interests. No great cost need be incurred if some countries decide not to participate in a given operation. When the former communists did come to power in Italy, in recent years the Italian commitment to NATO was barely mentioned and no one considered intervention. Nor are governments seriously concerned that a failure to maintain rigid intra-alliance compliance will lead to war among Western governments, as occurred in World War I, or to a failure of deterrence, as occurred with World War II. Instead, the major threat to concerted Western action is apathy; governments preoccupied with domestic matters may not act at all. Under such circumstances, governments welcome flexibility to create "coalitions of the willing" and to legitimate them through whatever international organizational form is most convenient, whether it is the EU, the United Nations, NATO, the Organization for Security and Cooperation in Europe (OSCE), the WEU, an ad hoc body such as a "G-25," or none at all. In striking contrast to cold war policy toward NATO, the redundancy and openendedness of these security commitments may constitute a virtue and increase our ability to achieve common policy goals. Beyond a minimum of uniformity required for military planning and logistical purposes, which recommends the maintenance of NATO as the preeminent organization for defense planning, flexibility in decisionmaking may well be a significant advantage.

The same lesson applies to economic matters. International institutions like the WTO or the North American Free Trade Agreement (NAFTA), with their binding dispute resolution procedures and regional human rights regimes, which have become deeply embedded in domestic institutions, increasingly function as forums and networks where we observe true political contestation among national officials, nongovernmental organizations, and the representatives of international organizations. Increasingly international courts, regulatory bodies, bureaucracies, and conferences resemble the messy, open-ended political world of national politics rather than the simpler, more restricted world of classical diplomacy.[79]

If this is even partly true, then the EU's current tensions—on the surface something uniquely European—are in fact a precursor of new problems and a source of new solutions for countries throughout the globe. As the EU struggles with the monumental challenges of the next decade and drifts farther away from the postwar vision of a federalist union dedicated primarily to the prevention of another European war, we must remember that Europe's trials are the price of success in establishing a true polity—an experience from which outsiders have much to learn.

79. Slaughter (1997).

Chapter 2

Economic and Monetary Union: Playing with Money

Erik Jones

The European Union's proposal to form an economic and monetary union (EMU) is one of the most ambitious gambits in international monetary history. If statesmen and pundits are to be believed, the reward for success will be Franco-German reconciliation and continental unity. The price of failure will be the weakening of the entire edifice of integration. A united Germany loosed from its bonds to the West could turn eastward, could become more assertive, could even become irrational. However, if Europe does manage to construct a continental currency, Germany will be anchored firmly to the values of liberal democracy and intergovernmental cooperation. In this sense, as Loukas Tsoukalis argues, EMU is really about the balance of power—and perhaps that is how it should be.[1] Perhaps.

The purpose of this chapter is to round out the discussion of EMU by bringing in two dimensions at work beneath the dramatic

This paper benefited from conversations with David Calleo, Simon Duke, Daniel Gros, Carsten Hefeker, Paul Heywood, Charles Kupchan, Kathleen McNamara, Andrew Moravcsik, Thomas Row, Joel Turkewitz, William Wallace, the CEPS (Centre for European Policy Studies) Economic Policy Group, and the W. Averell Harriman Study Group on Transatlantic Relations of the Council on Foreign Relations in New York. The views expressed in this essay are my own as, of course, are any mistakes of fact or logic.

1. Tsoukalis (1996). Tsoukalis's impression that EMU is more about high politics than economics is widely shared. See, for example, Tyrie (1991).

language of—for lack of a better term—European "high politics." My contention is that EMU directly implicates at least three levels of society: the national elites who plan for monetary integration, the populations who support them, and the leaders of industry and labor who bargain over wages and (by extension) prices. For monetary integration to be successful, all three levels must agree on the objectives and workings of EMU.

In Europe today, the three different levels are in contradiction to each other. Although there is broad agreement among governing elites on how a monetary union should work and what it should accomplish, this agreement is poorly understood or even misinterpreted by the general public and openly contradicted by the aspirations of economic elites, particularly those held by representatives of labor. Intergovernmental consensus suggests that EMU will happen. At the same time, however, public confusion means that EMU may be unpopular, and potential industrial conflict means it may prove unworkable.

This argument is presented in five sections. The first surveys conventional interpretations of the history of monetary integration and particularly why EMU has proven so difficult to bring about. The second analyzes the intergovernmental bargain at the heart of current plans for monetary integration. The third examines how national elites are trying to increase popular support for EMU. The fourth explains why the aspirations and concerns of economic elites, particularly on the side of labor, have been left out of the monetary integration process. Finally, the fifth section explains why EMU became the focus of controversy at the 1997 Amsterdam summit as well as how it should be expected to function in the future. As these conclusions are somewhat pessimistic, the final section also suggests possible directions for reform.

Bad Luck: A Brief History of Monetary Integration

Monetary integration has been a long time coming.[2] The first plan for a European monetary union, the Werner plan, was drafted in the

2. Much of this section parallels the thumbnail sketches of European monetary history provided by Jacquet (1993) and Eichengreen and Frieden (1994, pp. 2–5).

late 1960s. And the latest plan, embodied in the Maastricht Treaty, will permanently fix exchange rates in 1999. This thirty-year time period compares poorly with the two years required to take the European Coal and Steel Community from proposal to implementation, the ten years necessary to create a European customs union, and the six years allotted for the completion of the Single European Market.

An easy interpretation for the almost thirty years' delay is that monetary integration suffered from an extraordinary run of bad luck. Each time a plan for monetary union was announced, Europe experienced some economic or political crisis. This was not the case for other aspects of integration. For example, the Schuman plan was greeted first with the Korean War and then with the boom period of the mid-1950s, which eliminated concerns about overproduction of coal and steel and delivered a strong boost to Europe's economies.[3] The European Economic Community coincided with the rapid growth of the 1960s and the flood of American direct investment. Finally, the completion of the internal market came at the crest of Europe's recovery from the recession of the early 1980s and toward the end of disinflation.

Proposals for monetary integration had no such luck. For example, the 1969 Werner plan stumbled on the collapse of the Bretton Woods system (1971) and then collided with the first oil price shock (1973). The end of the Bretton Woods system undermined the institutional framework designed to support the transition to monetary union. The framers of the Werner plan had sought only to foster intra-European exchange rate coordination within the network of dollar exchange rate targets supported by the International Monetary Fund and the U.S. Federal Reserve System. Once the U.S. Federal Reserve stopped intervening in international currency markets, the dollar exchange rate targets became harder to maintain. European governments and central banks responded by bringing forward the transitional mechanism for intra-European exchange rate coordination, which they renamed the "snake in the tunnel." Their

3. By 1957 the High Authority of the ECSC had only been called on to spend about U.S. $4.5 million of the U.S. $12 million budgeted for adjustment assistance. Diebold (1959, p. 418). The High Authority concluded from this experience that integration is much easier when growth is high, and the costs and benefits of integration are shared in terms of relatively slower or faster improvement. Willis (1965, p. 228).

ambition was to minimize the fluctuations between European currencies (the snake), while at the same time returning exchange rate variations between Europe and the United States to within IMF norms (the tunnel).

Such interim measures were short lived. The differences in macroeconomic policies across Europe made it difficult for national governments to match each other's performance. And, in much the same way, macroeconomic differences and the refusal of American authorities to intervene made it difficult for the collection of European governments to maintain their joint currency parities against the dollar. The transitional mechanism provided for in the Werner plan was inadequate to cope with the change in the international environment—countries could not stay in the snake, and neither could they keep the snake in the tunnel.

The 1973 oil crisis and the recession of 1974–75 brought the inadequacies in Europe's plan for monetary integration into sharp relief. The countries of Europe dropped any pretense of macroeconomic coordination, with some, notably the smaller countries, gravitating toward Germany, and others, such as Italy and France, choosing to go it alone. The snake was taken out of the tunnel by 1974, and all but a few countries left the snake by 1976. Europe's first attempt at monetary integration had ended in failure.[4]

Nevertheless, the desire to build a monetary Europe remained. As the snake mechanism headed toward collapse, politicians and technocrats began planning for a more resilient institutional framework to support exchange stability within Europe while at the same time shielding Europe's economies from the fluctuations of the dollar. The result was the 1978 plan for a European Monetary System (EMS). Like the Werner plan, the EMS was intended ultimately to bring about an economic and monetary union. Unlike the Werner plan, however, the EMS emphasized the transition to monetary union far more than the end result. The exchange rate mechanism (ERM) for coordinating European currency movements could survive in a more turbulent world economy and would even promote

---

4. Perhaps the best analysis of this episode in European monetary history can be found in Tsoukalis (1977). For early views of the Werner proposal, see Coffey and Presley (1971) and Magnifico (1973).

greater coordination of macroeconomic policies across participating countries.[5]

Despite more careful preparation, the European Monetary System ran into difficulties within months of its March 1979 inauguration. Europe's economies skidded on the second oil price shock, tripped over the sudden rise in U.S. real interest rates, and plunged into recession.[6] The EMS survived, but only by becoming an end unto itself. Exchange rate coordination was the objective rather than the instrument to achieve deeper integration. Although the desire for monetary union continued to be fostered among national elites and European technocrats, concrete plans had to be put on hold until after the economic recovery.

During the 1980s, the member countries of the EMS perfected their participation in the exchange rate mechanism and began to search for more ambitious objectives. Monetary integration moved once again to the fore of debate. The 1988 Hanover summit opened discussions about Europe's monetary future that culminated in the 1989 Delors plan for monetary union. The Delors plan contained an equally strong understanding of the transition and of the end result, and was to build on the successes of the EMS in order to realize the ambitions of the Werner plan.

Bad luck comes in threes, however, and the experience of the Delors plan completed the triptych. The collapse of the Berlin Wall (1989) and the unification of Germany (1991) sent political and economic shock waves throughout Europe. As a result, national leaders began to revise their estimates of each other and of the process of integration. Meanwhile, a tightening of real interest rates and a recession in the United States combined to halt the recovery of Europe's economies and spark a new recession.

The monetary integration project survived by the thinnest of margins and only as a result of grim determination at the highest political levels. Although the Delors plan was agreed to as part of the Maastricht Treaty, the combination of political unease and economic malaise complicated first the ratification and then the implementation of the project. By the middle of the 1990s, the prospects for EMU remained uncertain. Another dose of bad luck—or so the

5. Ludlow (1982).
6. Cleveland (1990).

64   Erik Jones

argument runs—and it is doubtful that monetary union will come about.

The "bad luck" interpretation of past attempts at European monetary integration is attractive because it provides both an explanation and an agenda. It can be invoked to justify the collapse of well-laid plans as well as to show the means to improvement. By the mid-1990s, the Commission could draw on a much deeper pool of practical expertise and sophisticated analysis than ever before. Not only Europe had learned from the failures of the past three decades; macroeconomics as a social science had learned as well.[7]

For example, one interpretation of the period of exchange rate instability during the early years of the EMS says, essentially, that the key to warding off bad luck is a credible display of resolution. Governments must show their willingness to stick to a set of monetary objectives even when events in domestic politics or the world economy take a turn for the worse. Otherwise market speculators will try to profit from government inconstancy, whether real or imagined. Given the enormous volume of international financial transactions, even imaginary inconsistencies on the part of government economic policymakers can be translated into real and powerful speculative attacks.

Continued commitment to the Maastricht plan for monetary union provides a dual source of credibility. On the one hand, policymakers can claim to have been pursuing the same objective for the past several years. Thus to the extent to which credibility is earned through consistently following the same course of action, Europe's policymakers (at least those outside Great Britain) can be said to be credibly committed to EMU. On the other hand, the plan forces them into institutional commitments to the objectives of monetary integration—central bank independence, domestic price stability, fiscal solvency. Here the notion of credibility has more to do with taking steps to prevent a change in policy ("tying one's hands") than with past performance.[8]

Thus, in a sense at least, the bad luck interpretation is also a justification for EMU. Monetary union was held up by bad luck in the past. As a result, Europe's politicians have learned to remain reso-

7. The professional learning of economists is summarized in Tavlas (1993).
8. The importance of this point is emphasized in Cohen (1994).

lute in their policy objectives. Moreover, they have taken steps in the Maastricht Treaty to ensure that future leaders will have no choice but to continue along the same course of action. The continuance of monetary integration, so they claim, is essential to maintaining Europe's credibility. And such credibility is necessary to forestall bad luck.

Credibility and Commitment: The EMU as an Intergovernmental Bargain

What the "bad luck" interpretation lacks is any consideration for the constraints national leaders have themselves imposed on plans for monetary union.[9] The history of monetary integration is as much a story of negotiation between governments as it is a tale of Europe's wrestling with the forces of globalization. According to this "intergovernmental" interpretation of events, each phase in the history of European monetary integration locks in a different aspect of the bargain between countries.

During the first phase of the process, from the Werner plan to the collapse of the snake, the issue was whether the costs of monetary integration would be shared symmetrically across countries. In the jargon of monetary integration, the dispute was between "economists," meaning Germany and the Netherlands, and "monetarists," meaning France and Italy. The economists argued that aspirants to monetary union should converge on a common set of real economic structures before locking exchange rates. And the monetarists argued that locking exchange rates would promote the convergence of real economic structures. On the surface, this looks to be a rather dry chicken-and-egg debate. Taken more deeply, the issue is really about whether France would converge on German economic structures (the logical result of economist thinking) or whether France and Germany would meet at some middle ground (a possible outcome of the monetarist chain of reasoning).

The negotiation of the EMS signaled that France would converge on German economic structures. Put another way, the first phase of the intergovernmental bargain ended with agreement that Ger-

9. Much of this section is adapted from McNamara and Jones (1996).

many would not change its domestic economy to accommodate the process of monetary integration, and neither would it make economic sacrifices automatically so that other countries could change their economies. In practice, this meant that the EMS would be a subject of intergovernmental rather than supranational concern and that Germany would not guarantee financial support to participating countries, although it could provide assistance in exceptional circumstances. In exchange, German negotiators agreed to include in the design of the ERM a number of institutional supports for weaker currencies. This proved to be a minor concession. The very short-term financing facilities and other mechanisms were rarely used to great effect. However, the act of concession held an importance all its own and indicated a rebirth of the special relationship between France and Germany.

The EMS bargain was more about the transition to monetary integration than about any possible monetary union. Therefore the EMS period, from 1979 to 1988, could be interpreted as a proof of good faith by all parties. Germany's role was to reaffirm the virtues of its own economic structures as well as the importance of the Franco-German relationship, while the rest of Europe demonstrated both the willingness and the ability to converge on German norms.

This proof of good faith was mitigated by two important factors. The first of these was that the Franco-German relationship *was* important to both Germany and France, as symbolized by Mitterrand's 1983 speech to the German Bundestag as well as by Germany's willingness to participate in a Franco-German brigade.[10] And the second mitigating factor was that convergence on German economic performance helped European countries regain control over domestic inflation and, eventually, government accounts. Whether as an international "binding" commitment or as a visible monetary anchor, the EMS bargain helped national leaders outside Germany sell the virtues of austerity to the general public and to economic elites.

The third phase of European monetary integration, inaugurated with the 1988 Hanover summit, saw national governments reopen negotiations about what a monetary union would look like. The Delors plan represents a first attempt to seal a bargain within which

10. McCarthy (1990).

Germany agrees to play a more symmetrical role, while the other countries of Europe agree to build a set of institutions patterned on the German model and dedicated to the fulfillment of German economic objectives. The implications of this bargain are that European monetary integration can be brought within the supranational institutions of Europe, while at the same time the process of monetary integration is protected by a new set of institutions—an independent central bank and so on—to ensure the continuance of German-style economic performance. For this agreement to work, however, no asymmetry could develop against German economic interests. In other words, Germany refused to be implicated in any automatic system for sharing the economic costs of deviating from German-style economic performance: There would be no redistribution of fiscal resources and no bailing-out of the insolvent.

Following this intergovernmental interpretation of European monetary integration, the importance of German unification was simply that it *changed* Germany. Because both the EMS and the Delors plan relied on Germany as a reference, a new Germany—with different economic structures and potentially different priorities—threatened to undo the bargains. This explains why national reactions to German unification were so clumsy. Having spent the better part of two decades learning to converge on Germany as a constant, the other countries of Europe had no idea how to respond to Germany's sudden change.

The response to German unification was to lock the Delors bargain into the Maastricht Treaty in the hopes that the agreement would hold together until Germany could again fulfill its traditional role as "model." However, this solution to the problem of German unification posed problems of its own. To begin with, national governments had to adjust to the economic effects of German unification without changing their position in the EMS. Put another way, this time national leaders had to call for domestic austerity to support the European Monetary System, rather than invoking the European monetary system to support calls for domestic austerity. Second, national leaders had to justify using Germany as a reference for good economic behavior when it was obvious to anyone who read the newspaper that Germany was not doing particularly well or was at least experiencing exceptional circumstances.

The final problem raised by locking the Delors bargain into the Maastricht Treaty was that by doing so national politicians made monetary integration a subject of public concern. Where the Werner plan had been a largely technocratic venture and the EMS a subject of primarily intergovernmental concern, the Maastricht Treaty was inextricably bound to the democratization of the European Union. As a result, markets interpreted the Danish veto of the Maastricht Treaty as a popular rejection of monetary integration. When public opinion polls suggested a similar No vote in France, markets assumed this would mean the end of the EMS. Consequently, a series of speculative attacks began that eventually overwhelmed the ERM.[11] The EMS bargain appeared to have come unwound before it could be replaced, and the result was that few expected the Maastricht plan for EMU to have a future.

The Hard Sell: EMU as a Solution to Unemployment

Despite the setbacks of the early 1990s, the process of creating a single currency has proceeded much farther than EMU's doomsayers would like to believe. The European Monetary Institute, an institutional forerunner of the continental central bank, has begun to consolidate its position as the administrative and information center of monetary Europe. The technical details for introducing a single currency as a unit of account, store of value, and means of exchange have largely been worked out.[12] And, perhaps most significantly from the bureaucratic standpoint, Europe's central bankers have begun the internal reorganizations necessary to transform a collection of national central banks into a coherent system.[13] Much as the framers of the Maastricht Treaty hoped (and as the neofunctionalist theories of integration would predict), the Treaty on European Union conjured an institutional framework into being,

11. Cobham (1994).
12. The broad details for the introduction of a single currency were hammered out at the Madrid summit of December 1995 and are listed in the conclusions of the presidency. The European Commission's Green Paper, *On the Practical Arrangements for the Introduction of a Single Currency*, is reproduced in Torres (1996, pp. 303–78).
13. Interviews with officials at the Austrian National Bank, March 1996.

setting to work the expansionary forces of technocratic administration.[14]

The progress made toward EMU stems in part from the interaction between the EMS and the 1992 program for the completion of the internal market. The EMS promised to "broaden the zone of monetary stability" in Europe and thereby minimize the pernicious effects of exchange rate volatility on trade and investment. For its part, the 1992 program facilitated the mobility of goods, services, labor, and capital, in order to increase the efficiency and competitiveness of the European marketplace. The larger objectives of these two projects were complementary: to create a favorable environment for productive investment and economic growth. However, the mechanisms embedded in these projects were contradictory. The "fixed but adjustable" character of national exchange rates within the EMS gave rise to concern that national governments would abuse the power of realignment to make competitive devaluations. Meanwhile the market liberalization at the heart of the 1992 program—and particularly the liberalization of capital markets—greatly complicated the practice of exchange rate targeting by increasing the potential for speculative attacks on national currencies.

In this context, monetary integration was more than just an intergovernmental bargain—it was a policy response to market imperfections. In other words, it was a "good" idea that promised to de-

---

14. The hopes of the Maastricht Treaty's framers are hard to document precisely. Nevertheless, public statements by François Mitterrand and Helmut Kohl confirm their desire to force EMU into existence as well as their fear that future generations would lack the nerve or the stature to carry out such a project. This type of elite predetermination is a major part of neofunctionalist theories of integration, which argue that form precedes function: once an institution is established to serve a particular aspect of integration, the technocrats running it soon find that they must broaden their competencies if they are to achieve their objectives. Moreover, the institution attracts the political attention of functional interest groups, who see in it a new arena for lobbying activities. In this way institutions not only increase their competencies, they also create their own constituencies. This dynamic is supposed to lead inexorably to some equilibrium level of integration. As a model for understanding the European process, the neofunctionalist argument is woefully incomplete, as the example of Charles de Gaulle and a subsequent mountain of political science theorizing have come to demonstrate. Nevertheless, as a partial explanation of the dynamics at work, neofunctionalist theory does shed important insight. For a recent overview of integration theories, see Keohane and Hoffmann (1991) and Michelmann and Soldatos (1994).

liver economic benefits to the Union as a whole. The objective of having a single currency was to resolve the mechanical contradictions between the EMS and the completion of the single market; hence the official end result of monetary integration is to create an *economic* and monetary union. A single currency would put an end to exchange rate realignments even as it eliminated the possibility for speculative attacks. In this way, Europe would benefit from a more efficient marketplace as well as a broader zone of monetary stability. Moreover, a single currency would provide a one-time increase in Europe's gross domestic product (GDP) equal to about 0.4 percent through the elimination of transaction costs between national currencies.[15] In short, everyone wins. The trick, of course, is explaining this to the voting public.

The challenge of building support for monetary integration within national populations is daunting. Most members of the public do not have a technical understanding of what money actually is, let alone of the qualitative difference between fixed-but-adjustable exchange rates, irrevocably fixed exchange rates, and a common currency—respectively, stages II, III-a, and III-b of the Maastricht plan. Thus any argument that monetary union will improve the functioning of the single market raises obvious questions about what the single market is actually about and how much better monetary integration is likely to make it. Finally, as populist politicians in Germany, France, and Great Britain easily discovered, much of the voting public holds a strong attachment to its national currency for reasons having little to do with economics.[16] Thus the challenge is not only to explain the benefits of monetary union. National leaders also have to weigh those benefits against the alternative to monetary union as well as in relation to the less tangible aspects of money as an expression of national pride and national sovereignty.

15. The estimate for efficiency gains is taken from the annex prepared by Marc Vanheukelen for Emerson and others (1992). American readers may be interested to note that the figure corresponds to estimates of the increase in economic efficiency resulting from the introduction of the greenback in the United States during the late 1800s—somewhere between 0.4 and 1.1 percent of value added in 1878. See Sheridan (1995, pp. 21–22).

16. Dyson (1994).

The easy way out is to hope for a strong economic recovery. If bad luck can prevent monetary union from coming about, maybe good luck can hurry it along. Certainly there appears to be a strong correlation between economic well-being and the growth of favorable attitudes toward Europe. Periods of relatively strong performance, such as during the early-to-mid-1950s, the 1960s, and the late 1980s, all correspond to periods of dynamism in Europe.

Unfortunately for this flip side of the bad luck interpretation of European monetary history, however, the relationship between economic performance and popular support for monetary integration is at best only a partial one. As Richard Eichenberg and Russell Dalton have demonstrated, the recent correlation between popular support for the EU and economic performance is limited to government success at reining in price inflation.[17] During the period from 1973 to 1988, popular belief in the benefits of European integration decreased as inflation accelerated and increased as inflation rates declined.

Somewhat surprisingly, the correlation between popular support for Europe and economic performance does not hold true for indicators other than price inflation. During the same 1973 to 1988 period, Eichenberg and Dalton were able to find almost no correlation between belief in the benefits of European integration and the level of unemployment, for example. Eichenberg and Dalton speculate that the difference between inflation and unemployment—at least in the public's mind—is that politicians insisted during the 1980s that integration, and particularly EMS participation, would help bring down inflation rates. Politicians never claimed integration would bring down unemployment. In fact, as Wessel Visser and Rein Wijnhoven argue, conservative politicians were able to remain in power during the 1980s at least in part because they claimed *nothing* could be done to resolve unemployment directly.[18] The best (conservative) governments could hope for during the 1980s was to create the conditions within which unemployment would resolve itself as a "natural" outcome of market forces. Following this line of argument, the popular opinion toward Europe did not change with

17. Eichenberg and Dalton (1993).
18. Visser and Wijnhoven (1990).

changes in the unemployment rate during the 1980s and early 1990s because, in the public arena, the two issues were not usually linked.

The conservative strategy to dissociate unemployment from European monetary integration was probably more a result of the deep economic consensus on the matter than of some political sleight of hand. Simply put, unemployment and monetary integration are not often linked by economists either. Since the founding of the EMS in 1979, macroeconomic discussions of monetary integration have focused primarily on disinflation and fiscal consolidation, with unemployment being considered only as a side effect of these necessary adjustments. Therefore while it is possible to find a wide range of studies exploring almost any combination of factors—disinflation and unemployment, disinflation and fiscal consolidation, fiscal consolidation and unemployment, monetary integration and fiscal consolidation, and monetary integration and disinflation—it is difficult to find any analysis making a direct link between monetary integration and unemployment that does not pass through either fiscal consolidation or disinflation (see figure 2-1).

The link between monetary integration and unemployment is also absent from the Maastricht plan for monetary union. Article 109j of the Maastricht Treaty requires that national governments achieve relative performance targets for consumer price inflation, long-term interest rates, and exchange rate stability, and absolute performance targets for government deficits and outstanding public debt levels.[19] These are the "convergence criteria" for monetary integration. The "nominal" criteria—those relating to price inflation, long-term interest rates, and exchange rate stability—refer to the relationship between monetary integration and disinflation. The

___

19. The precise nature of these targets is so often reported it probably does not bear repeating. Nevertheless, for the interested, a combined reading of Article 109j, the protocol on convergence criteria, Article 104c, and the protocol on the excessive deficit procedure yields five criteria. To become a member of EMU, a government must (1) have an average rate of consumer price inflation which does not exceed that of the three best performers in the Union by more than 1.5 percent; (2) have an average long-term interest rate which does not exceed the three best performers in terms of price stability by more than 2 percent; (3) respect the normal fluctuation margins of the Exchange Rate Mechanism of the EMS for a period of two years and not devalue against any other ERM currency during that same period; (4) have a deficit to GDP ratio at or close to 3 percent—or at least a good reason not to have one; and (5) have a gross general government debt to GDP ratio below, at or declining toward 60 percent.

FIGURE 2-1. The Analytic Framework for EMU and Unemployment

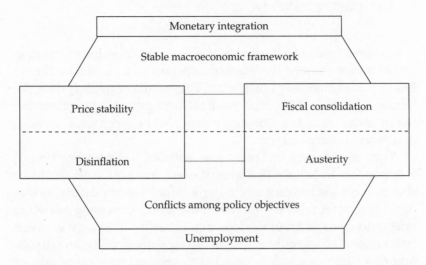

"fiscal" criteria—those relating to government deficits and public debts—refer to the relationship between monetary integration and fiscal consolidation. Moreover, it is clear from the treaty that the two sets of criteria are interrelated: fiscal consolidation supports disinflation, and disinflation supports fiscal consolidation.

Where the treaty does mention employment (article 2), the presumption is that the positive reinforcement between fiscal consolidation, disinflation, and monetary integration will somehow resolve the problem of unemployment. This presumption was reiterated in the 1993 White Paper *Growth, Competitiveness, Employment*:

> The main task facing macroeconomic policymakers is to eliminate the conflicts among policy objectives which have plagued the Community over the past 20 years and, more acutely, over recent years. Eliminating these conflicts will make growth, employment and real convergence compatible again with price stability and nominal convergence and will ensure that progress toward EMU will go hand in hand with stronger employment creation. In a stable and supportive macroeconomic framework market forces will be able to deploy themselves

unhindered and the possibilities opened up by the internal market will be realized.[20]

Interpreting this citation, the "stable . . . macroeconomic framework" means the positive interaction between stable money, sound finances, and monetary integration. The "conflicts among policy objectives" are the ambiguous (and often negative) interactions between disinflation and unemployment and between fiscal consolidation and unemployment.

When the Maastricht Treaty was initialed in December 1991, it was possible to believe that almost every member state would be able to meet the convergence criteria. More fundamentally, it was possible to accept that the analytic framework supporting monetary integration was an accurate depiction of reality. This logic explains how national elites could expect to call on popular discipline in support of austerity measures intended to prop up their proposals for EMU. Between the initialing and ratification of the Maastricht Treaty, Europe slipped into recession, and suddenly things began to look different. The problem was not that the recession broke apart the self-reinforcing relationships between fiscal consolidation, disinflation, and monetary integration. Rather the problem was that unemployment increased despite the achievement of a "stable macroeconomic framework."

Clearly the unemployment problem could not be addressed at the macroeconomic level alone. Indeed most economists believe the roots of the problem are microeconomic in nature.[21] Nevertheless, the rise in unemployment shook confidence in the intellectual framework for monetary union. And the exchange rate crises of 1992, 1993, and 1995 indicated that this loss of confidence was spreading to the markets as well. Although EMU is locked in by an act of treaty, even this might be insufficient to ensure that monetary integration will take place.

In September 1995 German finance minister Theo Waigel insisted that his European counterparts commit to a "stability pact" as a united front against assertions that convergence was somehow to blame for the recession. The rest of Europe consented (perhaps re-

---

20. Commission of the European Communities (1993, p. 50).
21. Layard, Nickell, and Jackman (1991).

luctantly). At the Madrid summit in December, the European Council reiterated the need to maintain a high degree of convergence between the member states' economies on a durable basis, and at the April 1996 meeting of finance ministers in Verona, the member states accepted most of Waigel's recommendations.[22]

Waigel's success in gaining initial acceptance for his stability pact is due in part to the ambiguity of the link between convergence measures and rising unemployment. In other words, Waigel could make a credible case that efforts to meet the nominal convergence criteria are largely unrelated to the mounting level of European unemployment. Nevertheless, the thrust of Waigel's stability pact is to ensure that governments continue with fiscal consolidation. And here it is more difficult to dispute the argument that efforts to meet the convergence criteria actually deepened the recession. Having tied their hands with the EMS in the 1980s, politicians are finding it difficult to claim they are not tying their hands with monetary unification in the 1990s.

Still, the evidence is unclear, primarily because Europe's public finance crisis would require resolution with or without the Maastricht Treaty. Thus while there is some plausibility in the argument that a well-timed fiscal expansion would have stabilized European demand, there is little evidence that Europe's national governments had the ability to make such an expansion. By the early 1990s, fiscal resources were already overstretched and in desperate need of deep structural reform.

The Maastricht criteria added little emphasis to the financial problems of western Europe, and almost no government adhered to the criteria—or even their own convergence programs—in any case. Despite the ambiguity of the relationship between the need for fiscal consolidation and Europe's plan to create an economic and monetary union, there appears to be a popular perception that convergence on the Maastricht criteria has worsened the recession and hampered the recovery. When French presidential candidate Jacques Chirac announced in the early months of 1995 that unem-

22. The citation is taken from the conclusions of the European Council Presidency as reproduced in *Agence Europe* 6629, December 17, 1995, p. 8. Acceptance of the stability pact by member state finance ministers was reported in both *Agence Europe* 6708, April 15/16, 1996, pp. 6–9, and *European Report* 2124, April 17, 1996, pp. II.2–II.3.

ployment and social exclusion would be his top priorities, speculation ran rampant that he was backing away from monetary union.[23] In October 1995, when President Chirac announced his commitment to monetary integration, he was accused of abandoning the unemployed. Finally, in November, when French prime minister Alain Juppé initiated legislation to curb early retirement and to reform the national health system, he not only incited massive protests against spending cuts but also rekindled opposition to EMU. In this context, Waigel's insistence on the stability pact represents an attempt to refute the existence of any link between unemployment and EMU. By extension, it is also an attempt to shore up the analytic framework wherein the creation of a stable macroeconomic environment sets the stage for resolving contradictions between policy objectives.

This two-pronged approach is evident in the December 1996 Dublin Declaration on Employment. The European Council appended this declaration to its call for the creation of a precise institutional mechanism to underwrite Waigel's stability pact in order to address concerns that Europe was doing nothing to help the unemployed. Yet while ostensibly a list of suggestions for labor market reforms, the declaration reiterates the linkages between monetary integration, a stable macroeconomic framework, and job creation. In its first seven paragraphs, the Dublin Declaration insists that "there are clear grounds for optimism [because] macroeconomic developments . . . are all creating the conditions for increased growth and employment"; that "it is necessary to continue with macroeconomic policies oriented toward stability, growth, and employment"; that "there is no conflict between sound macroeconomic and budget policies on the one hand and strong and sustainable growth in output and employment on the other"; and "that EMU and the euro will make an important contribution to generating the stable macroeconomic framework necessary for sustainable employment."[24] Regardless of whether the member states adhere to the Council's suggestions for increasing labor market efficiency, the message is clear: EMU is part of the solution and not part of the problem.

23. McCarthy (1996).
24. These citations are taken from "The Jobs Challenge: Dublin Declaration on Employment," *Dublin European Council (13 and 14 December 1996): Presidency Conclusions*, Annex II.

Nevertheless, Waigel's success in getting the other member states to commit to the terms of his stability pact has done little to eliminate the perceived link between monetary integration and poor economic performance. On the contrary, perceptions that monetary unification somehow worsens economic performance harden with every increase in the level or duration of unemployment. As Commission president Jacques Santer argued before the European Parliament, "Fears of unemployment . . . chip away at faith in the single currency. These fears are unjustified. But we know and you know that perceptions can make or break policies, even the best ones."[25]

Waigel's stability pact has failed to convince "public opinion" that monetary unification is not somehow linked to unemployment for the simple reason that unemployment is not everywhere the same. Provision of "a stable macroeconomic framework" seems to resolve "conflicts among economic objectives" better in some countries than others. Evidence for this is assembled in the three panels of figure 2-2, showing the evolution of unemployment by country from 1960 to the present. The countries are grouped by average performance during the 1990s, and it is startling to note that two of the seven countries most likely to be tapped for membership in 1998 fall in the group of worst performers: France and Ireland.[26]

The differences across countries are depicted in figure 2-3 in terms of the standard deviation of unemployment levels as a percentage of the total labor force. It is here that the disparate implications of "a stable macroeconomic framework" are most striking. Using the period from 1979 to 1983 as a benchmark for preference convergence around the principles of stable money and sound financing, we can see that the fate of Europe's economies have clearly diverged.

The explanation for this divergence in unemployment lies not in monetary integration per se but rather in the institutional differences played out against the background of monetary integration.

25. *European Report* 2104, February 3, 1996, p. II.10.
26. The Netherlands—arguably the strongest contender for EMU after Germany—should also be placed among the worst performers in terms of unemployment. The Dutch warrant a fourth-place ranking only if we believe that more than 10 percent of the work force can truly be worker-disabled and if we accept that a 49 percent participation rate measured in terms of annual hours worked corresponds with only 7 percent unemployment. Jones (1998).

FIGURE 2-2. Unemployment in the European Member States, 1960–97

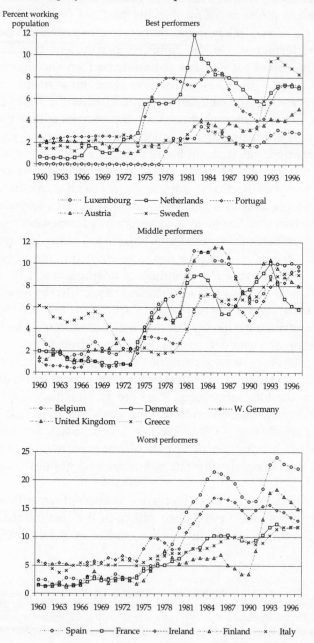

Source: European Commission.

FIGURE 2-3. European Unemployment, Variation across Countries, 1960–95

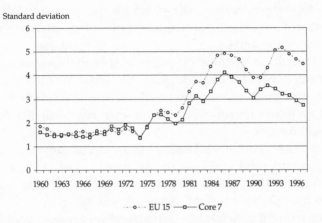

Source: Author's calculations based on Figure 2-2.

As mentioned earlier, economists have long argued that micro-economic factors such as wage bargaining regimes, social welfare programs, minimum wage schemes, and job security measures all have an impact on employment—ceteris paribus, or holding every-thing else constant. A possible interpretation of Europe's stable macroeconomic framework is that, like the ceteris paribus assump-tion, it holds everything else constant and allows us to see the differ-ent implications of varying institutional regimes. Such an interpre-tation reflects the prevailing wisdom with respect to unemployment, as embodied in the OECD *Jobs Study.* "While bad macroeconomic policy always results in bad economic perform-ance, good macroeconomic policy does not, by itself, guarantee good overall economic performance. Propitious economic condi-tions only offer a starting point in dealing with unemployment."[27] The real solution lies in institutional reform.

The danger to European monetary integration is that national populations will prefer to throw out the stable macroeconomic framework in an attempt to hold on to their social welfare institu-tions. A second-best alternative would be to recreate national insti-

27. Organization for Economic Cooperation and Development (1994, p. 32).

tutions at the European level—building a social Europe every bit as elaborate as the European welfare state. Both of these alternatives threaten to undermine the intergovernmental bargain underlying the Maastricht agreement. Eliminating the common macroeconomic framework offers little prospect of actually resolving unemployment and would undermine the price stability that Germany insists on as a prerequisite for its participation in EMU. At the same time, any attempt to erect a continental welfare state contradicts the principles of national control over, and national responsibility for, national fiscal resources.

Instead, such a continental welfare state would automatically implicate Germany (and the Netherlands, Austria, Denmark, and others) in financing the poor economic performance of less prosperous countries over the longer term. An automatic system of fiscal revenue sharing might also (almost perversely) pull money away from the poorer countries to cushion the effects of a temporary downturn in Germany, the Netherlands, Austria, or Denmark. Few national politicians are willing to stake their political capital in a system responsible for either outcome. For example, Austria and the Netherlands have reacted very strongly to their position as net contributors to European coffers, and Germany is showing considerable fatigue as Europe's perennial "cash cow." Similarly, one can only imagine the fallout if Spain were to find itself subsidizing German unemployment. Thus while discretionary financing through cohesion payments is acceptable, automatic financing is not.[28]

The European compromise is that national governments will retain control over the provision of social welfare and that the European model for social development will be preserved. Different economies will face the trade-off between social welfare institutions and unemployment according to national preferences and subject to a limited number of union-wide standards. Thus while the conclu-

28. Any system of automatic fiscal flows across countries or regions involves both the redistribution of resources over longer periods of time and the stabilization of income performance over shorter periods of time. If the system is progressive, the redistribution of resources will flow from richer regions or countries to poorer regions or countries. Nevertheless, the stabilization of income performance can force income to flow from poorer countries or regions to richer countries or regions even under a progressive fiscal system. For evidence of this perverse stabilization in Germany see McNamara and Jones (1996), and in the United States see Gros and Jones (1994).

sions of the Madrid (1995) and Turin (1995) summits both make reference to the necessity for structural labor market reforms, they also concede that much remains to be done to provide the basis for better cooperation and coordination in order to strengthen national policies.[29] However, this lack of coordination raises an obvious question: if national institutional differences are to remain, how will any disparate group of countries be able to accept a common monetary regime without some countries suffering more unemployment than others?

Rather than answering this question, Europe's leaders have opted for the "hard sell"—a strategy based on convincing national populations that EMU will mean more jobs. As then Italian prime minister Lamberto Dini explained at the start of the Italian presidency of the European Council, "monetary union and the creation of jobs must be seen as an entity so that one has the feeling Europe means opportunities, income, growth, and work."[30] This is a high-risk strategy in that it makes an explicit link between monetary union and unemployment that has not existed before. If successful, such a public relations campaign will harden job creation as the standard for assessing the merits of monetary union. Since almost no one expects a dramatic decline in unemployment over the near future, popular attitudes toward EMU are likely to worsen.

The Excluded Middle: EMU as a Source of Distributional Conflict

There is no direct link between monetary union and job creation. Therefore it is impossible to say for certain whether the net effect of EMU will be to create jobs or to destroy them. In different circumstances either outcome is possible. And given the varying conditions across European countries, neither outcome is certain. This explains, perhaps, why political scientists and economists have had such difficulty identifying stable coalitions for or against EMU at the sectoral level.[31]

29. The citation is taken from the Council Presidency conclusions to the Turin summit as published in *European Report* 2121, April 3, 1996, p. 3.

30. *Agence Europe* 6640, January 8/9, 1996, p. 3.

31. Giovannini (1993).

Where we can be certain with EMU is that there will be winners and there will be losers. The process of monetary integration will have different consequences across society, industry, regions within countries, and countries within the monetary union. Moreover, the fact that institutions differ across member states, and that these institutional differences have important implications for EMU's effects across markets, makes it difficult to identify exactly who the winners and losers will be. Following this line of reasoning, the Delors proposal to create an economic and monetary union had only one serious shortcoming—at least according to the economists responsible for preparing the background studies for the Intergovernmental Conference on EMU.[32] The suggested institutional framework made no provision for compensating sectors, regions, or countries that may be adversely affected under a common monetary policy.

The argument that monetary union will create winners and losers who should be compensated is hardly new to economic thinking or to European experience.[33] Peter Kenen published his "eclectic view" that monetary unions should compensate for the asymmetric effects of a common currency during the late 1960s.[34] In turn Kenen's analysis underlay much of the criticism leveled by the European "reflection group" during the mid-1970s, which concluded that the Werner Plan for monetary integration had failed in part because national governments proved unwilling to share the burdens of adjustment to the world monetary crisis and the 1973 oil price shock.[35] In other words, the importance of winners and losers to the success of monetary integration has been incorporated and underscored in Europe's history of bad luck.

Nevertheless, the negotiators at Maastricht relegated almost all of the economic analysis about the redistributive effects of EMU to the background of arguments about binding a unified Germany to the West and about refounding the Franco-German relationship at the core of European integration. The EMU was hardly uncontroversial, but the controversies did not include the redistributive effects of

32. Emerson and others (1992).
33. Indeed, the problems posed for regional economies from a common monetary policy were stressed in the December 1995 *Economic Outlook* of the OECD.
34. Kenen (1969).
35. Marjolin (1975, pp. 80–82).

monetary integration.[36] Greece, Portugal, and Spain were awarded cohesion payments to ease the strains of nominal and fiscal convergence, but no provision was made to share the burdens of adjusting within a common currency regime.[37]

This is hardly surprising. In fact, it parallels closely the pattern of negotiations over the EMS more than a decade earlier. German negotiators at both points in history insisted that national fiscal resources should remain subject to national control and national responsibility. Discussion of the distributional costs of monetary union contradicted this belief and promised to open a larger debate about the merits of fiscal federalism. Although economists disagree about how much compensation is likely to cost and how successful any institution is likely to be, there is a general suspicion among them that compensation for the redistributive consequences of EMU will require some centralization of finances at the European level.[38] For the negotiators at the Maastricht conference, however, any additional financial commitment to EMU beyond making side payments to ensure the support of the poorer member states was unacceptable both as a constraint on national sovereignty and as an impediment to national fiscal consolidation. Indeed the treaty authors went even farther to insist that there would be no bailout for member states who, for whatever reason, could not manage their domestic economies and public finances (article 104b).[39]

The major difference between the EMS and EMU negotiations was that as a result of the EMS experience, national elites shared a similar—although not identical—set of macroeconomic preferences for low price inflation, stable exchange rates, and sound budgetary finances. Such similarity was not evident during the 1970s, and the lesson drawn from the 1975 Marjolin Report was that preference

36. Sandholtz (1993); Morgan (1993).
37. Italianer (1993).
38. See, for example, MacDougal (1977); Sala-I-Martin and Sachs (1992); Italianer and Pisani-Ferry (1992). What is not clear is whether a set of common fiscal institutions would be either necessary—see Bayoumi and Masson (1995); Gros and Jones (1994); von Hagen (1991)—or effective.
39. Article 103a does open the possibility for a member state to receive transfers from the Union when that country is seriously threatened with severe difficulties caused by exceptional occurrences beyond its control. However the language of the treaty suggests that such assistance will only be forthcoming in the event of a natural disaster. See also Italianer (1993, p. 84).

convergence is a prerequisite for successful monetary integration. Therefore much of the technical discussion of monetary union at Maastricht was consumed with the development of mechanisms to test would-be participants for sufficient commitment to the guiding principles of EMU: stable money and sound finances. The multilateral surveillance and excessive deficit procedures constitute the mechanisms for evaluating such commitment, and the convergence criteria provide the basis for evaluation.[40]

The problem is that price stability depends on more than just national commitment. In part, at least, price stability depends on how the burdens of adjustment to economic change are distributed between wages and profits and between unemployment and disinvestment within the monetary union. This fact was largely hidden during the 1980s, when national elites were able to sell the asymmetries implicit in the EMS by focusing attention on national solutions to national problems; in other words, by selling tailor-made austerity measures and adjustment strategies to domestic economic elites. Those countries that were most successful with disinflation either succeeded in finding a means for capital and labor to work together or they sided with one group against the other. Germany and the Benelux countries succeeded with the more consensual strategy, while Britain sided with capital against labor, and Sweden sided with labor against capital. Countries such as France and Italy were less successful either in finding a compromise or in choosing sides.

The importance of establishing broadly acceptable adjustment mechanisms was obscured by the convergence of preferences on economic objectives as well as by the growing belief that credibility results largely from commitment. At Maastricht, European leaders could choose between three alternative systems for sharing adjustment costs:[41] they could integrate factor markets, allowing adjust-

40. For a discussion of this preference convergence, see Moravcsik (1991); Sandholtz (1993); McNamara (1998).

41. In this context, adjustment can be considered as a necessary change of institutions or behavior in response to changes in any number of factors, from government policies to raw material prices, productivity levels, consumer tastes, and market demand. Price stability is possible where there is agreement on (or at least acceptance of) how the burdens of adjustment are to be distributed, and price stability is not possible where there is disagreement or conflict over the distribution of burdens. In this sense, solidarity—or agreement on the distribution of adjustment costs—can be considered a necessary if insufficient condition for price stability.

ment to take place through movements of labor and capital; they could share fiscal resources; or they could let each member state fend for itself. In the event this did not prove to be much of a choice. The European Union has neither a common set of labor market institutions nor a fiscal regime capable of sharing adjustment costs. Moreover, European Union leaders have expressed little interest in creating either form of adjustment mechanism.[42]

Instead of striving to increase European factor mobility or creating a common set of fiscal institutions, the Maastricht plan for EMU assumes that economic adjustment can be dealt with on a piecemeal basis within existing national and even regional labor markets. According to this assumption, if all local factor markets work efficiently, then the diverse regions of the monetary union will be able to adjust rapidly to any change in the economic environment. In other words, local solidarity will replace solidarity across the Union.

Nevertheless, the "efficient local factor markets" assumption is open to question for two reasons. To begin with, it ignores the role of institutions in generating local solidarity; in other words, local acceptance of market rules. Under the Maastricht plan for EMU, industrial and labor organizations operating in different national institutional contexts must be persuaded to accept the same monetary policy—trade unions in Germany, France, and Great Britain will all be treated under the same rubric by the European system of central banks. However, so long as domestic institutions affect the way people do business, monetary integration will mean different things to similar groups from different countries.[43] Therefore finding a similar bargain that will appeal to all groups in all countries is an exceedingly complicated task.

A second reason to question belief in "efficient local factor markets" as a mechanism for adjustment is that it underestimates the in-

42. This preference for efficient local factor markets as the primary means of adjustment continued long after the signature of the Maastricht Treaty. In an attempt to "win over the Germans," Economics and Finance commissioner De Silguy noted that "differences in customs, lifestyles, and social protection hamper labor mobility in Europe" and that, while "Germany has a system of financial equalization that attempts to compensate for financial imbalances between Länder . . . [no] equivalent exists within European Monetary Union." See *European Report* 2066, September 13, 1995, p. II.5.
43. Richez-Battesti (1996).

teraction between diverse sets of local institutions. In many cases, as with the smaller countries, the mechanism for national economic adjustment during the 1980s relied on coordinated price-wage reductions in order to improve manufacturing export competitiveness.[44] In this way, successful adjustment for these smaller countries was dependent on the degree to which they succeeded in beggaring their larger German neighbor, using a forced increase in cost-competitiveness to shift unemployment from their own countries to Germany.[45] The declarations of the Madrid, Turin, and Florence summits argue against such competitive adjustment mechanisms, and yet this begs the question how the smaller countries are supposed to respond to economic crises in the future.

The European answer to this question lies in real-wage flexibility—in other words, local factor markets will change relative costs and prices in much the same way that government coalitions relied on statutory or corporatist price-incomes policies in the past. However, for real-wage flexibility to come about, trade unions will have to change their entire pattern of collective bargaining, both in the smaller countries and in their larger counterparts. Indeed a failure of the trade unions to change their ways would be detrimental to the entire process of monetary integration.

The best hope for EMU is that the completion of the Single European Market will weaken the power of trade unions at the national level and thereby force them to accept the dictates of local factor markets. Indeed this is what the economists working for the European Commission expected all along.[46] The assumption is that as product markets become more competitive across countries, national and local trade unions will have little power to force employers into making unrealistic wage increases. Thus to the extent to which trade unions are incapable of enforcing wage moderation on their own members, they will be forced to accept adjustment through labor mobility. This assumption has been confirmed through formal analysis by Jean-Pierre Danthine and Jennifer Hunt, who argue that "with tougher product market competition and converging prices, the room left open for diverging wage policies nar-

---

44. Jones (1994).
45. Jones, Frieden, and Torres (1998).
46. Emerson and others (1992, chapter 6).

rows: national unions, independently of the level at which bargaining takes place, are thus led to adopting increasingly similar courses of action."[47] Danthine and Hunt believe that the "similar courses of action" adopted by trade unions will take the form of efficient and competitive labor markets. If they are right, then the completion of the internal market should result in the competitive local factor markets anticipated by the framers of monetary union.

However, the danger is that trade unions will respond to the creation of an economic and monetary union by coordinating their wage bargaining strategies across countries. The argument here is that while it is difficult to determine who will win or lose from monetary union, it is easy to see that the Maastricht plan for economic and monetary integration represents a threat to organized labor as a whole. More specifically the process of integration threatens the core responsibility of the trade unions—collective bargaining.[48] The appropriate response from the trade union perspective, then, is to promote the informal coordination of wage bargaining across countries, both by sharing information about relative pay scales and by proposing the establishment of union-wide wage norms.

By coordinating their bargaining strategies, the trade unions can eliminate wage costs as a competitive factor across product markets. And while trade union leaders are careful to insist that such coordination will take regional productivity levels and labor market conditions into consideration, the implications for European adjustment are clear. Rather than seeing an increase in real-wage flexibility, Europe will face an increase in real-wage rigidity. As a result, Europe's economic and monetary union will find itself with no means for adjusting to differences in economic performance across regions. The implications here are unambiguously negative for EMU. Nevertheless, the trade union leadership will not accept a reduction in its organizational power over such a central issue as

47. Danthine and Hunt (1994, p. 540).
48. The possibility that the Maastricht plan for EMU will result in an informal coordination of wage bargaining across countries is reinforced by Driffill and Van der Ploeg (1995). In their analysis, Driffill and Van der Ploeg find that product market integration will *increase* rather than decrease the incentives for trade unions to coordinate their wage setting with unions in other countries.

wage bargaining even if this means damaging the adjustment mechanism at the heart of monetary integration.[49]

Before exploring this prospect in any detail, it is necessary to dispense with objections that the trade unions are too disorganized at the European level for any such coordination to come about. To begin with, while trade unions may hold different preferences with regard to maternity leave, pensions, and vacation pay, it is clear that wage bargaining is an issue they hold in common. Thus previous arguments that European labor was divided and ineffective in its promotion of social issues in Europe may no longer hold with the same force.[50] Second, for coordination in wage bargaining to succeed in upsetting the adjustment mechanism at the heart of EMU, it is unnecessary for the trade unions to create centralizing structures capable of disciplining rogue trade unions.[51] Centralization is only necessary for coordinated wage restraint. For coordinated wage increases, centralization is superfluous if not counterproductive.

If anything, monetary integration will increase the prospect for informal wage bargaining coordination across national lines. This is true for two reasons. To begin with, trade unions in one country will be able to compare their wages with trade unions in other countries more easily. For example, auto parts workers in Spain will know immediately that they are getting only a fraction of what similar workers in Germany are getting. Given the importance workers attach to relative pay scales, all it takes is for an aggressive trade union leader to point out the obvious in making the case for a wage claim or strike ballot.[52]

A second reason is that aggressive wage claims made in one part of the monetary union will have an impact on price levels throughout the monetary union. Thus for trade union leaders hoping to preserve real wages, it will be natural to ask their colleagues in other

49. In making this argument, I have drawn heavily on Gros and Jones (1996) and the other papers collected in the same volume.
50. Streeck and Schmitter (1991).
51. Reder and Ulman (1993).
52. Anecdotal evidence in support of this hypothesis comes from the recollections of politicians I have spoken with about their experiences on the stump in Spain and Portugal. One of the most common questions constituents ask about the single currency is how long it will take before they receive German-level wages. Clearly more sophisticated survey data are required to determine whether this concern is representative of the working population at large.

countries what they are planning to claim by way of increases. Any failure to seek such basic information would undermine the bargaining strategy of the union. Once sought, however, such information is more likely to put upward pressure on the wage claims made by more passive unions than downward pressure on the claims made by more aggressive ones. The effect will be an appearance of coordinated bargaining, even if no coordination was actually intended.[53]

For this line of analysis to be accepted, however, both of these factors for informal coordination should already be at work in existing monetary unions, and so it is useful to consider what the effects are. Evidence from regional data in European countries tends to support this line of analysis. Within existing national economies, there is a clear pattern of convergence around the wage setting in high-productivity sectors and high-income regions. For poorer regions, the result is rising real wages and rising unemployment—precisely what the framers of monetary union hope to avoid.[54] In other words, a European monetary union promises to be no more effective than national monetary unions in dealing with regional disparities in economic performance. Moreover, EMU will be unable to offer adversely affected regions the chance to adjust either through a sharing of fiscal resources or through the clearing of factor markets. In terms of adjustment, EMU may not be just as bad as existing monetary unions; it may be even worse.

Finally, there is the problem that informal wage bargaining coordination raises issues quite separate from the question of adjustment. If such coordination takes place, real-wage rigidity will increase across the monetary union, and unemployment will increase along with it. This possibility threatens the twin objectives of monetary integration. Any increase in unemployment will undermine attempts at fiscal consolidation, and continuous growth in real wages will undermine domestic price stability. Having chosen an adjustment strategy directly threatening to labor interests, national leaders will be forced into a showdown reminiscent of the 1970s.

53. This argument is suggested in a recent paper by Hefeker (1997).
54. Abraham (1994).

Playing with Money: Economic and Monetary Union

Nevertheless, the intergovernmental bargain at the heart of EMU leaves little choice but to rely on efficient local factor markets as the primary mechanism for economic adjustment. Europe's national leaders are unwilling to accept the full implications of fiscal federalism on a continental scale, and almost no one expects a large increase in European factor mobility. Implicit in the intergovernmental bargain, then, is the faith that local factor markets will adjust efficiently in the future.

The implications of this bargain are threefold. To begin with, some countries, regions, sectors, and social groups will fare better than others under EMU. Second, who wins and who loses will depend on the nature of the economic disturbance and on the domestic institutional context, a fact that makes the losers hard to identify or to compensate. Third, the promotion of efficient local factor markets will challenge the position of the trade unions in wage bargaining: the winners and losers from EMU may be hard to identify, but the losers from the promotion of real-wage flexibility and efficient local factor markets are not.

In a straightforward test of wills, it might be expected that Europe's national leaders would be able to ignore the complaints of the trade unions. However, in the grossly simplified debate over the merits of EMU as a source of employment, it is possible that the trade unions will prevail. National trade union representatives couch their arguments for wage coordination in terms of "social dumping" versus "Social Europe." The wage discipline that economists assume will result from monetary integration is social dumping—a negative spiral of competitive wage decreases that will undermine the gains labor has made during the postwar period. By contrast, the international coordination of wage bargaining is analogous to Social Europe—a preservation of the advances made by labor in Europe, combined with the extension of those benefits to less fortunate regions.

In this way, the trade unions have been able to take advantage of popular confusion over EMU in order to up the ante. It is not enough to claim that EMU will help resolve the problem of unemployment. EMU must do so without reducing the quality of existing employment. The success of this strategy lies in the fact that the debate over international wage coordination gives intellectual credibility to trade union concerns about social dumping. Although economists may debate whether trade integration leads to a downward competition in working conditions, they cannot deny that increased wage restraint is an intended result.

By forging a link between union-wide wage norms and European Commission claims that EMU offers a partial solution for unemployment, the trade unions have succeeded in underscoring the tension between Social Europe and Maastricht Europe. Along the way, the trade unions have threatened to deprive Maastricht Europe of its adjustment mechanism and to force national leaders into a reconsideration of the bargain at the heart of EMU. Finally, the trade unions have the advantage of time. The longer unemployment remains high in Europe, the more the public will begin to question Commission arguments that the Maastricht plan promises a solution.

The controversy over EMU following the 1997 French legislative elections and during the Amsterdam European Council summit illustrates the problem at hand.[55] While President Jacques Chirac's center-right coalition lost ground through a failure to tackle the dual problem of low wages and high unemployment, Lionel Jospin's center-left alternative failed to crystallize a coherent economic program of its own. The appointment of ministers such as Dominique Strauss-Kahn, Martin Aubrey, and Jean-Pierre Chevènement suggests vaguely Keynesian notions of employment growth through public spending but nothing more concrete. Nevertheless, there is a growing consensus that monetary union is somehow central to the distinction between Left and Right. For example, as one-time Socialist finance minister Michel Sapin suggests, while the Left regards EMU as a social instrument for the fight against unemployment, the Right views it as "an instrument for fiscal solidarity between countries."[56]

55. This reading of events stands in contrast to the conventional bad luck view that Chirac's decision to call snap elections precipitated the crisis over EMU. While it may be true that Chirac's timing lost him the elections, the controversy over EMU has much deeper roots. Indeed, by precipitating the crisis in 1997, Chirac may have forestalled an even greater controversy surrounding the selection of members in 1998.

56. Cited in Le Monde, April 29, 1997.

In the run-up to the Amsterdam Council summit, Jospin's vague suggestions of Keynesianism and his emphasis on unemployment promised to ignite a Franco-German conflict of epic proportions. The results, however, were less than dramatic. The "Resolution of the European Council on Growth and Employment" reiterates the role of EMU in providing the framework for economic growth and employment opportunities and calls for even further efforts "to strengthen the links between a successful and sustainable Economic and Monetary Union, a well-functioning internal market and employment." Such efforts focus on increasing labor market efficiency, reducing nonwage labor costs, and encouraging "the social partners to fully face their responsibilities within their respective spheres of activities."[57] In other words, very little has changed.

From the perspective of mid-1997, the future for EMU does not look bright. If discussions about monetary integration continue to pivot on unemployment, EMU will become increasingly unpopular. And if they continue to ignore the distributional consequences of monetary integration, EMU will be unsuccessful. What implications such a failure might hold for the process of European integration can only be a matter for speculation. Europe may be unmade by money, or it may not. It is still too early to tell. However, this analysis does not mean that a dim future is certain.

Perhaps Europe's obsession with unemployment will force national and European elites to face the distributional consequences of EMU and begin broadening the scope of the Maastricht bargain to take into consideration the concerns of the larger public and of economic elites. Under such conditions, it is conceivable that Europe will grow to encompass a set of continental institutions capable of generating fiscal solidarity across countries, regions, sectors, and social groups within the monetary union. Such institutions would inevitably prove controversial and bring heated political deliberations into the heart of European macroeconomic management. But such controversy at least holds the promise of being able to channel the economic tensions between the social partners and within the organized labor movement.

57. These citations are drawn from the first and last paragraphs of "Resolution of the European Council on Growth and Employment." *European Council, Amsterdam (16 and 17 June, 1997): Conclusions of the Presidency,* Annex 1.

Alternatively the peoples of Europe may be persuaded to embrace some form of market solidarity and to accept the fact that meaningful differences between national wage bargaining institutions are incompatible with the maintenance of stable money and sound finances at the European level. The decision to develop market solidarity would heighten the contrast between Maastricht Europe and aspirations to Social Europe, making clear who exactly must lose for monetary integration to succeed. Such a vision of Europe will be controversial as well. However, this controversy promises to deliver better-informed national decisions on participation in EMU.

In any case, until Europe's leaders are prepared to broaden the scope of their commitment to monetary integration so as to include other segments of society, they are also unprepared for EMU. Any attempt to force the pace of monetary integration will be playing for money. Proponents of EMU may be successful, but they are wagering high stakes. Should Europe's leaders succeed in creating EMU only to have it fail, the Maastricht plan may prove to be more than just another footnote in Europe's history of bad luck.

Chapter 3

State, Market, and Regulatory Competition in the European Union: Lessons for the Integrating World Economy

Giandomenico Majone

Since its beginning, the European Community (EC) has grappled with a problem that is also becoming increasingly important for the integrating world economy: how to reconcile the integration of national markets with the preservation of national sovereignty. This chapter explores different dimensions of this complex problem, examining solutions that have been tested in the course of European integration and attempting to distill some general lessons.

The Depoliticization of Europe's Common Market

The first and probably most important lesson is the rediscovery of the old liberal principle of the separation of politics and economics. This principle, which at the national level seemed to have been repealed after the Great Depression of the 1930s, was recognized by the European Community's founding fathers as an essential prerequisite for integrating the economies of sovereign states with their different legal orders, frontiers, and systems of administration and citizenship. The principle is firmly embedded in the 1957 Treaty of Rome, which created the European Economic Community (EEC), although traces of the interventionist philosophies prevailing at the time are also clearly visible.

A consistent application of the ideas of economic liberalism could hardly have been expected in a text produced by statesmen raised in the tradition of *dirigisme*; but despite the conceptual ambiguities of the founding treaty, the disjunction of state and market turned out to be the most striking characteristic of the process of European integration. It was also the root of the problem of democratic legitimacy that has always troubled European institutions.

It would be hard to find a clearer contemporary example of the separation of politics and economics than the way the Maastricht Treaty—the latest amendment of the Rome Treaty—defines the status and functions of the future European Central Bank (ECB). The ECB can make regulations that will become European and member states' law without the involvement of the EU Council of Ministers or of national parliaments. Its sweeping statutory powers include the right to impose penalties on credit institutions for failure to comply with its rules. The bank has a single objective—monetary stability—and the freedom to pursue this objective completely independently of the other European institutions and of national governments.

Moreover, since the governors of the central banks of the member states are members of the ECB Council, they too must be insulated from domestic political influences in the performance of their task; they can no longer be players in the old political game of pumping up the economy just before an election. In short, in the Economic and Monetary Union (EMU) issues of macroeconomic policy that have been the lifeblood of domestic politics, determined the rise and fall of governments, and affected the fate of national economies are to be decided by politically independent experts.[1]

Such extraordinary developments must be viewed against the background of a system of nation-states accustomed to using their powers to tax and spend to the limits of economic and political feasibility and extremely jealous of their political sovereignty. Even after the Maastricht Treaty, foreign and security policy, justice and home affairs, and health, education, fiscal, and social policy remain in the domain of intergovernmental, rather than supranational, re-

1. Nicoll (1993).

lations. In these core areas of state activity, the members of the EU are expected to establish systematic cooperation and close policy coordination. But in the language of European law, cooperation and coordination mean joint and interdependent actions without legal force: renegers cannot be taken to the European Court of Justice.

The strength of the commitment to preserve national sovereignty is indicated by a recent example. When a German citizen (and former EC official) challenged the constitutionality of the decision of his own government to join the Economic and Monetary Union (EMU), the German Constitutional Court rejected the challenge on the grounds that the Maastricht Treaty, like previous European treaties, was nothing more than an international agreement among sovereign states. The members of the Union, the Court argued, remain the "lords of the Treaties" (*Herren der Verträge*) and never surrendered their right to secede.

But if political integration remains as elusive as when the Rome Treaty was signed, economic integration is a very tangible reality, with intra-EC trade in goods growing from less than 40 percent of total foreign trade in 1960 to more than 60 percent in 1990. (Except for agricultural products, this growth is largely attributable to trade creation rather than trade diversion.) In 1989–90, for the first time, the total number of intra-EC mergers exceeded that of mergers taking place within national boundaries. Only a process of progressive depoliticization of the European market could achieve such far-reaching integration of the national economies without directly challenging the political sovereignty of the nation-states. This process of depoliticization of the economic sphere has not been a linear one, however. The temptation to replace national *dirigisme* by its supranational equivalent was strong in the early stages of European integration, and the ideology of interventionism continues to inspire recurrent proposals for a more activist role of the EC/EU in industrial, technology, and social policy.

The Legacy of Interventionism

As mentioned above, the framers of the founding treaties came from countries where public ownership of key industries, national planning, aggregate-demand management, and large-scale income redistribution were considered perfectly legitimate forms of state intervention in the economy. This ideological background is evident in the 1951 Treaty of Paris, which established the European Coal and Steel Community (ECSC).

Although the main objective of the treaty was the elimination of trade barriers and the encouragement of competition in the sectors of coal and steel, many specific provisions were hardly compatible with economic liberalism. Thus the High Authority, the supranational executive of the ECSC, was given extensive powers, including the right to levy taxes, to influence investment decisions, and even in some cases to impose minimum prices and production quotas. The creation of the European Atomic Energy Community (Euratom) is a further indication of widespread political support for an active industrial policy at the supranational level.

The treaties establishing the ECSC and Euratom dealt with particular sectors of the economy, albeit ones that at the time were considered to be strategically important. The 1957 Treaty of Rome creating the EEC had a much wider scope and greater ambitions, and for this reason its drafters could not avoid facing directly the issue of state-market relations. The emphasis on the freedom of movement for persons, services, and capital; the provisions for a forceful European competition policy along the lines of the U.S. antitrust model; the significant addition to this model of rules on state aid to national (often state-owned) enterprises and on national procurement policies having the effect of distorting competition within the common market; the equally significant requirements for the removal of the distortions of competition caused by state regulations or resulting from the existence of public undertakings and undertakings granted special or exclusive rights by the member states— all these rules point to a definitely more liberal economic approach than is found in the other two treaties.

In fact, neoliberal lawyers and economists have celebrated the Rome Treaty, which they consider the true economic constitution of Europe, as a great improvement over the constitutions of the member states since it embodies the principle of the separation of politics and economics. In this view, market integration is the guiding principle in the division of competencies between the Community and the member states and the only justification for delegating supranational powers to the European institutions.[2]

However, even the EEC Treaty contains several interventionist elements, most strikingly in the articles dealing with the common agricultural policy (CAP). The objectives of the CAP, as defined in the treaty, are complex and partly contradictory: to increase agricultural productivity; to ensure a fair standard of living for the agricultural population (which at the time represented more than one-fifth of the total labor force in the six founding member states); to stabilize markets; and to ensure regular supplies and reasonable consumer prices. More realistically, the European Court of Justice (ECJ) has interpreted the CAP objectives so as to give priority to maintaining farmers' income over increasing agricultural productivity or ensuring reasonable prices for consumers. Thus the Court has recognized the essentially redistributive character of the policy, which currently absorbs about 50 percent of all budget expenditures of the Union (down from about 75 percent in 1980).

These redistributive objectives are pursued by a variety of *dirigistic* and protectionistic means. The operational core of the CAP is the common organization of the markets for specific products, based on the instruments of common prices, Community preferences, and financial transfers. In addition to market organizations for specific products, horizontal regulations applying to all products have been adopted by the European Commission with regard to common questions such as licenses and export levies.

To understand the exceptional status of the CAP with respect to the general philosophy of the Rome Treaty, one must keep in mind that in postwar western Europe "agriculture became the equivalent of a large nationalized industry, managed by interventionist policies which sought to impose macroeconomic objectives in return for exemptions from the forces of open economic competition."[3] According to the same author, although agriculture was the most vulnerable of all elements in the postwar consensus, it has proved to be one of the most durable elements of that consensus, precisely because of its Europeanization: "The Common Agricultural Policy has lumbered on like some clumsy prehistoric mastodon, incapable of

2. Sauter (1995).
3. Milward (1992, p. 229).

evolution into the present world where the political influence of agriculture on parliamentary systems is small indeed, an awesome reminder of the strength which integration could add to the rescue of the nation-state."[4] In this connection, it should be noted that the way the policy developed did not correspond at all to the original proposals of the European Commission, which had envisaged a limited, self-financing, relatively low-price regime.[5]

The CAP is the most obvious, but not the only, sign of the influence of interventionist philosophies on the EEC Treaty. That influence can be detected even in the competition rules of the treaty. Thus article 85 deems inconsistent with the common market "all agreements between firms ... and all concerted practices likely to affect trade between Member States." As Frederic Scherer observes, the reference to "all agreements" has the ring of the per se prohibitions embodied in judicial interpretations of America's Sherman Anti-Trust Act.[6] However, article 85 goes on to permit exceptions for agreements and concerted practices that contribute "towards improving the production or distribution of goods or promoting technical or economic progress."

Despite such lapses from doctrinal purity, the interpretation of the Treaty of Rome as an economic constitution based on the separation of politics and economics is fundamentally correct. Additional supporting evidence is provided by the fact that the EEC Treaty, in contrast to the ECSC and Euratom treaties, does not include a common industrial policy. This omission suggests that the framers of the treaty considered a European industrial policy to be incompatible with a liberal economic constitution, while the rules on competition and on state aid were adequate to deal with the distortions that resulted from the industrial policies of the member states.[7] As will be seen later in this chapter, legal, judicial, and policy developments in the 1980s further emphasized the elements of economic liberalism inherent in the Rome Treaty. Recently, however, the separation of politics and economics has again been challenged in the name of "economic and social cohesion."

4. Milward (1992, p. 317).
5. Moravcsik (1993).
6. Scherer (1994, p. 35).
7. Sauter (1995).

A European Social Policy?

The advocates of a European welfare state, or at least of a significant role for the EU in transnational redistribution, are generally motivated by a historical analogy but particularly by concerns about the future of social entitlements in an integrated European economy. The analogy is to the integrative role of social policy in the formation of the nation-state in nineteenth-century Europe. Historically, social policy has made an essential contribution to the process of nation building by bridging the gap between state and society. It is argued that a supranational welfare state would provide an equally strong demonstration of Europe-wide solidarity. However, the very success of the national welfare state sets limits to an expanded social policy competence for the Union.[8]

The reluctance of the member states to surrender control of such a politically sensitive area of public policy explains the very modest role of social policy in the process of European integration. It is also likely that the development of welfare state institutions at EU level would reinforce popular feelings against centralization, bureaucratization, and technocratic management. Indeed the experience of both New Deal America and the European welfare states proves beyond doubt that the expansion of the redistributive function of the state has been one of the main causes of political and administrative centralization. On the other hand, the delicate value judgments about the appropriate balance of efficiency and equity that social policies express can be made legitimately only within national communities. It is difficult to see how politically acceptable levels of income redistribution could be determined centrally in a system of nation-states where political, legal, and economic conditions are still so different.

Again, since historic social and linguistic barriers reduce the mobility of European society, the diversity in state welfare policies is unlikely to produce the American phenomenon of "welfare magnets"—states with high benefits that attract the poor from other states.[9] Also for this reason, therefore, the case for harmonizing welfare standards at the EU level is weak.

8. Leibfried and Pierson (1995).
9. Peterson and Rom (1990).

According to some scholars, the recent impressive growth of resources allocated to the poorer regions of the EU proves that even if a full-fledged European welfare state is, at present, politically and economically unfeasible, it is at least possible to develop certain of its elements.[10] However, this argument overlooks the important distinction between reducing inequality among individuals and reducing disparities across regions. Since most regions contain a mix of poor and better-off people, a program aimed at redistributing resources to a region whose average income is low may simply result in a lowering of the tax rate and/or in a substantial increase in the number of well-paid jobs for the middle class. The main beneficiaries of the program will thus be rich individuals and members of the middle class rather than the poor—a phenomenon well known in developing countries and also in the Italian *Mezzogiorno*.

In sum, the regional programs of the EU should be viewed as side payments in larger intergovernmental bargains rather than as elements of a developing supranational welfare state or as a demonstration of Europe-wide solidarity. More precisely, interregional transfers are best understood as incentive-efficient mechanisms in the sense intended by Paul Milgrom and John Roberts; that is, as incentives to induce reluctant member states to support efficiency-enhancing policies such as the completion of the internal market or monetary union.[11]

If regional policy is, at best, an inefficient method for achieving a more equal redistribution of income at the individual level, the common agricultural policy has almost completely failed to meet earlier expectations regarding its redistributive role. Actually, the CAP has contributed through its operation to the worsening of regional and income inequalities inside the EC/EU. This, as Loukas Tsoukalis notes, was the unavoidable result of a policy that relied for years on price supports for unlimited quantities, thus favoring the large and efficient producers.[12]

In sum, the experience of the EC/EU shows that large-scale redistribution within a system of sovereign states is difficult and inefficient and also raises serious problems of democratic legitimacy.

10. See especially the collection of papers in Leibfried and Pierson (1995).
11. Milgrom and Roberts (1992).
12. Tsoukalis (1993, p. 267).

Moreover, it is wrong to assume, as many students of European integration do, that the increasing integration of national markets must eventually bring about common welfare policies and institutions. On the contrary, as long as the majority of Europeans reject a high level of political and administrative centralization, integration of national markets is only possible if efficiency and redistributive issues are carefully separated.

Market Integration and the Protection of Diffuse Interests

To say that the competencies of supranational institutions should be limited, by and large, to efficiency problems is not to suggest that noncommodity values must remain unprotected at the international level. Rather, efficient solutions are bound to balance economic and noncommodity values if the latter enter into the utility function of a sufficiently large number of people. In fact, the EC/EU has played an important and in some cases a pioneering role in environmental protection, consumer safety, equal rights for working men and women, and several other areas of social regulation.

It is important to note that while the member states have maintained their power to tax and spend, they have been quite willing to delegate far-reaching regulatory powers to the European level. In many cases, such powers extend well beyond the competencies assigned to the European institutions by the founding treaties and also beyond the functional needs of an increasingly integrated European market. For example, although environmental protection is not even mentioned in the Rome Treaty, well over 100 environmental regulations were introduced by the Commission and approved by the Council in the period from 1967 to 1987, when the Single European Act explicitly acknowledged the competence of the EC to legislate in this area.

Today European environmental regulation includes more than 200 pieces of legislation, and in many member states the corpus of environmental law of EC/EU origin outweighs that of purely domestic origin. Moreover, while the first environmental measures were for the most part concerned with *product* regulation and thus could be justified by the need to prevent the possibility that national standards would create nontariff barriers, later measures increasingly stressed *process* regulation (emission and ambient quality standards, control of waste disposal and land use, protection of flora and fauna, and so on), thus aiming explicitly at environmental rather than free-trade objectives.

Such regulatory growth appears all the more surprising in view of the fact that before the Maastricht Treaty, environmental regulations required unanimous approval by the Council of Ministers. Note that delegation to the supranational level was not the only strategy open to the member states. National governments could have responded to widespread concerns about environmental pollution in Europe by coordinating more closely their environmental policies. This is what they do in other important areas such as health, education, and social security. The problem with intergovernmental regulatory agreements, however, is that it is often difficult for the parties concerned to know whether or not the agreements are properly kept. In part, this is because regulatory enforcement involves a good deal of administrative discretion. In the case of an intergovernmental agreement about transboundary pollution, for example, national regulators will usually be unwilling to prosecute industrial polluters as rigorously if the level of enforcement is determined unilaterally rather than under supranational supervision. But when it is difficult to observe whether national governments are making an honest effort to enforce a cooperative agreement, the agreement is not credible. Hence the delegation of regulatory powers to a supranational authority like the European Commission is best understood as a means whereby the member states can commit themselves to regulatory strategies that would not be credible in the absence of such delegation.[13]

However, the delegation of rule-making authority to the European level has produced some consequences unanticipated by the national governments.[14] One of these unanticipated consequences is the development of an impressive body of legislation and judicial decisions protecting diffuse interests that lacked effective representation at the national level. Thus the European Commission and Court of Justice had considerable success in promoting and monitoring the rights of working women, forcing major revisions of na-

13. Gatsios and Seabright (1989).
14. Majone (1996).

tional practices.[15] Similarly, consumer-protection legislation and environmental regulation were poorly developed in many member states before the EC became active in these areas.

Political and institutional factors explain the different characteristics of domestic and European policies. On the one hand, because of the dominance of well-organized redistributive coalitions, European welfare states have historically favored producers—management, unionized workers, organized professions—at the expense of consumer welfare and individual rights. On the other hand, political systems characterized by party control of both executive and legislature, powerful central bureaucracies, and weak judicial review do not leave much room for either direct representation of diffuse interests or the emergence of independent policy entrepreneurs able to organize such interests.

The situation is quite different at the European level. The insulation of the Commission from partisan politics and the electoral cycle and its well-honed skills as a policy entrepreneur,[16] the activism of the Court of Justice, the interest of the European Parliament in finding a distinctive role of itself—all these factors explain why diffuse interests are generally better protected at the European than the national level. Note, too, that the small size of the EU budget (about 1.3 percent of the gross domestic product of the Union and less than 4 percent of the total expenditure of the central governments of the member states) severely limits the scope of redistributive programs. With the exception of agriculture and, more recently, regional aid, European policies do not provide a fertile ground for the growth of stable rent-seeking coalitions. Hence an apparent paradox: the same supranational institutions so often criticized for their lack of democratic legitimacy have become the guardians of diffuse interests that were long disregarded by the national welfare states.

From Harmonization to Mutual Recognition

The second part of this chapter examines the different strategies followed by the European institutions and the member states in

15. Ostner and Lewis (1995).
16. Majone (1996).

their search for a satisfactory equilibrium between the potentially conflicting requirements of market integration, the protection of diffuse interests, and the preservation of national sovereignty. A turning point is represented by the famous *Cassis de Dijon* decision of 1979. In this decision, the European Court of Justice determined that a member state could no longer prevent the marketing within its borders of a product lawfully manufactured and marketed in another member state. Current regulatory developments are still affected, in different and partly contradictory ways, by the *Cassis* judgment.

In 1992 the Treaty on European Union (Maastricht Treaty) added "subsidiarity" as another basic principle of regulatory policymaking in the EU. According to this principle, "the Community shall take action . . . only if and in so far as the objectives of the proposed action cannot be sufficiently achieved by the Member States and can therefore, by reason of the scale or effects of the proposed action, be better achieved by the Community."[17] The emphasis on subsidiarity in the EU Treaty reveals a widespread concern about the centralizing tendency of early modes of European policymaking. Contrary to the expectations of some member states, however, the logic of subsidiarity does not imply a renationalization of certain areas of policymaking but rather a larger role for subnational governments and also for new institutional arrangements independent of the national governments and even, to some extent, of the European authorities.

Before discussing future scenarios, however, we must examine recent policy developments. Since the early 1980s, the Commission has devoted a good deal of effort both to generalizing the principle of mutual recognition enunciated in the *Cassis* decision and to protecting consumers against the risks that an unconstrained application of the principle could entail. The 1985 White Paper on the completion of the internal market proposed a new approach to European regulation including, as one of its key elements, the strategy of mutual recognition of the rules, regulations, and standards of each member state by the other member states. The immediate reason for introducing this new strategy was to reduce the burden on the Commission of harmonizing national rules. Despite the impres-

---

17. Article 23b of the EU Treaty.

sive growth of Community regulation in the 1960s and 1970s, by 1985 the Commission had to acknowledge that the amount of work that remained to be done was such that the goal of completing the internal market by 1993 could not be achieved by relying exclusively on the traditional harmonization approach. In the words of the Commission, "Experience has shown that the alternative of relying on a strategy based totally on harmonization would be over-regulatory, would take a long time to implement, would be inflexible and could stifle innovation."[18]

Harmonization of national regulations had been the main objective of the European Community in its first twenty-five years. Harmonization is the adjustment of national rules to the requirements of a common market. Its characteristic instrument is the directive because this instrument specifies only the regulatory objectives to be achieved and leaves the choice of methods to the member states. This discretion, however, created persistent and pervasive implementation problems. In addition, it is easy to imagine the difficulties experienced by European regulators in attempting to harmonize the rules of six, nine, twelve, and finally fifteen countries with widely different legal, administrative, and political traditions.

The 1985 White Paper attempted to overcome the problems created by the traditional approach through a multipronged strategy: mutual recognition of national regulations and standards; legislative harmonization restricted, however, to laying down essential health and safety requirements obligatory on all member states; and gradual replacement of national product specifications by European standards issued by the Comité Européen de la Normalisation (CEN) or by sectoral European organizations such as the Committee for Electrotechnical Standardization CENELEC in the electrical sector and the European Telecommunications Standards Institute (ETSI) in the telecommunications sector. In essence, the White Paper proposed a conceptual distinction between matters where harmonization is essential and those where it is sufficient that there be mutual recognition of the equivalence of the various requirements laid down under national law. The rationale for mutual recognition is that, in the Commission's words, "the objectives of national legislation, such as the protection of human health and life and of the en-

18. Commission of the European Communities (1985, p. 18).

vironment, are more often than not identical," so that "the rules and controls developed to achieve these objectives, although they may take different forms, essentially come down to the same thing, and so should normally be accorded recognition in all Member States."[19]

To a large extent, the originality and value of the new approach depend on how the "essential requirements" are defined and on what is left to the sphere of mutual recognition of national rules or of voluntary technical norms. In the first practical application of the new approach (Directive 86/112 on simple pressure vessels), the Commission stated that the essential requirements should:

—create, after transformation into national law, legally binding obligations;

—grant the manufacturer the right to produce without following national or European standards, in which case the certification bodies should be able to check for conformity with the essential requirements;

—enable the Commission to confer on the European standards organizations mandates that are sufficiently precise.

The logic of the distinction introduced by the new approach becomes clearer if one recalls the familiar distinction between *specification* standards and *performance* standards. A regulation prescribing that ladders must have rungs at least one inch in diameter is using a specification standard, while one mandating that the rungs must be capable of withstanding a certain maximum weight is creating a performance standard. A new type of ladder made of lighter but stronger material might be impermissible under the specification standard but acceptable under the performance standard.

In the field of technical standardization, the new approach consists to a large extent of the replacement of a multitude of specification standards by a few performance standards that a product must satisfy in order to secure the right of free movement throughout the common market. For example, the 1988 Toy Safety Directive does not tell the toy manufacturers how they should produce their toys. Instead, annex II of the directive sets out broad performance standards concerning matters such as the flammability and toxicity of the toy. These essential safety requirements may be met by two different methods. First, a toy can be made in accordance with CEN

19. Commission of the European Communities (1985, p. 18).

standards. Alternatively, the manufacturer can seek approval for a toy that does not conform to CEN standards but that nonetheless claims to meet the overall performance level. Specifications worked out by the experts at the CEN normally provide the easiest way of proving conformity with the performance standards defined in the directive. Innovation remains possible even if a manufacturer relies on such specifications, since (a) the specifications are nonbinding; and (b) given the nongovernmental nature of the CEN, they can be easily adapted to technical progress. Moreover, since harmonization is limited to the safety aspects of the product, national and regional diversity is successfully preserved in the framework of a European regulation.

The system is completed by the mutual recognition of testing and certification procedures. According to the jurisprudence of the European Court of Justice, products covered by a directive harmonizing the essential requirements are presumed to conform to the directive if the importer demonstrates the approval of a recognized certification body. Accepted types of certification (typically, certificates issued by recognized laboratories) are defined in each directive. Thanks to the mutual recognition of certificates, products can circulate freely in the market of another member state on the basis of a single certificate issued in the country of production. At the same time, the Commission attempts to improve the quality of national certification bodies. Approved bodies must satisfy minimal requirements in terms of personnel, technical and financial resources, basic infrastructure, and so on.

Mutual Recognition in Practice

The new regulatory philosophy, initially developed for the free movement of goods, has also been applied to the free movement of services. A good illustration is provided by the important Second Banking Directive of 1989, which contains the leading principles of EU supervisory banking law. The directive is based on four principles:

—Harmonization of essential standards for prudential supervision;

—Mutual recognition of the way in which each member state applies those standards;

—Based on the first two principles, home-country control and supervision of credit institutions operating in other member states;

—Pursuant to the principle of home-country control, a single license for credit institutions granted by the home country and valid throughout the EU.

In addition, the directive lists permissible banking activities. The list is very broad, including activities such as dealing in and underwriting securities, and can be updated by the Commission to reflect the emergence of new banking services. As an important consequence of the new approach, there is no central European authority for the supervision of credit institutions: the control of banking business is to be carried out, to a large extent, by the national authorities. For certain issues, however, the directive additionally provides for cooperative solutions that include the member states' authorities as well as the Commission.

The most striking innovation introduced by the Second Banking Directive is the EU-wide control of a credit institution by its home-country authority. As a result, the competencies of national authorities have been considerably expanded, as they cover not only the domestic activities of credit institutions but also their business in other member states. This shows that the principle of mutual recognition, even though it does not involve the transfer of regulatory powers to the European level, does nonetheless challenge national sovereignty in the economic sphere by forcing the member states to accept a plurality of legal orderings within their own territory. Such legal pluralism was well known to medieval lawyers, who were accustomed to deal with overlapping systems of church, royal, merchant, and urban law, but is quite foreign to the principles of omni-competence and unrestricted territorial sovereignty on which the modern nation-state is based. Actually, it could be argued that the traditional method of harmonizing national laws, as practiced in pre–*Cassis de Dijon* days, posed a less serious threat to the received view of national sovereignty than mutual recognition and its corollaries, such as the principle of home-country control.

Article 18 of the Second Banking Directive requires member states to recognize that the competent authority of the home-member state shall be responsible for the prudential supervision of credit institutions—excluding, however, certain matters that remain within the responsibility of the authorities of the host-member state, in particular the liquidity of branches and measures to implement monetary policy. Thus this article introduces the principle of mutual recognition in two specific areas: authorization and prudential supervision. Host-member states may no longer require authorization for branches (as distinct from subsidiaries) of credit institutions already licensed in another member state. The single-license principle is meant to allow credit institutions to spread a network of branches throughout the Union. Branching in other member states should be comparable to domestic branching; however, a considerable amount of information has to be submitted to the home-country authority, which communicates the proposed establishment to the host country within three months. Within two months of receipt, the host-state authorities are obliged to prepare for the supervision of the credit institution, in accordance with article 21 of the directive. They shall, if necessary, indicate the conditions under which those activities are to be carried out in the host-member state.

Finally, the host-country authority has to report any infringement of provisions subject to its competency, while the authority of the institution's home country must take the necessary steps to bring such infringement to an end. Only in urgent cases, or where the measures taken by the home-member state are inadequate, is the host country competent to enforce the termination of the irregularities.

The twin principles of mutual recognition and prudential supervision by the authorities of the country of origin also inspired a group of recent directives regulating insurance and investment services: Directives 92/49 and 92/96 on nonlife and life insurance, and Directive 93/22 on investment services. Their underlying philosophy is that every supplier of services legally established in one member state may pursue his or her professional activity in all other member states provided he or she follows European rules and those of the country of origin. The supplier is free to do so either by establishing branches in other countries or through the free provision of services across national borders. The EU limits itself to establishing uniform rules to protect the basic economic interests of consumers, notably in the areas of capital adequacy and solvency. At the same time, the host state loses its autonomous power to control professional activities coming from other member states: regulatory responsibility for the entire territory is vested in the regulator of the country of origin.

It is clear that such an arrangement may create problems for the protection of consumers in the host country. In recognition of this possibility, article 31 of Directive 92/49 requires an insurance company to inform policyholders about the applicable contract law and about arrangements for the handling of complaints. Directive 92/96 goes even further: it contains a right of cancellation for policyholders fourteen to thirty days after conclusion of the contract and imposes certain information obligations concerning such items as the means of terminating the contract, means of payment of premiums and duration of payments, the extent to which benefits are guaranteed, the premiums for each benefit, the tax arrangements applicable to the type of policy, and so on.

The principle of mutual recognition also has been applied to the difficult area of professional mobility. In the 1970s, the Commission had proposed sectoral directives meant to facilitate professional mobility by harmonizing the conditions for access to, and the exercise of, various professions. This approach was relatively successful for the medical and paramedical professions, but little progress was made in other areas such as law, architecture, engineering, and the pharmaceutical profession. The new strategy outlined in the 1985 White Paper aimed at a general (rather than sectoral) system of recognition based on the following elements:

—The principle of mutual trust between the member states;

—The principle of comparability of university studies between the member states;

—Mutual recognition of degrees and diplomas without prior harmonization of the conditions for access to, and the exercise of, professions;

—The extension of the general system to salary earners.

These principles find concrete application in Directive 89/48 on "a general system for the recognition of higher education diplomas awarded on completion of vocational courses of at least three years' duration." The system introduced by the directive is general in the sense that it applies to all "regulated" professions and to employed professionals as well as to the self-employed, and that it deals with both entry into and the exercise of a profession. Unlike the older sectoral directives, the new directive does not attempt to harmonize the length and subject matters of professional education or even the range of activities in which professionals can engage. It is well known that all these factors vary considerably from country to country. Instead, the directive introduces a system by which the states can compensate for such differences, without restricting the freedom of movement of professionals. Thus if in country A training for a certain profession is shorter by at least one year than in country B, the latter can require that an applicant from country A have practical professional experience in addition to formal education; the required professional experience cannot, however, exceed four years.

If the differences concern not the length but the contents of the professional curriculum, the host country can demand that the applicant take a test or else acquire practical experience for a period not exceeding three years. The applicant is free to choose between these two "compensation methods," while the competent authority of the host country has the burden of showing in detail the deficiencies in the diploma of the applicant. The procedure must be concluded within four months and end with a reasoned decision that may be appealed in the courts of the host-member state.

Directive 89/48 creates, for the first time in Europe, a single market for the regulated professions. A member state no longer can deny access to, or the exercise of, a regulated profession on its territory to EU citizens who already exercise or could legitimately exercise the same profession in another member state. In addition to facilitating professional mobility, the directive helps raise the level of professional education throughout the Union. This is because the citizens of a country that does not regulate adequately a certain profession are at a competitive disadvantage if they wish to use their professional skills beyond the national borders. There are indications that professional education and regulation are already changing in several countries in anticipation of greater professional mobility in the future.

Regulatory Competition

As the above examples suggest, mutual recognition provides a framework of general rules within which different regulatory approaches can compete. Competition is an efficient way of assessing the costs and benefits not only of goods and services but also of different methods of regulation. By providing opportunities for experimentation and policy learning, competition among rules can raise the standard of all regulation and drive out rules that offer protection consumers do not in fact require. The end result is *ex post*, or bottom-up, harmonization achieved through market-like processes rather than through imposition by public authorities as in the case of *ex ante*, or top-down, harmonization.

Ex ante harmonization may still be needed in order to avoid excessive competition among rules or a race to the bottom leading to a general deterioration of health, safety, or prudential standards; but, as we saw, it should be limited to a few essential requirements and should clearly distinguish between policy objectives and means for achieving such objectives.

However, it is important to recognize that mutual recognition makes heavy demands on the good faith and loyal cooperation of the national governments. An American scholar has rightly observed that the principle presupposes a higher degree of comity among the member states of the EU than the commerce clause of the U.S. Constitution requires among individual American states. The commerce clause has been interpreted by the U.S. Supreme Court as allowing each state to insist on its own quality standards for goods and services unless the subject matter has been preempted by federal legislation or unless state standards would unduly burden interstate commerce.[20] The European Court of Justice (ECJ), for its part, has required the member states to acknowledge the validity within their borders of safety and prudential standards emanating from different legal systems.

Such a complex system of overlapping jurisdictions cannot operate without mutual trust and loyal cooperation. That is why the Commission listed mutual trust as the first element of the new approach for the mutual recognition of diplomas. Article 5 of the Rome Treaty requires member states to "take all appropriate measures ... to ensure fulfillment of the obligations arising out of this treaty or resulting from action taken by the institutions of the Community" and to abstain from any measure that could jeopardize the attainment of the objectives of the treaty.

20. Hufbauer (1990).

The ECJ has interpreted article 5, going well beyond the principle of international law that *pacta sunt servanda* (pacts must be kept), in a way that approaches the principle of *Bundestreue*, or federal comity, in German constitutional law.[21] In the interpretation of the Court, this article of the treaty imposes a duty of mutual trust and loyal cooperation not only between member states and European institutions but also among national governments and administrative institutions.

Unfortunately, this normative principle is often violated in practice. An illuminating example is provided by the failure of early attempts to harmonize national regulations for the approval of new medical drugs. The old procedure included a set of harmonized criteria for testing new products and the mutual recognition of toxicological and clinical trials, provided they were conducted according to EC rules. In order to speed up the process of mutual recognition, a multistate drug application procedure (MSAP) was introduced in 1975. Under the MSAP, a company that had received a marketing authorization from the regulatory agency of a member state could ask for mutual recognition of that approval by at least five other countries. The agencies of the countries nominated by the company had to approve or raise objections within 120 days. In case of objections, the Committee for Proprietary Medicinal Products (CPMP)— a group that includes experts from member states and Commission representatives—had to be notified. The CPMP would express its opinion within 60 days and could be overruled by the national agency that had raised objections.

The procedure did not work well. Actual decision times were much longer than those prescribed by the 1975 directive, and national regulators did not appear to be bound either by decisions of other regulatory bodies or by the opinions of the CPMP. Because of these disappointing results the procedure was revised in 1983. Now only two countries had to be nominated in order to be able to apply for a multistate approval. But even the new procedure did not succeed in streamlining the approval process since national regulators continued to raise objections against each other almost routinely.[22] These difficulties finally induced the Commission, with the full sup-

---

21. Due (1992).
22. Kaufer (1990).

port of the European pharmaceutical industry, to propose the establishment of a European Agency for the Evaluation of Medicinal Products and the creation of a new centralized procedure. Compulsory for biotechnology products and certain types of veterinary medicines and available on an optional basis for other products, the procedure would lead to EU-wide authorization. Both the agency and the centralized procedure have been established by Council Regulation 2309/93 of July 22, 1993.

In an interesting paper on the political economy of centralization, Roland Vaubel examines several variables that may explain why most federal states have experienced a secular trend toward centralization. He shows that many influential political actors are interested in bringing about a more centralized system of government than is warranted on efficiency grounds: federal legislators; political executives and bureaucrats; federal judges; pressure groups representing regionally homogeneous interests; even politicians and bureaucrats operating at lower levels of government, since expansion of the central government need not be at the expense of the lower-level governments.[23] The example just given and many others that could be chosen from both recent EC/EU history and from the history of mature federal systems show that the trend toward greater centralization may also be explained by motivation factors such as lack of trust and of incentives to cooperate loyally.

Another factor not sufficiently considered by the advocates of subsidiarity and mutual recognition is the possibility that lower-level governments use regulations strategically, that is, to benefit their own jurisdiction at the expense of other jurisdictions. Such a possibility arises even in the case of purely local market failures. For instance, problems of safety regulation in the construction of local buildings create no transboundary externalities and thus, according to the principle of subsidiarity, should be left to the local authorities. However, if safety regulations specify a particular building material produced only in that locality, they amount to a nontariff barrier and thus have negative effects on interstate or international trade. Hence local regulation of a local market failure may create an international policy externality. Similarly, local authorities have sometimes controlled air pollution by requiring extremely tall smoke-

23. Vaubel (1994).

stacks on industrial facilities. With tall stacks, by the time the emissions descend to ground level they are usually in the next city, region, or country and so of no concern to the jurisdiction where they were emitted.

Thus every multilevel system of government faces a serious dilemma. Local governments are more attuned to individual preferences, but they are unlikely to make a clear separation between providing public goods to their citizens and engaging in policies designed to advantage their jurisdiction at the expense of their neighbors.[24] Centralization of regulatory authority at a higher level of government can correct such negative policy externalities, but its cost is the homogenization of policy across jurisdictions that may be dissimilar with respect to underlying preferences or needs.

The history of European integration provides a clear illustration of this dilemma of regulatory federalism. For more than two decades, the Commission tried to achieve market integration by means of harmonizing directives that effectively replace national regulations. As we saw, the 1985 White Paper recognized that a strategy based wholly on harmonization was overregulatory and too insensitive to national and regional differences. Hence the decision to rely extensively on mutual recognition, restricting harmonization to essential health, safety, and prudential requirements. Problems remain, however, as shown by the failure of the decentralized process for the EC-wide approval of new medical drugs and the subsequent centralization of testing procedures in the new European Agency for the Evaluation of Medicinal Products.

I argue that the problems are caused, at least in part, by the tendency of national and subnational governments to use regulation strategically. Decentralized procedures would be more credible if regulators were free to decide issues on their merit rather than on grounds of political expediency. Also, close cooperation among politically independent regulators would reduce the need for top-down harmonization at the European level. There are indications that this is the direction regulatory reform in the EU is now taking.

24. Noll (1990).

Transnational Regulatory Networks

The rise of regulatory agencies operating outside the line of hierarchical control or oversight by the central administration is a new phenomenon in Europe.[25] Hence the independence of such agencies still lacks a clear legal basis. Even if national regulators are personally committed to the statutory objectives assigned to their agency, that commitment lacks credibility as long as the agency remains isolated and politically too weak to withstand ministerial interference.

However, commitments may be strengthened through teamwork. Although people may be weak on their own, they can build resolve by forming a group or network.[26] Similarly, a regulatory agency that sees itself as part of a transnational network of institutions pursuing similar objectives and facing analogous problems, rather than as a new and often marginal addition to a huge central bureaucracy, is more motivated to resist political pressures. Because the regulator has an incentive to maintain his or her reputation in the eyes of fellow regulators in other countries, a politically motivated decision would compromise the regulator's credibility and make cooperation more difficult to achieve in the future.

The European system of central banks, as outlined in the Maastricht Treaty, provides one example of a highly formalized transnational network. More informal networks are emerging in other policy areas. The Commission's Competition Directorate (DG IV) recently initiated a decentralization project with the long-term goal of having one European competition statute applied throughout the EU by a network including DG IV itself, national competition authorities, and national courts. Direct links already exist between Commission inspectors and national competition authorities concerning any investigation carried out by the Commission. Moreover, a high level of harmonization of national competition laws has already occurred spontaneously in the member states, while national competition authorities everywhere are becoming more professional and increasingly jealous of their independence.[27]

25. Majone (1994).
26. Dixit and Nalebuff (1991).
27. Laudati (1996).

A high level of professionalization is crucial to the viability of a transnational network model. Professionals are oriented by goals, standards of conduct, cognitive beliefs, and career opportunities that derive from their professional community and that give them strong reasons for resisting interference and directions from political outsiders.[28] In turn, political independence is important because basic ideological differences concerning, for example, the role of competition principles in economic policy are likely to persist among the member states. However, such differences are much less pronounced among professional competition regulators from different countries, just as the commitment to price stability tends to be stronger among central bankers from different countries than among a random sample of politicians from the same country. Without a common basis of shared beliefs and commitments, a cooperative partnership of national and supranational regulators could not function effectively.

There is no reason why the network model, given the right conditions, could not be extended to other areas of economic and social regulation and indeed to all administrative activities where mutual trust and reputation are the key to greater effectiveness. An example of the latter type is the emerging pattern of coordinated partnership between the EU statistical office, Eurostat, and the national statistical offices of the member states.[29] The heads of the national offices see the partnership as a means of protecting the professional integrity of their organizations from politically motivated interference.

Another indication of the same trend came from a meeting of the Council of the Ministers of the Environment in 1991. It was agreed that member states should establish an informal network of national enforcement offices concerned with environmental law. Moreover, the recent creation of a number of specialized European agencies may be seen as a significant step in the same direction.[30] The list of the new bodies includes, in addition to the European Monetary Institute (the forerunner of the European Central Bank), the European Environmental Agency, the Office of Veterinary and Phytosanitary Inspection and Control, the European Centre for the

28. Moe (1987).
29. McLennan (1995).
30. *Agence Europe* 6098 (October 31, 1993).

Control of Drugs and Drug Addiction, the European Agency for the Evaluation of Medicinal Products, and the European Agency for Health and Safety at Work. These bodies are not (yet) full-fledged regulatory agencies. They neither make nor implement regulatory policies. For the time being, their functions are essentially limited to the collection, processing, and dissemination of policy-relevant data and information.

The future activities of the agencies need not be limited to such functions, however. First, the need to develop uniform assessment criteria for monitoring the implementation of Community regulations is at least as urgent as the development of common methodologies of data collection and analysis. Such matters can only be partially addressed in the formal texts of European legislation. Rather the development of criteria for monitoring implementation is a task that only the new agencies can adequately perform.

Second, these agencies cannot be the passive and uncritical receivers of data supplied by the national administrations. Sooner or later their offices will have to be given powers to visit member states to verify the accuracy and consistency of the methods followed by national and subnational governments.

Finally, as the House of Lords Select Committee on the European Communities argued in its 1992 report *Implementation and Enforcement of Environmental Legislation* , a strong case exists for some form of Community oversight of the measures taken by the member states to monitor and enforce compliance.[31] In fact, common regulations lose credibility if they are not consistently implemented throughout the EU. Hence the Committee suggested the creation of an "audit" inspectorate to examine the policies and performance of national authorities—rather than seeking to supplant them—and publicly report its findings to the member states, the Commission, and the European Parliament. Such an "inspectorate of inspectorates" would also report on shortcomings in administrative arrangements, such as inadequacies of training or resources that lead to insufficient regulatory activity.

The Committee rightly insists that these functions and powers should be formally distinguished from the Commission's own duty to enforce Community policies in the event of failure to do so by the member states. Thus the environmental inspectorate should not be

31. House of Lords (1992).

part of DG XI, the Commission's directorate responsible for environmental law. Rather the "logical home for an environmental inspectorate on the lines indicated is the European Environmental Agency, with whose functions the inspectorate would neatly dovetail."[32]

The transformation of the new European agencies into full-fledged regulatory bodies would have a number of significant advantages. It would limit the growth in size of the Commission, despite an expanding EU membership. Although the Commission would retain all the political responsibilities entrusted to it by the treaties, technical tasks would be delegated to the agencies. The latter would not operate in a political and institutional vacuum. National and EU representatives and experts would sit on the Management Board and on the Scientific Committee of each agency, as they already do now. The Management Board, whose task it is to provide strategic guidance to the agency, would comprise, as at present, one person from each country with membership in the agency as well as representatives from the Commission and the European Parliament. Note that membership in the agencies is already open to European countries that are not yet members of the EU. Thus Hungary, Poland, and the Czech Republic already take active part in the work of the European Environmental Agency. Finally, each European agency would operate in close partnership with the corresponding national regulatory bodies; indeed, it would form the central node of a regulatory network extending even beyond the borders of the European Union.

In sum, there are good reasons to believe that regulatory policy in Europe will be increasingly developed and implemented by specialized transnational networks, independent from both national governments and central European institutions, at least in their day-to-day decisionmaking.

Conclusions

Despite repeated setbacks and lingering problems, the EC/EU has achieved results that even optimists would have considered unattainable a few decades ago. The integration of national markets

32. House of Lords (1992, p. 41).

divided not only by history and geography but even more by protectionist legislation, by national monopolies and cartels, and by the state-centered politics of rent-seeking coalitions is, of course, an achievement of epochal significance. Yet the single market is not the only, and in the long run perhaps not even the most important, result of European integration.

For the first time since the model of state sovereignty that emerged after the peace of Westphalia (1648), Europeans live in a polity characterized by legal pluralism, multiple competing centers of authority, and the dispersion of state functions formerly concentrated at a single location.[33] The loosening of the Westphalian model has provided unprecedented opportunities for institutional and regulatory competition, policy learning, and the protection of individual rights and diffuse interests.

I have argued that market integration, and its economic and noneconomic consequences, have been made possible by a far-reaching depoliticization of transnational economic relations. As the framers of the economic constitution of Europe clearly saw, only in this way could market integration coexist with national sovereignty. Hence they reintroduced at the supranational level the liberal principle of the separation of politics and economics—and its corollary, the separation of efficiency and redistributive issues—that the interventionist welfare state had rejected at the national level.

Given the ideological temper of the decades immediately following the end of the Second World War, it is not surprising that this principle was not always consistently applied. The costs of this inconsistency are revealed, for example, by the failure of the major redistributive program of the Union, the common agricultural policy. However, the likely reform of the CAP, made necessary by the enlargement of the Union in Eastern Europe, will vindicate the wisdom of the original insight. Farm support will be treated as income support, with much of the cost falling on national budgets, and the Commission will assume the role it has always played in other policy areas, namely, monitoring national aid programs to see that they do not lead to subsidized competition.

33. Caporaso (1996).

Now, the separation of politics and economics has been achieved by means of two key strategies: first, by restricting the freedom of member states to intervene in national economies when such interventions interfered with the smooth functioning of the single European market; and second, by delegating extensive powers of rule-making and adjudication to supranational institutions enjoying a considerable degree of independence from the national governments as well as from the European Parliament. Although the first strategy, also known as "negative integration," does not pose any serious normative problem (the member states having freely accepted the rules of the game), the delegation of important regulatory powers to nonelected (or "nonmajoritarian") institutions immediately raises the issue of democratic accountability.

As already mentioned, the "democratic deficit" of the European institutions, and especially of the Commission, is a recurrent theme in the debate on European integration. The problem is quite general, however, and is becoming increasingly important as the integration of the world economy leads to the creation of international agencies with regulatory responsibilities. For example, the issue of democratic accountability has figured prominently in the arguments of U.S. environmentalists and other groups opposed to the North American Free Trade Agreement and again in connection with the establishment of the World Trade Organization. The legitimacy of European and international standardization bodies has also been repeatedly questioned.

An adequate discussion of the legitimacy problem of nonmajoritarian institutions, whether national or international, would require another chapter. Here I can only attempt to sketch, by way of conclusion, the outline of a possible solution. To begin with, note that the problem is, by definition, insoluble if one assumes that the only standard of legitimacy is the one derived from the pure or "Westminster" model of majoritarian democracy—direct accountability to the voters or to their elected representatives. In practice, however, it has always been understood that for many purposes, reliance upon qualities such as expertise, professionalism, policy continuity, or fairness is more important than reliance upon direct political accountability. In order to define such purposes more precisely, we have to go back to the fundamental distinction between efficiency and redistribution. Redistributive issues, I argue, are inherently political, and hence cannot be delegated to independent experts. Like other issues over which there is unavoidable conflict, redistributive issues can only be settled, in a democracy, by majority vote. This is the theoretical reason for asserting earlier that the assignment of redistributive functions to a technocratic body like the European Commission raises serious questions of democratic legitimacy. The same argument holds a fortiori for international agencies such as the World Trade Organization.

Efficiency problems, on the other hand, may be thought of as positive-sum games in which everybody can gain, although some people may gain more than others. Here the objective is not to favor one group of individuals, regions, or countries at the expense of another group but to find solutions that increase aggregate welfare. Hence the search for efficient solutions may be delegated to independent experts as long as the delegation is sufficiently precise to make accountability by results possible. When this condition is met and procedural requirements to ensure transparency and some form of judicial review are present, political independence and democratic accountability can be complementary and mutually supporting, rather than antithetical, values.

The possibility of separating, not only conceptually but also institutionally, the efficiency and redistributive aspects of public problems is arguably the greatest advantage of delegating certain decisionmaking powers to independent supranational bodies. Thus the distance of the European Commission from narrow sectional interests and its insulation from domestic politics explain why it is sometimes possible in Brussels to reach efficient solutions that powerful redistributive coalitions had blocked for a long time at the national level.

Conversely, the discontent produced by the attempt to pursue redistributive objectives at the European level, as in the case of agriculture, demonstrates the serious consequences of the failure to match correctly the level of governance with the nature of the problem at hand.

Chapter 4

Social Policy and European Integration

Paul Pierson

Debates over the complex relationship between the process of European integration and the evolution of social policy often generate more heat than light. On the one hand, there has been intense focus on the European Union's efforts to develop a "social dimension." National actors often suggest that matters of fundamental importance are at stake in struggles over the details of proposed legislation. On the other hand, most accounts of European social policy present a minimalist interpretation of European Union (EU) involvement.[1] Although the EU has become a central site for policymaking in diverse arenas, the welfare state is typically regarded as an area where national policy systems remain intact. Thus conventional wisdom holds that in contrast to most areas of government activity, the welfare state remains essentially national.

Much depends, however, on one's baseline for comparison. Relative to the scope of national social policy regimes, European Union social policy structures remain extremely rudimentary. Furthermore, compared with European Union activity in areas such as trade, industrial policy, or agriculture, the EU's social policy activity is also limited. Yet the conventional wisdom errs in suggesting that despite its great economic and political significance, the welfare state can remain largely insulated from the dramatic process of

1. DeSwaan (1992, 1994); Lange (1992).

European integration. Like other aspects of national polities, welfare states are now caught up in a loose, fragmented, but increasingly interdependent and multilevel system of European governance. I argue that the new linkages between national social policies and the EU operate in two directions. On the one hand, the character of social policy is increasingly influenced and constrained by developments "from above"—that is, at the EU level. At the same time, and somewhat more speculatively, I suggest that efforts to restructure national systems of social provision to cope with the mounting fiscal pressures confronting all welfare states will have increasing implications for the development of the EU.

European Integration and the Development of Social Policy

National welfare states remain the primary institutions of European social policy.[2] Moreover, the quite extensive barriers to EU action have prevented, and will continue to prevent, any true federalization of European social policy. Images of a potential European welfare state should be laid to rest. Yet at the same time, the dynamics of creating a single market do make it increasingly difficult to exclude social issues from the EU's agenda. The process of European integration has eroded both the *sovereignty* (that is, legal authority) and *autonomy* (de facto capacity) of member states in the realm of social policy. Many of these constraints unfold only as the process of integration moves forward, and many of the implications for social policy are indirect or must be tracked through their distinctive effects on particular programs in each of the EU's fifteen member states. For all these reasons, it is difficult to gauge the magnitude of the European Union's impact. Nonetheless, a balanced appraisal of European social policy must simultaneously acknowledge both the weak capacity for centrally guided initiatives and the growing role of the European Union in constraining national policy options.

---

2. This section provides a condensed and revised version of arguments originally developed in Leibfried and Pierson (1995).

Why Social Policy Remains Primarily National

The list of obstacles to an activist social policy at the EU level is long and must be underlined. Among the most important factors circumscribing new initiatives are the preexistence of distinctive national welfare states, the skepticism of member states concerning European endeavors in this realm, the unfavorable balance of power among social actors, and the institutional constraints operative in EU decisionmaking. Each of these points requires further elaboration.

EU policy is made in the context of an extensive, diverse array of preexisting, territorially based social policies. Each member state of the European Union has its own welfare state; its patterns of intervention in the lives of its citizens are already well established. These preexisting policy structures pose considerable barriers to an expanded social policy competence at the EU level. First, the sheer diversity of national regimes makes any simple process of harmonization unthinkable. In 1991 expenditures on social protection ranged from 19.4 percent of gross domestic product (GDP) in Portugal to 32.4 percent in the Netherlands. German spending per capita was four and a half times the Portuguese level in 1992. These aggregate statistics, while striking, only hint at the true diversity of national social policy regimes. Even similar overall expenditure levels may mask major differences in how money is spent. In 1992 Italy devoted 63 percent of its social protection budget to pensions, while the pension share in Ireland was only 27 percent. Greece spent less than 2 percent of its social protection budget on family and maternity policies, while Denmark spent 12 percent.[3]

The differences among national policy structures make any attempt at social policy integration exceptionally difficult. The Single European Act (SEA) facilitated the creation of an integrated market for goods and services by introducing the principle of mutual recognition. This success, however, was predicated on lowest-common-denominator, deregulatory policies—precisely the agenda most feared by advocates of a European social dimension. No simplifying rule similar to mutual recognition is likely to prove politically acceptable for social policy integration.

3. Eurostat (1996).

Exacerbating the barriers that structural diversity poses to European social policy integration is the sheer magnitude of national initiatives. In contrast to those pushing for the development of national welfare states in the nineteenth and early twentieth centuries, EU actors find that a great deal of the "space" for social policy is already occupied. Welfare state development was often a central component of national state-building processes on the Continent, promoting both political legitimacy and centralized control over economic resources. Because of member-state preemptions, however, development in the European Union has not mirrored this process. The central components of national welfare states—provision of education, health care, and retirement security—are likely to remain primarily under direct national control. EU initiatives are most evident around the edges of these national cores, in policy domains that are unoccupied or that the integration process renders particularly fragile. Alternatively, redistributive programs may operate quietly, under the cover of policy initiatives somewhat remote from traditional social policy; important examples are the common agricultural policy (CAP) and regional policy.

The EU's limited resources constitute a further barrier to legislative action. National programs preempt not only policy space but administrative and fiscal space. The EU lacks the administrative capacity to implement ambitious policies without turning to national bureaucracies. Any system of extensive service provision or individualized transfers would have to rely heavily on existing structures of national administration. The EU is similarly constrained fiscally. EU expenditures represent a little more than 1 percent of the European Community's gross national product and less than 4 percent of the central government spending of member states. Furthermore, the CAP and the structural funds preempt over 80 percent of EU expenditures. In short, the preexisting structures of national welfare states leave EU policymakers with a weak administrative and fiscal base and with limited access to core welfare state functions.

Institutional arrangements create further barriers to policy activity. EU institutions make it much easier to block reforms than to enact them. Rules governing social policy in particular have generally offered only narrow, market-related openings for legislation. Even on this limited terrain, moreover, reform requires a qualified majority. Assembling such a broad consensus is extremely difficult. The member states themselves, which serve as gatekeepers for initiatives that require Council approval, have jealously guarded their social policy prerogatives. Economic and geopolitical changes since the Second World War have gradually diminished the scope of national sovereignty in a variety of domains. The welfare state remains one of the few key realms of policy competence where national governments still appear to reign supreme. Given the popularity of most social programs, national executives have generally resisted losses of social policy authority. Even where some states do see the need for coordinated action, assembling a favorable coalition is difficult. For instance, in the domain of social policy the EU often exhibits sharp conflicts between the interests of high-wage and low-wage member states. These divisions among the member states make it difficult to reach a consensus on social policy.

A further barrier is the relative weakness of the social democratic forces most interested in a strong social dimension. Unions have lost influence in the past fifteen years in most of Europe, especially among the founding members of the EU. At the European level, organizational difficulties and profound conflicts of interest between high-wage and low-wage areas of the EU limit labor's influence. At the same time, business power has grown considerably, in part because of the increasing capital mobility that European integration has fostered. Thus the balance of power among social interests has further hindered efforts that institutional blockages, limited fiscal resources, and the tremendous difficulties of harmonizing widely divergent and deeply institutionalized national social policies would have rendered highly problematic in any event.

For all these reasons, national welfare states remain the primary sites of social policy initiatives. Nonetheless, I wish to argue that they do so in the context of increasing constraints from above. Much of this transformation has been missed because most discussions of social policy in the EU have focused on the high-profile but largely unsuccessful attempts to construct a "social dimension" of EU expenditures and, especially, regulations. Where the EU has become significant for social policy, however, this has been less the result of welfare state–building ambitions of Eurocrats than it is an indirect consequence of the effort to construct a single market.

The completion of the internal market produces growing pressures for the EU to invade the domain of social policy. The single-market initiative was based on a deregulatory agenda and assumed that initiatives to ensure free movement of goods, services, capital, and labor could be insulated from social policy issues, which would remain the provenance of member states. Yet for anyone familiar with the twentieth-century experience of the most developed mixed economies, this should have been recognized as a dubious assumption.[4] Already there is significant evidence that the tidy separation between "market issues" and "social issues" is unsustainable. Irrespective of the results of "high politics" struggles over social charters and treaty revisions, the movement toward market integration will carry with it a gradual erosion of national welfare state autonomy and sovereignty, increasingly embedding national regimes in a complex, multitiered web of social policy.

This transformation of sovereign welfare states into parts of a multitiered system of social policy occurs through three processes. "Positive," activist reform results from social policy initiatives taken at the "center" by the European Commission and Council of Ministers, along with the European Court of Justice's (ECJ) determinations of what those initiatives require. "Negative" reform occurs through the ECJ's imposition of "market compatibility requirements" that restrict and redefine the social policies of member states. Finally, the process of European integration creates a range of indirect pressures that do not legally require but nonetheless strongly encourage adaptations of national welfare states.

The Limited Success of Activist Social Policy

The European Commission's direct attempts to construct a significant social dimension—areas of social policy competence where uniform or at least minimum standards are set at the EU level—have occurred in fits and starts. It has been a saga of high aspirations and modest results, marked by cheap talk produced in the

4. It is worth noting that it runs directly contrary to the central tenets of political economy, which stresses precisely the embeddedness of economic action within dense networks of social and political institutions. Hall (1986); North (1990).

confident knowledge that the requirements of unanimous European Council votes meant that ambitious blueprints would remain unexecuted. This story has been well told elsewhere.[5] Here I review only the broadest outlines because the standard focus on these largely failed efforts to foist an activist social dimension on a reluctant Council presents a very partial view of what is happening. Where European integration has in fact eroded national welfare state sovereignty, this has occurred largely through quite different mechanisms.

Given the context described above—the diversity of national welfare states, the balance of power among social actors, the character of EU decision rules, the desire of member states to preserve discretion, and the conflicting interests among them—it is hardly surprising that the Council's substantive social policy enactments have occurred infrequently. That so much journalistic and academic ink has been spilled on the issue is more indicative of the nature of symbolic politics than the true prospects for anything like a European welfare state. Expansive visions of Community social policy have had far lower priority than initiatives for an integrated market.

Only in a few areas where the Treaty of Rome allowed more significant latitude—most notably through the gender equality provisions of article 119—has the EU legislated extensively. Even in this area, the European Court of Justice has played a crucial activist role, through its expansive interpretations of EU initiatives. To take just one example, ECJ decisions have had a dramatic impact on public and private pension schemes. The court's insistence on equal retirement ages in public pension systems forced Britain to level ages up or down. By choosing to raise the retirement age for women, the government will save billions of pounds while avoiding much of the blame for the lost benefits. When in the *Barber* case the ECJ made a similar ruling for occupational pensions, fear that the ruling might be applied retroactively to private pensions (at a cost estimated at up to £40 billion in Britain and 35 billion DM in Germany) fueled "what is probably the most intense lobbying campaign yet seen in Brussels."[6] Although this pressure led the Maastricht Treaty negotiators to explicitly limit retroactivity, the prospective impact of the

5. Mosley (1990); Streeck and Schmitter (1991); Lange (1992).
6. Mazey and Richardson (1993, p. 15).

court's rulings remains dramatic.[7] Even on gender issues, however, the market-oriented nature of the Community and its restricted focus on the paid labor market has tightly circumscribed the EU's interventions.

In the past decade, the institutional restrictions on social policy initiatives have loosened somewhat. The Single European Act's introduction of qualified majority voting in some domains has made social policy the focus of a sharp conflict, which Martin Rhodes has aptly dubbed the "treaty-base game."[8] There have been significant struggles to determine the range of issues that can be treated on a majority vote basis, either under article 100a (covering distortions of competition) or under the SEA's exception for proposals governing the health and safety of workers. Members of the Commission, the European Parliament, and the European labor organization ETUC (European Trade Union Confederation) have pushed with some success for expansive readings of these clauses, while the Union of Industrial and Employers' Confederations of Europe (UNICE), the main employers' organization, has strongly opposed such a move.[9] One indication of the growing room for social policy initiatives, however, was the enactment of the Maternity Directive of October 1992, passed under the "health and safety" provisions allowing qualified majority voting. This legislation both requires more generous policies in several EU countries and—significantly given the current pressure for austerity at the national level—prohibits other countries from cutting back their existing regimes. Although many proposals connected to the Social Charter, a "solemn declaration" signed by all the member states except Britain in 1989, have been watered down or stalled, the combined impact of what has been passed is not trivial.[10]

---

7. The retroactivity of *Barber* was thought sufficiently important (and costly) to warrant the attention of the Maastricht Treaty writers. In Maastricht a somewhat less costly, but not the least costly, version of retroactivity was chosen. It took a lot—a unanimous Treaty change—to recoup the initiative from the ECJ, and the ECJ upheld the solution found in Maastricht in *Ten Oever* (Case 109/91 of October 6, 1993). Estimated costs of full retroactivity for Germany are from Berenz (1994, pp. 385–90, 433–38); for Britain from Mazey and Richardson (1993, p. 15).

8. Rhodes (1995).

9. Lange (1992, pp. 235–56).

10. For some estimates of the impact on firms and governments—particularly emphasizing the effects on Britain—see Addison and Siebert (1993), pp. 13–28).

There has also been a considerable extension of regulations governing health and safety in the workplace under the terms of article 118a. The single-market initiative allowed qualified majority voting in this area out of fear that national regulations could be used as nontariff barriers to trade. Surprisingly, policymaking has produced neither stalemate nor lowest-common-denominator regulations. Instead, extensive regulations have generally produced quite a high level of standards. Furthermore, EC regulators moved beyond the regulation of *products* to the regulation of production *processes*, where the concerns about barriers to trade would seem to be inapplicable. As Volker Eichener has documented, the Commission's role as a "process manager" appears to have been critical in this complex and low-profile policy environment.[11] Much of the crucial decisionmaking took place in committees composed of policy experts. Some of these experts were linked to business and labor groups, but business interests did not have the option of simply refusing to participate, since regulatory action was likely to proceed without them. Representatives within these committees were often interested in innovation, having gravitated toward Brussels because in regulatory issues it seemed to be "where the action is." In this technocratic context, "best practices" from many member states (and from outside the EU) were pieced together to form a quite interventionist structure of social regulation.

The Maastricht Treaty may also have lowered the institutional barriers to social policy enactments, although the creation of a separate institutional track for social policy has also generated tremendous uncertainty. Faced with an impasse between British unwillingness to expand majority voting to social policy and France's refusal to sign a treaty that did not do so, the Netherlands and Germany together with the Commission's Jacques Delors engineered a complex compromise.[12] All member states agreed to allow the member states other than Britain to go forward on social policy issues under a new "Social Protocol," which expands the scope for qualified majority voting.[13] Britain would not participate in such deci-

11. Eichener (1993).
12. Lange (1993); Ross (1994).
13. Qualified majority will now be satisfactory for "improvement in particular of the working environment to protect worker's health and safety; working conditions; the information and consultation of workers; equality of treatment between

sionmaking, nor would it be governed by any policies taken in this framework.

With the election of a Labour government committed to joining the Social Protocol, this complex and unprecedented solution becomes moot. Under the terms of the protocol, the range of social initiatives that can be decided by qualified majority vote expands considerably, although major restrictions remain. In principle, efforts to implement new social policy initiatives should be facilitated, as Britain's capacity to obstruct legislation will have diminished and the four "poor" states (Greece, Ireland, Portugal, and Spain) do not command enough votes to block reform under qualified majority voting. Indeed, a European Works Council directive and a directive on parental leave have already been approved under these procedures.

Yet further activism seems likely to be modest in the near future. The Commission is itself involved in intensive soul-searching concerning the EU's proper social policy role.[14] Efforts to combat stubbornly high European unemployment have taken center stage, and the Commission seems to have accepted at least some of the British case about the need to promote "flexibility." The Commission's 1993 White Paper *Growth, Competitiveness, Employment* revealed a change in emphasis toward reducing labor costs, calling for tax reforms that would generate "a substantial reduction of nonwage labor costs (between 1 and 2 percentage points of GDP), particularly for the least-skilled workers."[15] The member states seem unlikely to allow the Commission to take the lead on such issues, suggesting that the immediate prospect is for consolidation with the completion of current agenda items but few new initiatives.

The dismissal of claims that a significant EU role exists in social policy are largely based on examination of the high politics struggles over positive, center-imposed social policies through devices like the Social Charter. Developments such as the Maternity Directive suggest that there may now be room for some European initiatives, and EU legislative activity is probably as extensive as, for ex-

men and women with regard to labour market opportunities and treatment at work; the integration of persons excluded from the labour market."Social Protocol, Article 2 (1, 2).

14. Ross (1995, pp. 221–26).

15. European Communities-Commission (1993, pp. 136ff.).

ample, federal social policy activity in the United States on the eve of the New Deal.[16] Yet if member states have lost considerable control over social policy in the European Union, this is primarily because of processes other than the efforts of Union officials to develop social policy legislation.

Social Policy and Market Compatibility Requirements

Lost amid the noisy fights over social charters and social protocols has been the quiet accumulation of EC constraints on social policy connected with market integration. The past three decades have witnessed a gradual if incremental expansion of Community-produced regulations and court decisions that have eroded national welfare state sovereignties. Political scientists, entranced by the world of high politics and grand bargains, have paid scant attention to this area of "low politics." The topic has been left to a small set of European welfare lawyers who have monitored another center of policymaking: the courts.

The ECJ has delivered more than 300 decisions on social security coordination and more than 100 on other social policy matters within the scope of articles 117–125—enough to incite pleas for a specialized EC welfare court for which the ECJ would function as a court of appeals. The ECJ's overall case load has been growing rapidly, from 34 cases filed in 1968 to 280 in 1980 and 553 in 1992. Social policy cases account for a growing share of this rising total. A comparison with core common-market topics like the customs union and free movement of goods, competition (including taxation), and agriculture is instructive. Although social cases accounted for only 6.3 percent of the total in these four categories in 1968, that share had increased to 22.8 percent in 1992. By 1992 only competition cases arose with higher frequency, and the rate of growth for social policy cases was far greater.[17]

16. Robertson (1989). This comparison is not meant to imply that we should expect European social policy to expand the way the American national welfare state did after 1929. For reasons indicated above—especially the fact that European policymakers, unlike New Deal reformers, operate in a context where preexisting welfare states are a critical part of the policy terrain—this is not a plausible scenario.
17. Caporaso and Keeler (1993, table 1).

The EC's social dimension is usually discussed as a potential corrective or counter to market building. Instead, it has proceeded largely as part of a market-building process which has spurred the demand for court decisions. The nexus between the market and social policy was at least partially acknowledged at the outset, when social policy in the Community was addressed largely in relation to the problem of reducing restrictions of labor mobility (articles 48–51). In recent years, cases associated with the free movement of services (articles 59-66) have become increasingly important.

One of the crucial points of tension between national welfare states and the developing common market has concerned regulations governing the mobility of labor across the jurisdictional boundaries of member states. Intra-European migration—compared with that within the United States—is small; there are only five million workers, including their dependents, who actually exercise this freedom. But these numbers have surpassed the "critical mass" necessary to generate continuously increasing litigation at the ECJ level. In legal terms, the adaptation of social policy to a developed context of "interstate commerce" does not require a quantum leap in European migration itself. A relatively small flow of migrants can trigger legal rulings affecting significant features of national welfare states. Individuals as litigants and national courts who refer cases to the ECJ are, together with the ECJ itself, the central actors in shaping this multitiered EC policy domain.

A detailed review of this case law cannot be attempted here.[18] Over a period of thirty years, a complex patchwork of regulations and court decisions has partially suspended the principle of member-state sovereignty over social policy in the interest of European labor market mobility, limiting national capacities to contain transfers "by territory." To take just one example, attempts to create a minimum pension benefit in Germany during the 1980s foundered in part because of concerns that the benefit would be "exportable" to non-German EC citizens who had worked for some time in Germany.[19] As a result of developing understandings of European law, member states are increasingly constrained in their capacity to: (1) limit social benefits exclusively to their citizens; (2) insist that

18. Leibfried and Pierson (1995).
19. Zuleeg (1989).

benefits can only be consumed on their territory; (3) prevent other social policy systems from directly competing on their territory (for example, the controversial situation of posted and seconded workers, especially in the German construction industry); and (4) maintain exclusive control over the administration of social welfare claims. If complete de jure authority in these respects is what sovereignty is all about, it has already ceased to exist in the EU.

Coordination has become the entering wedge for an incremental, rights-based homogenization of social policy. Neither "supranationalization" nor "harmonization" seems an appropriate label for this dynamic, since each implies more policy control at the center than currently exists. The process is more like a marketplace of "coordination," with the ECJ acting as market police, enforcing the boundaries of national autonomy. It structures the interfaces of fifteen national social policy systems, with potentially far-reaching consequences for the range of policy options available to national welfare states.

Nor do these new constraints stem only from free movement of labor considerations. The free movement of services doctrine also directly affects national welfare states, although the scope of this influence remains relatively opaque. While labor mobility issues have been worked out in hundreds of ECJ decisions spanning almost four decades, the influence of the free movement of services doctrine really surfaced only with the passage of the Single European Act in 1986. So far, it has generated only a few leading cases and comparatively little secondary Community law. Nevertheless, judging from the clear potential influence of the single market on the now common private insurance market, there appear to be significant prospects for a remolding of national policies in the social services, especially in the area of health care.

In principle, at least so it used to be thought, each state may choose its own policies for social services. However, the freedom of services doctrine may have considerable effects on national service delivery systems. Here, as Karl-Jurgen Bieback has argued, the divergent characteristics of member-state policy structures become crucial. For example, some member states (for example, Britain and Italy) have national health care systems with marginalized markets or nonmarket systems. Others (Germany, France, and the Netherlands) have insurance systems in which the state only supplies financing and a regulatory structure for goods and services that are provided by private providers. As Bieback observes,

> According to the ECJ the free movement of services clause in Article 59 of the Treaty of Rome applies only to services dealt with in markets and supplied for money, but not for services which are usually delivered as part of a "national service." Thus countries which organize their health-service systems on the basis of private markets where public and private suppliers may compete and access is free, like the systems of social insurance in France and Germany, are open for competition from suppliers from other countries, whereas the "National Health" systems are closed, except if they incorporate competitive structures like parts of the British system.[20]

Whereas the access of foreign providers to nonmarket systems is a nonissue, in quasi-market systems the access of foreign private deliverers is buttressed by EC law. This may create a deregulatory dynamic, especially when regimes rely on closed national producer markets for social services.

The emerging free market of services can be seen in most dramatic form in the rapidly evolving private insurance market. As of July 1, 1994, national private insurance has been drawn into the common market of the EU. The furious pace of cross-border mergers and acquisitions is creating a heavily concentrated insurance sector operating at the European level. Integrated European insurance markets allow for a greater differentiation of policyholders by risk groups, and thus for cheaper, more profitable policies with lower operational costs. Such an integrated private sector would confront fifteen national, internally segmented, public insurance domains. Insurance providers with the option of relocating to more lenient member states will have increased influence over national social regulation. At the same time, the clash between particular national regulatory styles and the quite different traditions of competing insurers from other member states is likely to be intense.

The results of public/private interplay in the context of a radically altered private sector are difficult to anticipate. There is, how-

20. Bieback (1991).

ever, considerable evidence from earlier studies of national welfare states that the reform of private-sector markets can have dramatic effects on public-service provision.[21] Public and private insurance compete mainly in areas like occupational pensions, life insurance, and supplemental health insurance. Permanent turf quarrels between public and private sectors seem likely concerning where "basic" (public) coverage should end and "additional" (private) insurance may begin. This is part of a broader process in which movement toward the single market challenges existing demarcations between the public and private spheres. The welfare state, which has traditionally been a key area for establishing these demarcations, is bound to be affected by the gradual and often indirect redrawing of boundaries.

Thus the balance between a free market (of services) and institutionally autonomous national welfare states, two principles embedded in the EU Constitution, is not a static but a dynamic one. Here is open terrain for Brussels, with a large potential for restructuring national service delivery regimes. This problem is likely to be particularly severe for Sweden and Finland, the two Nordic countries that entered the Union in 1995, since they have systematically pursued a policy of marginalizing competitive pressures in social service provision. As Kare Hagen argues:

> Political ambitions of providing high- and equal-quality health care to all segments of the population have required the extensive use of public monopolies that may militate against enterprise freedoms guaranteed by Community legislation. The same applies to state restrictions on private pension insurance and on how their funds are to be managed. In general, any kind of state welfare policy which is deliberately designed to prevent private purchasing power from being reproduced in the consumption of welfare goods supplied by the market, will run counter to the freedoms of the common market.[22]

Since the two principles of a free market in services and national autonomy over social policy contradict each other, it is up to the EU to fix, again and again, an ever-shifting demarcation line. While

21. See, for example, Rein and Rainwater (1986).
22. Hagen (1992).

labor-market coordination has been the main social policy item for
the ECJ in the past three decades, issues concerning freedom to sup-
ply and consume social services are coming to the fore. As Bieback
notes,

> As long as the Community opens the free market for social
> services there are only three options. Either the competence of
> the EC is extended to control and regulate the market for social
> services, or the Member States coordinate and harmonise their
> systems voluntarily, or finally all national systems of social
> services opt out of market systems into "national" systems.
> Evidently, all options tend to increase the pressure towards
> harmonisation.[23]

To summarize, even by looking only at issues of labor mobility
and freedom of services, one can see a wide range of market compatibility requirements through which either EC regulations or ECJ decisions impinge on the design and reform of national social policy. Examples related to the single market could easily be multiplied—for
example, restrictions on the degree of firm subsidies in regional policy. In Italy, for instance, the central government has been using
abatements of social insurance taxes as a strategy to attract investment to the *Mezzogiorno*. While the Commission agreed to permit this
until the end of 1993, it then initiated ECJ proceedings against the
continuation of the practice on grounds of "unfair competition."
Similarly, changes in Germany's social insurance system for farmers
requires Brussels's approval since such insurance is considered a sectoral subsidy. The broader point is clear: as rules related to the single
market are developed and enforced, the line demarcating economic
policy from social policy breaks down. As a result, a range of social
policy designs that would be available to sovereign welfare states are
prohibited to member states within the EU.

European Integration and De Facto Pressures on National Welfare States

The European Union now intervenes directly in the social policies of member states in two ways: by enacting significant social

23. Bieback (1991, p. 932).

policy initiatives of its own and by striking down features of national systems that are deemed incompatible with the development of the single market. In addition, the process of European integration has less direct but nonetheless consequential effects on member-state social policies. Both the economic policies of the European Union and the responses of social actors to those policies put pressures on national welfare states. Because these effects are indirect they are difficult to measure; nonetheless, they add to the general picture of increasing supranational constraints on the development of national social policy.

The most frequently cited source of pressure on welfare states within the EU is the possibility that heightened integration may lead to "social dumping." The term refers to the prospect that firms operating where "social wages" are low may be able to undercut the prices of competitors, forcing higher-cost firms to either go out of business, relocate to low–social wage areas, or pressure their governments to reduce social wage costs. In the more extreme scenarios, these actions could fuel a downward spiral in social provision, eventually producing very rudimentary, lowest-common-denominator national welfare states.

There is some evidence that these kinds of pressures have indeed restricted social expenditures in the United States, where labor (and capital) mobility is far greater than is currently the case in the EC.[24] Despite widespread attention to this issue, however, the evidence that European integration will fuel a process of social dumping remains limited. As a number of observers have noted, the social wage is only one factor in investment decisions, and firms will not invest in low–social wage countries unless worker productivity (relative to wages) justifies such investments. Neoclassical trade theory suggests that high–social wage countries should be able to continue their policies as long as overall conditions allow profitable investment.[25] One sign of the ambiguous consequences of integration is the fact that Northern Europe's concerns about "sunbelt effects" are mirrored by Southern Europe's concerns about "agglom-

24. Peterson and Rom (1990).
25. Though nominal wage costs vary dramatically, with the Netherlands and Portugal marking the two extremes, unit labor costs and therefore productivity diverge much less, pointing toward some advantages for low-wage periphery member states. Tsoukalis (1993, figure 6.1, p. 145).

eration effects" in which investment would flow toward the superior infrastructures and high-skilled work forces of Europe's most developed regions.[26]

Some analysts have criticized the neoclassical perspective for ignoring the fragility of the institutional networks that sustain the high-wage, high-productivity economies.[27] Rather than leading to a flood of investment in the periphery countries and a race to the bottom in social regulation, economic integration may lead to a more gradual and indirect process of national social policy erosion. There is little doubt that the enhanced exit options for businesses strengthen their hand in bargaining with governments and employees. Furthermore, even if maintenance of existing standards (which create a level playing field and reduce uncertainty) might be collectively rational for groups of employers, it may not be rational for individual firms. Increased mobility may encourage free riding. Emboldened firms may use the threat of "regime shopping" to force the renegotiation of national or local bargains with unions and governments. In turn, such efforts could introduce a dynamic that gradually undermines tightly coupled systems of social policy and industrial relations like the German one. This is a more restricted scenario for social dumping, but it nonetheless implies growing pressure on national welfare state regimes.

Social dumping may generate greater fears than current evidence warrants; the opposite could be the case for some of the other ways that economic integration creates indirect constraints on national social policy systems. The single market is forcing a gradual movement toward a narrowed band of value-added tax (VAT) rates.[28] In theory, governments finding that their VAT revenues have been lowered will be free to increase other taxes, but this may be no sim-

26. Streeck (1989); Petersen (1991, pp. 511–13); Lange (1992, pp. 239–44). In the third Yearly Report of the Commission on the Community's Employment Situation, Social Policy commissioner Vasso Papandreou stressed in July 1991 that regional disparities in the Single Market between center ("north") and periphery have slightly increased. This is attributed to two factors in the periphery: stronger demographic growth and job loss in the agricultural sector. Buying power per capita in Ireland, Portugal, Spain, and Greece is less than 70 percent of the northern average, a return to the distributional situation of 1975. *Frankfurter Allgemeine Zeitung*, July 19, 1991, p. 12.

27. Streeck (1995).

28. Kosonen (1994, pp. 15–21).

ple task. Because it is politically easier to sustain indirect taxes than direct levies, the new rules may create growing constraints on member-state budgets, with clear implications for national social policies.[29] This is likely to be a particular problem for Denmark, which relies heavily on indirect taxes rather than payroll taxes to finance its generous welfare state.[30] To take two extremes, in 1992 only 12 percent of Danish social protection expenditures were financed by payroll taxes, while in Germany 75 percent were.[31]

Of far greater importance is the move toward monetary union, with its tough requirements for budgetary discipline. Monetary integration may encourage downward adjustments in welfare provision. For example, to participate in the final stage of monetary union, Italy would have to reduce its budget deficit from 10 percent of GDP to 3 percent by the end of the decade. This served to legitimate the intense pursuit of major cuts in old-age pensions and other social benefits by the governments of Silvio Berlusconi and Lamberto Dini. Although the efforts of the Berlusconi government were largely blocked by popular protests, the Dini government was able to introduce considerable retrenchment in the health care and pension sectors.[32] Further cutbacks are currently under consideration.

While other countries face less radical adjustments, the convergence criteria present formidable problems for almost all of them. In France, pressures to meet the convergence criteria played a central role in the development of Prime Minister Juppé's tough austerity plans. As in Italy, these initiatives sparked intense public discontent and the withdrawal of some proposals. The government's cuts in welfare state programs were widely viewed as a key factor in the French left's surprising victory in the 1997 parliamentary elections. Despite these political setbacks, significant parts of the Juppé government's reforms have been implemented. As in Italy, more cutbacks are planned.[33]

Here again, there is tremendous uncertainty about the effects of monetary integration on national welfare states. Since governments would have faced pressure for austerity in any event, analysts are

29. Wilensky (1976); Hibbs and Madsen (1981).
30. Petersen, (1991, pp. 514–22; 1993); Falkner (1993).
31. Eurostat (1996, p. 137).
32. On France see Bonoli and Palier (1995).
33. Ferrera (forthcoming) and Regini and Regalia (forthcoming).

faced with the difficult counterfactual task of estimating what would have happened in the absence of the push for monetary union. The convergence criteria, finally, do not of course *require* budget cuts—tax increases would also be possible. Yet there can be little doubt that the new context created by the EMU considerably strengthens the hand of those seeking such cuts.[34] This complex issue, including its potential impact on popular support for European integration, is explored in greater depth in the second part of this chapter.

It is difficult to evaluate the consequences of these various indirect pressures for national welfare states. Many of the possible problem areas lie in the future, and some of the others, such as social dumping, are difficult to measure even if they might be occurring now. Furthermore, one has to weigh the pressures for reform against the welfare state's considerable sources of resilience.[35] Yet the picture that emerges is one where national governments possess diminished control over many of the policies that have traditionally supported national welfare states—macroeconomic policies, tax policies, perhaps even industrial relations systems. Again, these developments challenge the dominant view of a market-building process at the European level that supposedly advances relentlessly while leaving the development of welfare states a purely national affair.

Summary: Social Policy in Europe's Emerging Multitiered System

The affairs of welfare states remain primarily national in scope, but this is slowly changing as a new political framework takes

34. Monetary union would not only put pressures on national social programs; it could prod the Union into a more active role in efforts to combat unemployment. Analysis of the prospects for monetary integration in Europe has frequently been coupled with discussion of the need for accompanying social policies to address the likely emergence of regional imbalances. Monetary union would strip national governments of significant macroeconomic policy levers, and a Community-wide macroeconomic stance will create significant regional unemployment problems. Should monetary union occur, there are certain to be demands for a greater level of fiscal federalism, although the obstacles to implementing such a reform would also be formidable. See Eichengreen (1992). As Ross notes, the Spanish stressed this implication of monetary union during the run-up to Maastricht and made it clear that they would not sign a new treaty unless a major expansion of regional redistribution was included. Ross (1995, pp. 152-53).

35. Pierson (1996a).

shape in Europe. Although the case is easier to make for issue arenas such as regional policy or agriculture, even in the traditional areas of social policy the member states of the European Union now constitute part of a multitiered system. Scholarly attention has focused largely on Commission efforts to establish a social dimension of Community-wide policies or at least minimum standards. To date, these efforts have modified member-state social policies in relatively few areas. More important, although far less visible, have been the social policy effects of the single market's development. These have occurred either indirectly (through pressures on national welfare states) or directly, as the Commission, national courts, and the ECJ have sought to fashion rules that attempt to reconcile member-state policy autonomy with the effort to create a unified economic space.

What is emerging in Europe is a unique multitiered system of social policy, with three distinctive characteristics: a "hollow core," a prominent role for courts in policy development, and an unusually tight coupling to market-making processes. In speaking of Europe's "hollow core" I mean to convey both that the EU's social policymaking apparatus is extremely bottom-heavy compared with any existing federal system and that the capacity for policy innovation, either national or supranational, is diminishing. The quite weak center has limited capacity to formulate positive social policy. As a result, social policy evolution is likely to be more the result of mutual adjustment and incremental accommodation than a consequence of central guidance.[36] From the center comes a variety of pressures and constraints on social policy development but much less in the way of clear mandates for positive action.

The influence of the constituent member states, their incentives to maintain control over the legitimacy-sustaining aspects of social policy, and the widely divergent legacies of preexisting national welfare states are likely to remain all important in this context. Yet the hollow core depiction of the EU reflects a weakening of the member states' position in key respects as well. With the gravitation of authority, even of a largely negative kind, to the European level, the capacity of member states to design their welfare states as they choose is also diminishing. The role of the member states at this

36. For a useful if somewhat polemical discussion, see Streeck (1995).

juncture is multifaceted if not contradictory. Significant losses of autonomy and sovereignty occurred without member states paying a great deal of attention. Although member states currently resist some of the single market's implications for their own power, their capacity to do so is limited by their fear of jeopardizing the hard-won benefits of European integration.[37]

Member states are placed in a position of choosing from an increasingly restricted menu. It has been suggested that this dynamic strengthens national executives at the expense of domestic opponents, and (as I discuss in the next section) this may sometimes be the case.[38] Yet in the process of escaping from domestic constraints, national executives have created new ones that profoundly limit their options. Political authorities at *both* the national and supranational level suffer from a "hollowness" that limits their capacity for social policy intervention.

The second distinctive characteristic of social policymaking in the EU is that the legal prohibitions and requirements that do develop from the center are unusually court driven. It is as much a series of rulings from the ECJ as the process of Commission and Council initiatives that has directly impinged on national welfare states. The ECJ's institutional design fosters activism. In contrast to the Council or Commission, the ECJ cannot, once confronted with litigation, escape making what are essentially policy decisions as a matter of routine. The Court relies on secret majority votes, which shelter it from the political immobility typical of other European actors. ECJ decisions can generally be undone only by unanimous votes of the Council.[39]

Thus the structure of EU institutions puts the ECJ on center stage. Attempts at corporatist policymaking may have generated most of the drama surrounding Europe's social dimension, but businesses and unions have had little direct involvement in the decisions that have actually created legally binding requirements for the social policies of member states.[40] It should be stressed that such a court-

---

37. For a more general argument about some of these processes, see Pierson (1996a).

38. Milward (1992); Moravcsik (1994).

39. Eichenhofer (1992).

40. This is not to say that the activities of economic actors are irrelevant to the development of Community social policy. The influence of business has, for example,

led process of social policy development is likely to have its own logic, reflecting demands for doctrinal coherence as much or more than substantive debates about the desirability of various social policy outcomes. Legal systems have their own internal standards for judging the appropriateness of policy designs. Reforms built around a judicial logic may have less capacity to achieve substantive goals. They may also be more insulated from certain kinds of political processes, such as electoral ones, that have been central in the formation of national welfare states.

Finally, this multitiered system of social policy is uniquely connected to a process of market building. Of course, in mixed economies social policies always intersect in a variety of complex ways with market systems. Nowhere else, however, has the construction of markets so visibly and intensively shaped the development of social policy initiatives. The EU's interventions in the traditional spheres of social policy have not, on the whole, taken the form of what Karl Polanyi famously called a "protective reaction" against the expansion of market relations.[41] Indeed initiatives of this form (such as the Social Charter) have usually been dismal failures. Instead, as the centrality of decisions regarding labor mobility and free service markets reveals, European Union social policy interventions have grown up as part of the process of market building itself. These interventions have been extensive. They have created a structure in which national welfare state regimes are now part of a larger, multitiered system of social policy. This is a peculiar arrangement, quite different in crucial respects from that of traditional federal welfare states. It is, however, clearly one where the governance of social policy occurs at multiple levels. Member states profoundly influence this structure, but they no longer control it.

The Contemporary Welfare State and the Politics of European Integration

The first section of this chapter has given a somewhat unorthodox answer to an orthodox question: how has the process of Euro-

been considerable in restricting Commission efforts to pursue a more activist social dimension, and in advancing the deregulatory agenda that has set the framework for ECJ decisions.

41. Polanyi (1944).

pean integration altered the character of policymaking related to social issues and the welfare state? This section focuses, more tentatively, on a question that is rarely asked but which is of increasing significance: what implications does the character of contemporary welfare state politics have for the process of European integration? I suggest that the growing connections between the welfare state and European-level decisionmaking have repercussions in both directions. Not only does the movement toward European integration influence national welfare states, but national politics surrounding the welfare state are likely to have mounting consequences for European integration.

The headline of an article on France in the *Economist* posed the question bluntly: "EMU without tear-gas?" The headline referred to the Juppé government's efforts to move toward meeting the convergence criteria without repeating the traumatic experience of 1995. At that time, the Juppé government's plan to cut large deficits in the social security system provoked paralyzing public sector strikes, an embarrassing government retreat, and a sharp fall in the government's popularity. This series of events was mirrored by similarly tense dramas in other countries. In Italy, for instance, the Berlusconi government was severely damaged by attempts to impose cuts in pension and health care programs as part of its push to reduce the Italian deficit. The subsequent Dini government later introduced a more modest set of reforms following arduous negotiations with Italy's unions and employers.[42] These events signal the growing links between painful and politically treacherous discussions of the national welfare state and plans for further European integration. I explore these important linkages in three steps. First, I briefly highlight the prominence of the welfare state in West European polities. Second, I discuss the growing fiscal pressures on the welfare state and the difficult politics accompanying that fiscal transition. Finally, I discuss how the process of European integration is increasingly implicated in these political struggles and the risks this may pose for the integration process.

---

42. On France see Bonoli and Palier (1995); on Italy see Ferrera (forthcoming) and Regini and Regalia (forthcoming).

148   Paul Pierson

The Role of the Welfare State in West European Polities

It is difficult to exaggerate the impact of the welfare state on the evolving character of the postwar Western European market democracies. Although the process took various forms and arrived at different destinations in different countries, all Western Europe experienced a massive expansion of public social provisions after World War II. The development of generous public retirement and disability systems along with universal health care were the core elements of these welfare states, but they were flanked to varying extents by major public initiatives in family policy (child allowances, parental leave, and child care), housing, and labor market policy. By the mid-1980s, most European countries allocated 20 to 25 percent of their GDP to such programs, and laggards (such as Greece, Portugal, and Spain) were rapidly catching up.

These programs are now deeply embedded in the economic, social, and political structures of the Western European countries. Social practices, such as schooling, child rearing, the organization of local communities, and retirement, are all heavily influenced by systems of social policy. Patterns of labor market participation, especially for women, vary considerably across Europe in significant degree as a result of the different designs of national welfare states.[43] Business structures and strategies in Europe have adapted to particular institutional contexts, in which the incentives and disincentives associated with labor market and social insurance policies loom large.[44]

The extension of the welfare state has also had a tremendous impact on domestic politics. The massive postwar expansion of "social citizenship" was extremely popular. Especially in the period before 1973, the Keynesian wisdom that increased social spending, high wage growth, and low unemployment were not only compatible but mutually reinforcing created a powerful political formula. To an extent that was not appreciated at the time, governments during the postwar boom also benefited from favorable demographic conditions and from the opportunities that pay-as-you-go financing of pensions creates for the provision of immediate benefits and the de-

43. Esping-Anderson (1990).
44. Soskice (1991).

ferral of major costs.[45] The nation-state's assumption of guaranteed social security provided a considerable boost in the political standing of governments. For much of the postwar period, political parties competed to develop new social programs and promise more generous social benefits.

As these programs matured, they also created dense networks of political support. With the growing significance of transfer payments, recipients have had an increasing stake in expanding or at least maintaining existing benefits. Social service programs—in health care, child care, and so on—create two distinct and politically significant clienteles: benefit recipients and benefit providers. In most European countries, social service provision accounts for a significant share of total employment. In many countries, public services have accounted for most or all employment growth since 1973.

Thus to a significantly greater extent than is true in the United States, public social provision has been woven deeply into the fabric of European societies and is of tremendous political salience. As I argued in the first section, it is hardly surprising that major changes in the economic and political structure of Europe would have an impact on national welfare states. What also seems increasingly likely is that the opposite will hold as well: emerging pressures on national welfare states will have implications for the process of European integration. To understand why, one must briefly review the mounting difficulties facing national systems of social provision.

Increasing Fiscal Pressures and Contemporary Welfare State Politics

The welfare state's golden age ended abruptly in 1973. Worsening economic performance created pressures on the welfare state from two directions: revenue flows were undermined while demands on social programs increased. Changes in the global economy, and in particular an increase in capital mobility, heightened calls to contain social expenditures. Yet problems associated with low growth were greatly exacerbated by demographic trends, as an aging population and the maturation of programs enacted earlier

45. Pierson (1997).

150   Paul Pierson

led to steadily rising expenditures. Indeed it is easy to focus too much on the impact of globalization. In fact, the scale of the welfare state's commitment had reached a point where such pressures were inevitable in any event.[46]

Although fiscal strains on the welfare state have become more severe over the past two decades, the worst is yet to come. The interaction of an aging population with the considerable entitlements built up by those retiring suggest formidable pressures on public budgets over the next thirty to forty years.[47] There is considerable variation across countries, but the burdens associated with aging are likely to be especially severe in the "Christian Democratic" countries of continental Europe (such as Germany and Italy), which share the characteristics of rapid population aging, low labor force participation rates (especially among women), and generous public pension schemes.[48] While public pension payments are expected to peak at less than 8 percent of GDP in the United States, Great Britain, and Canada, under current projections they will reach between 13 and 20 percent of GDP in France, Germany, and Italy.[49] The latter systems are also the most severely underfunded, despite already high payroll taxes. And while pension payments represent the greatest single source of spending pressures, there will be additional cost increases as well, associated particularly with health care.

Thus the welfare state has entered a new era of austerity. This era is certain to last a very long time, and indeed the pressures for austerity are likely to get considerably worse before they get better. Given the centrality of the welfare state to existing social relations in Western Europe, it is thus crucial to examine the implications of these changing circumstances for democratic politics.

For two reasons, the new politics of the welfare state is quite different from the old.[50] First, the political goals of policymakers are

46. Klein and others (1996).
47. OECD (1995).
48. Esping-Andersen (1996). Under current law in France, for instance, most workers are entitled to full pension benefits at age sixty, which provide a benefit of two-thirds to three-fourths of final salary, all paid for by current workers under a pay-as-you-go arrangement. Roughly one-third of public sector workers can retire at full pension before age sixty. Public pension spending in France currently totals 10.9 percent of GDP. *The Economist*, February 15, 1997, pp. 47–48.
49. OECD (1995).
50. For a detailed discussion see Pierson (1996a).

different; second, there have been dramatic changes in the political context. Each of these points requires elaboration. There is a profound difference between extending benefits to large numbers of people and taking those benefits away. For the past half century, expanding social benefits was generally a process of political credit claiming. Reformers needed only to overcome diffuse concerns about tax rates (often sidestepped through the use of social insurance "'contributions'") and the frequently important resistance of entrenched interests. Not surprisingly, the expansion of social programs was, until recently, a favored political activity, contributing greatly to both state-building projects and the popularity of reform-minded politicians.[51]

The new policy agenda of austerity stands in sharp contrast to the credit-claiming initiatives pursued during the long period of welfare state expansion. The politics of retrenchment is typically treacherous. On very rare occasions, policymakers may be able to transform retrenchment into an electorally attractive proposition. More often, the best they can hope to do is to minimize the political costs involved. Advocates of retrenchment must persuade wavering supporters that the price of reform is manageable, a task that a substantial public outcry makes almost impossible.

In short, retrenchment is generally an exercise in what R. Kent Weaver has termed the politics of blame avoidance.[52] A crucial reason is that the costs of retrenchment are relatively concentrated (and often immediate), while the benefits are not. That concentrated interests will be in a stronger political position than diffuse ones is a standard proposition in political science.[53] As interests become more concentrated, the prospect that individuals will find it worth their while to engage in collective action improves. Furthermore, concentrated groups are more likely to be linked to organizational networks that keep them informed about how policies affect their interests. These informational networks also facilitate political action.

An additional reason that politicians rarely get credit for program cutbacks concerns the well-documented asymmetry in how

51. Flora and Heidenheimer (1981).
52. Weaver (1986).
53. Olson (1965); Wilson (1973).

voters react to losses and gains. Extensive experiments in social psychology have shown that individuals respond differently to positive and negative risks. Individuals exhibit a *negativity bias*: they will take more chances—seeking conflict and accepting the possibility of even greater losses—to prevent any worsening of their current position.[54] Studies of electoral behavior, at least in the United States, confirm these findings. Negative attitudes toward candidates are more strongly linked with a range of voter behaviors (for example, turning out to desert one's normal party choice) than are positive attitudes.[55]

While the sources of this negativity bias remain unclear, the constraints that it imposes on elected officials are not. When added to the imbalance between concentrated and diffuse interests, the message for advocates of retrenchment is straightforward. A simple redistributive transfer of resources from program beneficiaries to taxpayers, engineered through cuts in social programs, is generally a losing proposition. The concentrated beneficiary groups are more likely to be cognizant of the change and easier to mobilize, and because they are experiencing losses rather than gains are more likely to incorporate the change in their voting calculations. Retrenchment advocates thus confront a potential clash between their policy preferences and their electoral ambitions.

All these tendencies are reinforced by the second broad characteristic of the new era of welfare state politics. While the shift in *goals* from expansion to cutbacks creates new political dynamics, so does the emergence of a new *context*: the development of the welfare state itself. As Peter Flora has noted, "Including the recipients of [pensions,] unemployment benefits and social assistance—and the persons employed in education, health and the social services—in many countries today almost 1/2 of the electorate receive transfer or work income from the welfare state."[56] With these massive programs have come dense interest-group networks and strong popular attachments to particular policies, which present considerable obstacles to reform.

54. Kahneman and Tversky (1979, 1984).
55. Bloom and Price (1975); Kernell (1977); Lau (1985).
56. Flora (1989, p. 154).

The maturation of the welfare state fundamentally transforms the nature of interest-group politics. The emergence of powerful groups surrounding social programs can make the welfare state less dependent on the political parties, social movements, and labor organizations that expanded social programs in the first place. This helps to explain why neither the significant decline in the power of organized labor since 1973 nor the rightward shift in electoral politics in many countries during the 1980s has led to anything like a dismantling of the modern welfare state.

In short, the shift in goals and context creates a new politics marked by pressures to avoid blame for unpopular policies. This new politics dictates new political strategies.[57] Retrenchment advocates will try to play off one group of beneficiaries against another and will often develop reforms that compensate politically crucial groups for lost benefits. Because of the political costs associated with retrenchment, policymakers will seek to spread the blame by achieving broad consensus on reform wherever possible. Perhaps most important, those favoring cutbacks will attempt to lower the visibility of reforms, either by making the effects of policies more difficult to detect or by making it hard for voters to trace responsibility for those effects back to particular policymakers.[58]

This last point deserves emphasis. What distinguishes democratic polities is the central role of elections in determining who wields political authority. This institutional structure provides voters with a crude but strong instrument for protecting their interests. Yet they can do so only if the relevant activities of policymakers are visible. The role of "visibility" in politics is often mentioned, casually, but little understood. All political actors posssess imperfect information about issues relevant to their interests. Furthermore, the distribution of information is usually highly unequal. In particular, mass publics often have limited information about the impact of changes in public policy. In this context, it may be possible for policymakers to lower the political costs of retrenchment actions by raising the costs to possible opponents of obtaining relevant information—that is to say, by lowering the visibility of their actions.

---

57. See Weaver (1986); and Pierson (1994).
58. Arnold (1990).

As Douglas Arnold has argued, electoral retribution against incumbents for unpopular policies requires three things.[59] First, voters must be able to discern that they have experienced particular negative outcomes. Second, they must be able to trace those outcomes to specific government policies. Third, they must be able to identify the policymakers responsible for the undesired policies. These conditions are not easily fulfilled, and policymakers may possess tools to lower the visibility of their actions in each respect.

In the contemporary era of relative austerity, those pursuing retrenchment will attempt to avoid blame by obscuring the negative consequences of their initiatives or by obscuring their own responsibility for these initiatives. It is here that the EU becomes a potentially important part of the new politics of the welfare state. National politicians, faced with the unenviable task of presenting voters with painful policies, can be expected to shift the blame whenever possible—and "Europe" will be an attractive target.

Austerity Politics and the European Union

Analysts have typically assumed that national politicians would resist efforts to "Europeanize" social policy because of the authority and legitimacy-building opportunities associated with social provision. As I argued in the first part of this chapter, for most of the history of the EU this assumption has proven sound. Considerable social policy authority has drifted away from member states, but they have generally resisted overt efforts to transfer policymaking power to the EU level.

At a time when control over social policy often means responsibility for announcing unpopular cutbacks, however, member-state governments sometimes are happy to accept arrangements that constrain their own options. Given the unpopularity of retrenchment, governments may find that the growing ability to blame the EU allows changes that they would otherwise be afraid to contemplate. Indeed national politicians may feel that the emerging political arrangements offer the best of both worlds—continued consid-

59. Arnold (1990).

erable discretion over policy development with substantial opportunities to use the EU as a scapegoat for unpopular policies.

The movement toward a multitiered political system opens up major new avenues for the politics of blame avoidance. Retrenchment advocates may be able to shift the balance of political power domestically if they can restructure the ways in which trade-offs among taxes, spending, and deficits are presented, evaluated, and decided. In Europe, the increasing policy significance of the European Union may alter the terrain for struggles over the welfare state. If reforms can be presented as legally required or economically imperative because of the single market or the need to participate in monetary union, national governments may be freed from some blame for welfare state cutbacks. Indeed it has been suggested that a principal cause of the EU's growing policy role is the way in which it shelters national executives from domestic political forces. In this view, far from eroding national sovereignty, the EU actually "strengthens the state."[60]

For the welfare state, the most important site for this dynamic is the move toward economic and monetary union (EMU). EMU, with its tough convergence criteria, has provided an impetus for significant austerity initiatives in some countries, including France and Italy. The criteria will require considerably tighter fiscal policies in states that hope to participate in monetary union. In this context, member states may be able to use the EU to provide political cover for reforms that they have been afraid to pursue.

This appears to have been the case in Italy, for instance. Political elites, especially within the Treasury (*Tesoro*), Central Bank (*Banca d'Italia*), and the Foreign Ministry saw monetary union as an attractive vehicle for overcoming the obstacles to austerity at home.[61] EMU would create an "external constraint" (*vincolo esterno*), allowing economic discipline to be imposed despite the opposition of domestic actors. Indeed Italy has made considerable progress in achieving fiscal consolidation over the past few years, including budget cuts and new revenues (the so-called tax for Europe).

As the French experience suggests, however, the creation of this external constraint may be a two-edged sword. Efforts to meet the

60. Moravcsik (1994).
61. Dyson and Featherstone (1996).

convergence criteria require rather rapid adjustments in fiscal policy. Yet there is considerable evidence that austerity measures are best pursued gradually; that it is far easier to moderate political reactions if painful reforms are introduced incrementally, with the most significant changes pushed beyond the time horizons of most voters.[62] This was the strategy employed by the successful German pension reforms in the 1980s and in the recent Swedish pension reform. Efforts to meet the convergence criteria, however, push governments toward precisely the short-term, painful initiatives that are most likely to raise the visibility of retrenchment efforts and provoke political trouble. France's attempt to lower its budget deficit from 5 percent of GDP to 3 percent from 1995 to 1997 was a recipe for political disaster. Given that the largest expressions of popular discontent in Western Europe over the past few years have regularly revolved around cuts in social benefits—the French protests against Juppé, Italian demonstrations against Berlusconi, and large demonstrations in Germany against recent proposed cutbacks in sickness pay—this interaction between European-level and national politics presents a source of considerable social turbulence.[63]

There is a more diffuse but more profound danger as well—that efforts to scapegoat the EU for painful austerity measures, even if successful in the short run, will considerably weaken the mass public's already modest support for European integration. Here there is a considerable mismatch between the short-term incentives facing national politicians and the long-term requirements for sustaining popular support for the integration process. By necessity, politicians tend to have short time horizons. The more salient an integrated Europe becomes within national electoral politics, the more decisionmaking on European issues will reflect these time horizons. With strong incentives to concentrate on the next election and recognizing that austerity can easily jeopardize reelection chances, politicials will often face irresistable temptations to blame Europe.

---

62. Pierson (1996a).

63. Again, analysis on this point requires the employment of difficult counterfactuals. What would have happened in the absence of the move toward EMU? It seems likely that France and other countries have achieved greater austerity than would otherwise have been possible, but that this has also been accompanied by greater social unrest.

It is hard to tell exactly how significant these dynamics will be, but we do know several things. First, as any examination of recent electoral politics would reveal, there are few issues of greater significance for voters than the fate of the welfare state. The track record of parties who lose favor with the public on this issue is poor.[64] Thus blame-avoidance pressures are likely to remain intense, and success in such efforts is likely to have significant negative consequences for the unlucky scapegoat. Second, we know that the mass public is becoming increasingly relevant to the whole integration process, as signaled both by the events surrounding the Maastricht referenda and growing elite concern about the dangers of Europe's "democratic deficit." Thus if efforts to scapegoat the EU for budget cuts imposed at the national level lead to declining public support for Europe, this is likely to have considerable repercussions.

Finally, we know that the public, never enthusiastic about a European role in social policy, is becoming increasingly skeptical about the social dimension of European integration. Evidence for this last proposition can be found in public opinion data. Since the late 1980s, Eurobarometer surveys have asked whether voters favored a significant EU role across a range of policy domains. Support for social policy integration has always been relatively low. On a range of issues, polls have shown some decline in support for integration. The drop, however has been sharper in the case of social policy than in other domains—a result which is especially striking because of the already low level of enthusiasm for social policy integration. Skepticism is particularly high in countries with well-developed welfare states, such as Denmark.[65]

There are probably several reasons for this relatively sharp decline in public support for an EU role in social policy. The recession, which has heightened concerns about economic vulnerability, has very likely contributed to the trend. Shifting perceptions of the connection between "Europe" and "social policy" have probably been important as well. Although in the late 1980s discussions of European social policy focused on the relatively popular idea of new European-level rights and standards, the EU has recently argued for the need to make social policy more flexible. In addition, social pol-

64. Pierson (1996a).
65. Dalton and Eichenberg (1996).

icy is increasingly discussed in connection with EMU, where the issue is how to impose the necessary budgetary stringency. Thus Europe seems to be increasingly perceived as an additional threat to very popular national social programs rather than as a new buttress for the welfare state. This is a dangerous development in a context where social programs are certain to come under growing fiscal pressure, politicians have incentives to find scapegoats, and the EU's popularity is already precarious.

The character of European politics and policymaking has undergone a considerable transformation as the European Union has taken shape. Compared with some other policy spheres, the transformation in the field of social policy has been rather halting and remains difficult to pin down. Because a number of the most relevant processes operate indirectly or are only now beginning to appear, claims about the most important dynamics are necessarily somewhat speculative. What does seem clear, however, is that "social policy development" and "European integration" can no longer be treated as largely separate processes. European integration is becoming an important influence on the character of social policy development, and the politics of national social policy reform has serious implications for the process of European integration.

Chapter 5

The Limits of Europe's Common Foreign and Security Policy

Philip H. Gordon

For more than three decades now, and in particular since the 1991 Treaty on European Union (TEU, or Maastricht Treaty), the European Union (EU) has been trying to enhance its effectiveness as a global diplomatic and military actor. This chapter places foreign and security policy integration within the framework of competing theories of European integration, reviews the recent functioning and effectiveness of the common foreign security policy (CFSP), assesses the results of the 1996–97 EU Intergovernmental Conference (IGC), and analyzes the prospects for successful progress toward a common European foreign and security policy in the coming decades. Is the European Union on its way, however slowly, to becoming an organized and unified foreign policy actor with increasingly common global interests and the means—including military means—to protect those interests? Or will a CFSP continue to prove elusive, the victim of historical and cultural differences among European states, diverging national interests after the end of the cold war, and the unwillingness of Europe's individual states and citizenries to relinquish control over foreign policy decisionmaking? What are the preconditions for further foreign policy integration and to what extent are those conditions currently being fulfilled or likely to be fulfilled?

I argue that the CFSP set up by the Treaty on European Union has not had a significant effect on European foreign policy cohesion or effectiveness. The CFSP has been useful as a forum in which European governments regularly discuss international affairs and seek consensus among themselves, but it has not been significantly better at producing consensus than the European political cooperation that came before it, and it has not endowed the European Union with the capacity to deal quickly and effectively with external crises. The European Union is highly effective in determining and implementing common external aid and trade policies that promote its members' long-term, nonmilitary interests. As I argue below, however, these are just some of the possible goals of a CFSP and not the ones most often in mind when its strengthening is discussed.

I also argue that the prospects for significant improvements in the functioning and effectiveness of the CFSP are limited. As I seek to demonstrate, past patterns and the most convincing theories of European integration suggest that integration takes place only when its perceived benefits exceed the perceived costs of lost sovereignty and prestige, and that this condition applies only when perceived national interests and government preferences converge to the point that the risks of ceding sovereignty are minimal. Because there is little evidence that these conditions currently hold, I predict that the member states of the EU will continue to be reluctant to adopt the institutional adjustments that would be necessary to enhance significantly the effectiveness of the CFSP. I argue that over the longer term, because of the end of the cold war, the likely enlargement of the European Union to include states with diverse and particular backgrounds and interests, and the unlikelihood that a common European identity will emerge, the external interests of EU member states are not likely to converge sufficiently to allow for significantly more pooled sovereignty. In the military domain, because of competing domestic priorities and the culture of dependence fostered by the cold war, Europeans will be unwilling to make the necessary institutional changes and spend the necessary sums of money that an independent strategic role would require.

Competing Theories of European Integration and Their Implications for a CFSP

To assess the prospects for integration in the area of foreign and security policy, it is useful to reflect on past patterns of European integration and on the theories that best explain the conditions under which integration proceeds in different areas. The coming years may possibly see a sharp departure from previous patterns of European integration, but it is unlikely; and in the absence of compelling reasons to believe these past patterns will not hold, the best way to know what to expect in the future is to try to understand what has happened in the past and why.

In the theoretical literature on the European Community, there are two broadly competing explanations—they might be called *functionalist* (or *neofunctionalist*) and *intergovernmentalist*—of how and why the process of integration proceeds.[1] The *functionalist* set of theories emphasizes the process by which power is gradually transferred to a "new center" as integration in some areas makes it more necessary in others; institutions, once set up, push to expand their power; leaders and people call for integration in new domains as they see its success in others; and transnational elites and interest groups tend to "socialize" and develop common views and interests. Ultimately, as power is transferred to the new, central institutions, people come to transfer their expectations and loyalty to the new institutions. Such functionalist theories dominated explanations of European integration during the 1960s, when the European Economic Community (EEC) was first moving forward but largely went out of fashion during the 1970s as European integration stalled.[2]

The second set of theories—*intergovernmentalist*—emphasizes national interests, bargaining, lowest-common-denominator deals, and the unwillingness of states (or at least large states) to compromise their core national interests. The intergovernmental paradigm has been predominant since the 1980s, when the limits of functionalism became clear and alternative explanations for the European Community's unexpected revival in the mid-1980s were required.

1. Here "integration" is defined as either the delegation of sovereignty to new central institutions or the sharing, or "pooling," of sovereignty in common institutions.
2. A more detailed discussion of functionalism would distinguish between "functional spillover," in which successful integration in one area leads to demands for integration in other areas, and "political spillover," in which success in institution building leads to greater supranational entrepreneurship and more cooperation. For a concise explanation and discussion of the literature on functionalism, see Moravcsik (1993).

162   Philip H. Gordon

Although the success of the 1987 Single European Act (SEA) and the decision at Maastricht in 1991 to proceed with monetary union has stimulated renewed scholarly interest in new versions of the old functionalist theories, the dominant explanation of the Community's recent revival has emphasized the importance of states.³

Functionalism and intergovernmentalism are not only competing descriptions of integration processes; they carry policy implications as well, particularly where the building of institutions is concerned. Confidence in functionalist explanations for integration leads to the belief that the setting up of institutions itself should be a goal because those institutions will be used, confidence in them will grow, their legitimacy will become established, and the ideology and momentum of integration will be maintained. In response to the intergovernmentalists' view that institutions cannot work unless common goals are shared, functionalists have faith that the institutions themselves can have an effect on the perception of common goals. Intergovernmentalists, thus, tend to take a pragmatic view of what is possible and seek to keep institution-building within those limits, while functionalists believe that the European integration process is about *changing* what is possible and *stretching* the limits. This debate about vision and momentum on one hand, and pragmatism on the other, has often marked the difference between French and British views about the European integration process.⁴

Which set of theories explains more? Despite the recent preference for intergovernmental approaches (which, as argued below, are more relevant to the CFSP), it must be admitted that functionalism still has a certain logic and that functionalist pressures do exist, even if they are not always strong enough to bring about spreading integration. Functionalism has been badly served by the ultimate

3. For the renewed interest in functionalism—but also the emphasis on states and governments—see Keohane and Hoffmann (1991) and the discussion in Moravcsik (1991).

4. French leaders (including Jean Monnet, Valéry Giscard d'Estaing, François Mitterrand, and Jacques Delors) have often explicitly supported the setting up of institutions—like the European Coal and Steel Community, the European Monetary System, or the Eurocorps—on the grounds that their very existence would propel the process of integration forward and keep the notion of "Europe" alive, whereas British leaders have tended to oppose institutions—including all of above—unless their immediate usefulness could be demonstrated.

expectation of a transfer of loyalties to a new center that has not happened. That failed expectation, however, should not discredit the theory. The process has hardly been rapid or complete, but it does seem, as functionalists expected, that the formation of a customs union led to pressures for a completed single market; that the creation of a single market led to increased calls for monetary union; that monetary union and other forms of integration have led to calls for further democratization of the EU; and that the common interests and perspectives resulting from all this integration increases pressure for a common foreign and security policy to represent and pursue the interests of the Union. All along, EU elites and institutions have pushed to expand their power, and the perceived successes in some areas (like the single market and common commercial policy) and perceived failures in others (like monetary and foreign policy) have led to calls for integration in new domains. These pressures have not always led to further integration, but it is worth noting that they exist.[5]

It is also clear from the past forty years, however, that the member states of the European Community have proven eminently capable of resisting the pressures and incentives of integration as well as the lobbying of institutions and interest groups, and that integration only moves forward when member states have sufficiently common perceived interests (government-preference convergence) that the potential gains of integration (through increased scale and the absence of interstate friction) are greater than the costs of lost sovereignty. As a general rule, only when it is in the mutual interests of the large states of the Community are common arrangements set up, and only when it is in those states' interest are those arrangements abided by in times of difficulty. In the mid-1960s, for example, the French government concluded that it was not in its interest to allow the strengthening of the European Commission or the increased use of majority voting, and it provoked the "Luxembourg Compromise," a de facto national veto on legislation that nearly all member states found useful to employ in the coming decades.[6] In the early 1970s, despite the pressures for—and setting up of—an in-

5. On the pressures toward integration and the process of "spillover," see Haas (1958, pp. 243, 283–317); and the discussion in Keohane and Hoffmann (1991, pp. 18–22).
6. For details, see Nicoll (1984).

164   Philip H. Gordon

strument to coordinate monetary policy (the "snake") and calls for a full monetary union, the oil crisis and Middle East War of 1973 drove EC economic policies apart and forced the dismantling of the monetary arrangements. European integration moved forward again in the 1980s with the SEA but only, as Andrew Moravcsik has shown, because the preferences and perceived interests of the main EC governments converged at that time and on that issue and integration proceeded in such a way as to meet the minimum requirements of the major EC States.[7] In the early 1990s, just as scholars had begun once again to pay close attention to regional integration theory, the diverging national interests of the main EC states led some of them to abandon their revived attempts to harmonize monetary policy and exchange rates (the exchange rate mechanism of the European Monetary System), and voters in France and Denmark showed in referenda that the popularity of even limited integration was not widespread. The fledgling CFSP showed its limits as soon as it was announced when member states were divided over how to deal with the conflict in former Yugoslavia.

The conclusion from even this brief sketch of the apparent processes of and prerequisites for European integration thus seems clear and is relevant to any assessment of the prospects for further integration in the area of foreign and security policy: states only share their sovereignty, let alone *surrender* sovereignty to a new institution, when the following conditions hold:

1. The perceived gains of common action through the advantages of scale outweigh the potential costs of lost sovereignty or national prestige.[8]

2. Government-preferences or perceived national interests have converged sufficiently so that the first condition holds (because lost sovereignty is likely to matter less when EC member governments have similar interests and ideologies).

7. See Moravcsik (1991). Also see Cameron (1992).
8. The advantages of scale include the added leverage that comes from a unified bargaining position; the benefits that derive from avoiding EU states pursuing *competing* interests; and the possibility of using Community prestige, means, institutions, and financing, which can enhance leverage and possibly facilitate more efficient implementation, for the pursuit of certain objectives. For a discussion of why common action might enhance leverage, see Ginsberg (1989, pp. 3, 154).

3. Very particular interests of large states remain protected either through the application of strict limits or conditions to the terms of integration, or through the opting-out of the state with the particular interests.

These conditions have held in the area of commercial policy, where the gains of scale in internal free trade and through a common external bargaining position outweighed the costs of giving up national commercial policies (condition one), and the particular interest of French agriculture was protected (condition three). They have held for the completion of the internal market, where the abandonment of the national veto was seen as necessary to pass important single-market legislation (condition one). Since by the mid-1980s all EC governments had accepted the virtues of economic liberalism and deregulation, the risks of sacrificed sovereignty were perceived as small, even by the British government at the time (condition two). And more recently, all three conditions played important roles in the area of monetary policy: the perceived gains of unity were greater than the lost-sovereignty cost of all the governments that agreed to participate (condition one); the first condition held because all those governments had come to accept the virtues of independent central banks and anti-inflationary currency policies (condition two); and Germany protected its particular interest in a stable currency by requiring strict criteria for joining the Economic and Monetary Union (EMU), while Britain and Denmark reserved the right not to participate because for them the first condition did not apply (condition three).

A similar analysis could be made of the agreement to allow open borders among the signatories of the Schengen Agreement as well as of the social chapter of the Maastricht Treaty, but not yet for foreign and security policy, in which the states have insisted on preserving national autonomy.

It is also worth noting what the past record says about when integration does *not* happen: it does not happen simply because states want to keep up the momentum toward functional integration. Institutions are important in forming common perceptions, and there is certainly a bias toward EU cooperation and political solidarity whenever possible. But the record suggests that states take only cosmetic steps toward integration when their perceived interests are not served by accepting real integration. European states may well

one day accept a fully integrated foreign policy simply for the sake
of creating a true union, but that would be breaking with a pattern
of functional cooperation that has evolved over the decades.

From the preceding analysis, it seems clear that the prerequisite
for the development of foreign and security policy integration is a
convergence of the perceived interests of the main member states, at
least to the point where they either (1) no longer fear that the common policy will diverge significantly from their national policy; or
(2) are compelled by the development of an important common interest to believe that a common policy is worth the sacrifice of national autonomy. States will only take the difficult and self-denying
decision to "share" their sovereignty if the gains of common action
are seen to be so great that sacrificing sovereignty is worth it or if
their interests converge to the point that little loss of sovereignty is
entailed.

I argue below that these conditions have not held in the past, do
not currently hold, and are not likely to hold in the foreseeable future. In foreign and security policy, the perceived benefits of institutionalized cooperation seem so low that governments still feel they
can indulge cultural, historical, or domestic political imperatives.
Before showing why, however, it is necessary to make clear just
what is understood here by common foreign and security policy, for
the discussion of the CFSP is often plagued by ambiguity and confusion about just what is being discussed. Indeed many apparent "disagreements" about the CFSP—both prescriptive and descrip-
tive—are not really disagreements at all but simply reflections of a
failure to agree on terms and state them clearly.

The first ambiguity with the CFSP is that it potentially covers a
wide range of different things, from long-term economic aid to crisis reaction and potential military interventions. Thus if one analyst
has in mind the EU's long-term approach to Sub-Saharan Africa or
Ukraine and another is thinking about the Gulf War or the Yugoslav
crisis, it is not surprising that they can come to very different conclusions about how successful the CFSP has been, what its prospects are, and how best to fix it.[9] As noted earlier, the EU is in fact

9. See, for example, Philip Zelikow's sharp critique of CFSP, based on the (un-
stated) assumption that it is primarily about military crisis response (like the Gulf
and Bosnia wars, the two cases he uses). The critique is trenchant if crisis response is
the issue at hand; if long-term foreign orientation is the issue the critique misses the
mark. And contrast this with the view of Eberhard Rhein of the European Commis-

highly effective at using trade and foreign aid in support of its long-term economic interests, but it is less good at crisis reaction or diplomatic and military intervention. I define "foreign and security policy" broadly and focus on the diplomatic and security aspects more than economic ones, since these are the areas the CFSP was designed to improve. It is true that the Maastricht Treaty makes a distinction between "external action" (in which the European Commission and other communitarian bodies have a leading role) and "foreign and security policy" (which is primarily intergovernmental), but it also states that the CFSP deals with "all questions related to the security of the Union" and sets forth goals no less ambitious than the "safeguarding of the common values, fundamental interests and independence of the Union"; "strengthening the security of the Union and its member states in all ways"; and "preserving peace and strengthening international security" (article J.1.2). These—and not just the institutional mechanisms laid out in title V of the Maastricht Treaty—are the objectives against which its contributions should primarily be analyzed and judged.

The second potential ambiguity is about what "strengthening the CFSP"—a goal of all the member states of the EU—really means. "Progress toward CFSP" could conceivably be judged according to how integrated (as opposed to intergovernmental) the policy is, how global (as opposed to regional) it is, how military (as opposed to civilian) it is, how well articulated (as opposed to poorly explained) it is, or how well it can deal with immediate crises (as opposed to pursuing long-term goals). There is no "right" or "wrong" definition of progress, but it is important to be clear just which definition one has in mind. Along any of these axes, I believe the notion of "making progress" toward a CFSP must involve the creation of institutional, legal, or political mechanisms to promote and implement common perspectives or actions. For the word *cooperation* to have meaning, it must to some degree entail getting states to do what they otherwise would not have done, either through mechanisms to promote convergence of views (through common analysis and consultation), through deals in the expectation of mutual gain, or, most significantly, through binding decisionmaking institutions.

sion, who, in listing the means available to a state for foreign policy—treaty policy; economic cooperation; and diplomatic measures—does not even mention military force. Not surprisingly, Rhein's judgement of CFSP is more positive than Zelikow's. See Zelikow (1996, pp. 9–10); and Rhein (1996, p. 55).

Simply happening to agree on the same policy—say, to support democracy in South Africa—is very important, but it does not require a common foreign and security policy to bring it about.[10]

Finally, the CFSP can be ambiguous because any normative judgment of it depends on the perspective of the judge. Depending on the level of analysis—the EU itself, one or another EU member state, outside actors such as the United States, or world order in general—the CFSP will have different merits and drawbacks. Foreign policy integration might, for example, be in the interest of the EU as an organization or of small member states with little independence to lose, but it might not be in the interest of other states or of outside actors. Rather than assert categorically that the CFSP is or is not a good thing, it is important to keep in mind the different ways integration would affect different actors in the process and the way in which these differences could affect the outcome of negotiations. Different actors will make different assessments of whether the CFSP would be in their interest, and opposing views will not necessarily be "wrong."

From EPC to CFSP: The Record of Foreign Policy Cooperation So Far

The CFSP created in the 1991 Treaty on European Union is but the latest in a long series of attempts over the past forty years to coordinate the foreign policies of the members of the European Community. The first successful attempt to do so—after the failed European Defense Community of the early 1950s and the failed Fouchet plans of the early 1960s—was "European political cooperation (EPC)," which was conceived at the Hague EEC summit of 1969 and

10. It might be worth noting that when the Community uses the word "common" in other functional areas ("common agricultural policy," "common currency," "common fisheries policy"), it normally refers to policies that are under the authority of Community institutions (such as the European Commission and Parliament or a European Central Bank), which go beyond simple intergovernmental coordination and genuinely imply joint implementation and binding central decisions. The reason the United States (or any other state) has a true "CFSP" is not because its "member states" have the same interests and always agree on what to do, but because it has legitimate, centralized institutions with the authority to make binding decisions.

came into being in 1970.[11] EPC was a network of European foreign ministers, political directors, and other diplomats who sought to meet regularly to exchange information and coordinate their foreign policies as much as possible.[12] It had no formal status in the EEC treaties and was entirely intergovernmental. EPC was a recognition by European leaders that in the absence of a more integrated approach, regularly meeting and talking about foreign policy was better than nothing.

The 1987 Single European Act gave EPC a place in the EC treaties for the first time. It assigned the European Commission a role in the "political and economic aspects of security" and called on EC governments not to block, wherever possible, "the formation of a consensus" (article 30.1). Yet even with these strengthened provisions, EPC played a limited role in European foreign policymaking in the late 1980s. Its outcomes were mostly declaratory, always based on consensus, and usually focused on relatively peripheral or uncontroversial issues (such as the Conference on Security and Cooperation in Europe, problems in the horn of Africa, and the Iran-Iraq War) rather than on core issues (such as the Soviet Union, Central Europe, the Mediterranean, or defense). At times EPC even seemed to get in the way of rapid EC foreign policy decisionmaking, as when European leaders took weeks before even making a statement on the 1979 Soviet invasion of Afghanistan or when they failed to find anything at all to say about the U.S. invasion of Grenada in 1983.[13] One of the most successful areas for EPC was its role in coordinating European policy toward the Middle East, beginning with the "Euro-Arab" dialogue of the late 1970s and culminating with the June 1980 Venice Declaration on the Arab-Israeli peace process.[14] Even in this area, however, although EC policies were fairly

11. The EDC was rejected by the French National Assembly in 1954 largely because it was too integrated and too Atlanticist, and the Fouchet plans were rejected by the Belgians and Dutch in 1962 because they were not integrated and not Atlanticist enough. This intra-European debate over integration and Atlanticism was one of the main reasons for the inability to agree on foreign policy cooperation for so long, and it still divides Europeans today.

12. For an excellent study of EPC written by an "insider," see Nutall (1992).

13. See Délégation de l'Assemblée Nationale (1994, p. 14).

14. The Venice declaration distinguished EU policy from U.S. policy by emphasizing the "legitimate rights of the Palestinian people" and calling for a Palestine Liberation Organization to have a role in the peace process. See Conseil Européen (1980); and Marschall (1994).

well coordinated, they were primarily declaratory and had little actual effect. When the Middle East peace process finally got off the ground in October 1991 after the Gulf War, its official sponsors were the United States and the moribund Soviet Union, and the EU played hardly any role.

The EPC was not without purpose or effect, however, and European diplomats noted over the years that regular contacts led to better understanding of each others' positions and facilitated a common approach.[15] EPC also helped to harmonize EC member state positions on a range of issues in regions such as Latin America and Asia, where local actors were unable to play one EC state off another because all members were following the same line. But if a habit of seeking common positions existed it was limited, and a common foreign and security policy did not result, as became sorely evident in Europe's responses to the Gulf War and the Yugoslav crisis. EC member states had national constituencies and interests, and EPC did not. Nor did the Community have the institutional means to impose a common position, or to back up its diplomacy with military force. As the 1990s began, European foreign policies were still nationally made, with EPC playing little more than a consultative function.

The CFSP was a response to EPC's perceived inadequacy in the face of the momentous change that took place in Europe in the late 1980s and early 1990s. With the cold war's end and German unification, France became convinced that the EC's foreign policy process had to be strengthened, if only to "tie in" a now fully sovereign Germany—and Germany, long a strong proponent of all aspects of European integration, readily agreed.[16] The result was the 1990–91 European Intergovernmental Conference (IGC) on political union, which was added to the IGC on monetary union already scheduled for that year and which concluded at the Maastricht summit of December 1991. Britain, until November 1990 under Prime Minister Margaret Thatcher, had opposed the holding of a conference on political union but was overruled by a majority of member states.

---

15. See Hill (1990, p. 33).
16. On the developments leading up to the CFSP agreement at the Maastricht summit of December 1991, see Jopp (1994, pp. 6–12); and Steinberg (1993, pp. 50–60).

Like many previous steps on the road to European integration, the CFSP created at Maastricht reflected a lowest-common-denominator compromise among the competing visions and interests of the EC's member states. In this case, the compromise was between one group of states, led by France and Germany, that sought to strengthen the existing EPC significantly and to give it more of an integrated and binding character, and another group, led by Great Britain, that was more cautious about giving up its national foreign policy prerogatives and sought to avoid any possible threat to the cohesion of the Atlantic alliance.

The Maastricht Treaty created a new, three-pillar structure for the European Union—with the European Community as the first pillar, the CFSP as the second, and Home and Justice Affairs as the third. Only the first pillar would be governed by the integrated community institutions (the European Commission, Parliament, and Court of Justice) while the other two would remain almost exclusively intergovernmental. This was a disappointment for those states that supported foreign policy integration within the European Community, but it reflected the unwillingness of a number of member states (not only Britain but also others including France) to abandon to the Commission their right of foreign policy initiative. Under the Treaty on European Union, the Commission is "associated" with the work of the CFSP (article J.9) and now has, along with member states, a right of initiative in foreign policy (article J.8), but the Council of Ministers remains the deciding body and the member states the key actors. Unlike in EC affairs (the first pillar), the European Parliament is only "consulted or informed about the fundamental aspects of CFSP" (article J.7), and the European Court of Justice has no role at all.

Like EPC, the CFSP foresees the "systematic cooperation of member states" (article J.1), and calls on them to consult in the Council and seek to coordinate their positions and statements on any question of foreign and security policy "representing a general interest." Going further than EPC, however, the CFSP provides for the possibility of moving beyond mere consultations to the adoption of "common positions" (article J.2) and "joint actions" (article J.3). Common positions on functional or regional issues may be declared by the Council "each time it deems necessary," and "joint actions" actually commit the member states to the joint implementation, including in some cases joint financing, of foreign policy decisions. While some aspects of implementing a joint action may be decided by qualified majority voting (QMV), the joint action itself must be decided by unanimity.

Finally, the CFSP went beyond EPC in bringing defense policy formally into the scope of EU affairs but only in a very limited fashion, reflecting the great divergence among member states about the role the Union should play in this area. Title V, article J.4, of the Maastricht Treaty reflects the lowest-common-denominator compromise nature of the treaty in stating, awkwardly, that the CFSP deals with "all questions related to the security of the Union, including the eventual framing of a common defense policy, which might in time lead to a common defense." The treaty also states that the EU can request the "WEU [the Western European Union], which is an integral part of the development of the Union, to elaborate and implement decisions and actions of the Union which have defense implications" (article J.4.2). In all of these areas related to defense, however, unanimity is the rule, and the integrated Community bodies have no role.

The result of the Maastricht negotiations on the CFSP is thus a good demonstration of the theory of European integration described earlier, that integration is only accepted when the perceived gains of scale clearly outweigh the costs of lost sovereignty, at least for the large member states. EC leaders came together at Maastricht to negotiate a common foreign and security policy in the wake of momentous international change, but despite the ostensible French and German enthusiasm for the project (and their mutual goal of an ever-closer Europe), they agreed only on limited institutional change, not a qualitative leap forward. The prerequisites for integration had not been met.

How effective has the CFSP been under the Maastricht provisions? Even the most enthusiastic supporters of a CFSP would accept the EU Commission's own assessment that "the aim of a substantial improvement has not been achieved."[17] The EU has, it is true, established more than twenty-five so-called common posi-

17. See European Commission (1995, p. 63). A recent French analysis has also admitted that CFSP "has not been able to play a determining role." See Institut Français des Relations Internationales (1996, p. 320).

tions, including one on economic relations with Libya, Sudan, Haiti, and former Yugoslavia; on general policy objectives or a common approach toward Ukraine, Rwanda, Burundi, Angola, and East Timor; and on functional subjects such as blinding lasers, the biological and chemical weapons convention, and the co-location of diplomatic missions. It has made an unprecedented number of joint declarations on foreign policy (roughly two per week) and taken more than three dozen "joint actions," including supervising elections in South Africa and Russia, delivering aid to the Palestinian Authority, organizing humanitarian aid in Bosnia and administering the Bosnian city of Mostar, supporting the indefinite extension of the Nuclear Non-Proliferation Treaty, and negotiating and implementing the Stability Pact (or Balladur plan) to ensure stability in Central Europe.[18]

But the CFSP has been absent from other, more important (or more controversial), aspects of European foreign and security policy. Intelligence collection and analysis is still a national responsibility, and common EU representation in international bodies such as the UN Security Council is not even considered, although the Amsterdam Treaty does call for "coordinated action in international organizations" (article J.9). In the Middle East, the EU has continued to seek a greater diplomatic role and in October 1996 appointed its own special representative there, but analysts agree that Europe's diplomatic role remains extremely limited relative to its economic presence and assistance to the region and that EU member states cannot agree on how the EU should interact with the United States in the peace process.[19] Even those states supposedly most enthusiastic about developing a united EU capacity for action, such as France, have been unwilling to abandon their own freedom of maneuver in areas of national importance. France's unilateral intervention in Rwanda in June 1994, its decision later that year to conduct a final series of nuclear tests (condemned at the United Nations by eleven of the sixteen EU member states), and its immediate dispatch of its foreign minister to Lebanon in the April 1996 crisis in the Middle East provided some recent evidence of the CFSP's inability either to

18. On the common positions and joint actions, see European Commission (1997, pp. 18–20); and Ryba (1995).
19. See Hollis (1997); International Institute for Strategic Studies (1996); and Stein (1996).

constrain continued national foreign policy behavior or to offer an acceptable alternative to it. Greece's 1994–95 economic embargo of the former Yugoslav republic of Macedonia, Britain's isolated support for U.S. air strikes on Iraq in September 1996, and France and Germany's unwillingness to agree to an April 1997 EU resolution critical of China's human rights record (lest it imperil their economic contracts with Beijing) were all further examples of cases in which certain EU states had distinct perceived national interests and pursued national foreign and security policies to protect those interests. Most recently, Italy's April 1997 decision to organize a peace enforcement mission to Albania *outside* the context of either the EU or WEU, because of a lack of consensus or ability in those organizations to compel joint action, demonstrated the enduring limits of the CFSP.

Close consultations among member states have been pursued through the CFSP, and the general bias toward "systematic cooperation among member states," while difficult to measure, does seem to exist. But in the areas that the Maastricht Treaty was supposed to strengthen—the areas in which the Community was not already competent through its effective first pillar—the CFSP has been ineffective. Judged by any of the possible criteria for "progress" discussed earlier—degree of unity of member states, ability to act globally, ability to act militarily, crisis reaction, or even presentation of policy—the CFSP has not been significantly better than EPC. Unless and until EU member states agree that there is more to be gained than lost from binding institutional integration, these weaknesses are unlikely to disappear.

Assessing the Amsterdam IGC

At the EU 1996–97 intergovernmental conference (concluded in Amsterdam in June 1997), called by the Maastricht Treaty partly to reassess and strengthen the CFSP, member states considered a wide range of institutional proposals for improving foreign policy cooperation. As noted above, the consensus among observers and officials alike was that the CFSP had not been effective, and some member states went into the IGC determined to make bold moves in the foreign policy area. Spurred on by the admitted failure in Bosnia, the need to find some functional area in which to pursue integration lest momentum be slowed, and ongoing uncertainty about the American role in Europe, many EU leaders thought foreign policy might be the most promising area for further EU integration, especially as the monetary union project seemed to be in trouble.

The Amsterdam summit made institutional or legal changes in four main areas.[20] None of the changes, however, is likely to lead to significant improvement in the functioning of the CFSP.

A Policy Planning and Analysis Cell

The one institutional change on which there was general agreement among all EU members, including Great Britain, was the setting up of an EU foreign policy planning and analysis cell. Despite the current existence of a foreign policy unit at the Commission and a CFSP secretariat, most European leaders agree that foreign policy analysis is currently done primarily at the national level, with the result that national positions can become hardened before a "European" analysis can be formed. A stronger capacity for EU planning and analysis—through a sizable and autonomous multinational grouping—was designed to alleviate this problem.

Strengthening the CFSP's planning and analysis is probably a useful initiative, but its likely usefulness should not be exaggerated. Indeed whatever failures the CFSP may have encountered in the past few years, their origin has been not so much that European leaders did not know what was going on, but rather that they could not agree on what to do about it. It will certainly not hurt to have a multinational European team in Brussels seeking to reach a common analysis of common problems, but many policies in important areas are made on the basis of national interests and public perceptions, not on the analysis of planning cells, national or otherwise. With the new planning and analysis cell, the leaders of EU member states will have at their disposal a more "common" analysis of for-

20. For the specifics of what was agreed on at Amsterdam, see Intergovernmental Conference, Amsterdam European Council, *An Effective and Coherent External Policy*, chapter 12, "The Common Foreign and Security Policy," available from the European Union website (http://europa.eu.int/abc-en.htm).

eign policy issues; the question that remains is whether they will use it.

A "High Representative" for Foreign Policy

EU leaders also agreed at Amsterdam to create the new post of "high representative" for the common foreign and security policy to assist the presidency in articulating and explaining EU foreign policy both within Europe and in the world at large. The holder of the new position will be the secretary general of the Council of Ministers and will be seconded by a deputy secretary general responsible for the running of the General Secretariat (so that the high representative can focus on foreign policy). This was a step back from an initial French proposal to create a "Mr./Ms. CFSP"—a leading political figure who would presumably carry more weight than a civil servant—but it was all that could be agreed on given opposition to the more ambitious version of the plan. Less integrationist states like Britain opposed the more political Mr./Ms. CFSP because they thought an independent figure might be difficult for the member states to control; some of the smaller member states opposed it because they feared Mr./Ms. CFSP would always come from a big country (or that the big countries would not heed him or her anyway); and the Commission itself opposed the plan because it believed its own external relations officials should be responsible for representing the Union abroad. Thus the high representative idea was a compromise to give a more personalized voice to the CFSP—but not too much more.

The appointment of a high representative for the CFSP will probably not do any harm, and there are cases in which it may help. In theory, the high representative—even if not a leading political figure—could provide coordination, continuity, and visibility to the leadership of the CFSP, and he or she could seek to persuade national governments to adopt common positions and then articulate those positions throughout the EU and to the wider world. Giving more visibility to the high representative—or to various EU special representatives, also allowed for in the Amsterdam Treaty—might also eliminate some of the flaws in the current "troika" system of EU representation, whereby the current, previous, and forthcoming holder of the rotating EU presidency represents the Union abroad.[21]

Even the most competent representative of an EU foreign policy, however, will have difficulty "representing" a common interest that does not exist and will run up against the same sort of intra-EU differences that have plagued the troika and Commission in their own efforts to represent the Union. It is worth remembering, after all, that throughout the Balkan crises, the EC/EU had respected, competent, and energetic policy representatives—Lord Carrington until 1992 and Lord Owen from 1992 to 1995. That Carrington and Owen were not able to prevent European foreign policy from being decided in national capitals (Carrington, for example, advised strongly against the recognition of Croatia and Slovenia in late 1991 but could not prevent a unilateral German promise to Zagreb and Ljubjana to do so) was no fault of their own, and it is unlikely that without further changes states will heed more closely the advice of their representative. So long as EU member states reserve the right to decide nationally whom they will aid financially, recognize diplomatically, sanction politically, or attack militarily, the high representative will have limited room for maneuver and little credibility as a representative. This will be particularly the case as long as the job is held by an unknown civil servant rather than a more prominent political figure. A high representative for foreign policy will only be able to do his or her job if there is something to represent.

21. Among the many drawbacks of the Troika system is the risk that at times none of the big countries is represented in international crises. At the time of the Iraqi invasion of Kuwait, for example, the Troika consisted of Ireland, Italy, and Luxembourg, and was snubbed as irrelevant by Iraq. When war in Yugoslavia broke out, the Troika comprised Luxembourg, Italy, and the Netherlands, a group that did not include the major European players in the Balkans. And during the April 1996 crisis in South Lebanon, the Troika consisted of Italy, Spain and Ireland, the first two of which were operating under caretaker governments, and the last of which had hardly any interests, experience, or influence in the Middle East. Without taking anything away from the able diplomats in the small European countries, the credibility, continuity, and unity necessary effectively to represent EU foreign policy—let alone to make it—surely does not exist under the current system. On the Troika in the Gulf, see Zaldivar and Ortega (1992, p. 131). On former Yugoslavia, see Silber and Little (1995, pp. 174–84).

Qualified Majority Voting

In the run-up to the IGC, a number of important actors and analysts argued that abandoning the national veto is an essential step toward a true CFSP. A high-level expert group led by Commissioner for External Political Relations Hans van den Broek, for example, concluded that "it is indispensable to liberate [the CFSP] from the paralysis of the veto." According to the group, "Unanimity must disappear, except for the practical organization of military interventions."[22] Similarly, Karl Lamers, the foreign policy spokesman of the German Christian Democratic Union/Christian Social Union parliamentary group, argued that "only majority voting engenders a capacity for effective action. Everything else is an illusion. Hence, majority voting must also be introduced in the field of foreign and security policy."[23] For Nicole Gnesotto of the Institut Français des Relations Internationales and a former French policy planner, it was essential to reform CFSP decisionmaking procedures "so that a majority of states can not be prevented from taking a Union action by the veto of a single state."[24] Expanding the use of QMV for the CFSP in one way or another was officially supported by all EU governments except Denmark, Finland, Ireland, Portugal, Sweden, and Great Britain.

Despite these arguments and the ostensible member-state support, however, EU leaders at Amsterdam failed to agree on any significant extension of qualified majority voting. Article J.13 of the Amsterdam draft treaty does allow for the use of QMV for the adoption or implementation of joint actions or common positions (once the "common strategy" is decided unanimously) but also notes that any member state can prevent such a vote if, "for important and stated reasons of national policy," it opposes the measure in question. The draft treaty also adopts the principle of "constructive abstention," which would allow a member state to abstain from imple-

22. See the report "La politique de sécurité de l'Europe à l'horizon 2000: les voies et les moyens d'une vraie crédibilité," *Agence Europe* no. 6,408, January 28, 1995, p. 3.
23. Lamers (1996, p. 81) also supports "putting an end to the unfortunate pillar structure." p. 81. Also see the Schäuble-Lamers document of the CDU/CSU of September 1, 1994; and the second CDU-CSU document, "Die Europäische Union Aussen- und Sicherheitspolitisch handlungsfähiger machen," Pressedienst CDU-CSU, Bonn, June 13, 1995. Available from the CDU/CSU press office, Bonn.
24. See Gnesotto (1996, p. 122).

menting an EU decision even while it accepts that the decision commits the Union. None of these provisions, however, go much further than those already existing in the Maastricht Treaty, which already allowed for QMV on the implementation of policies agreed unanimously and which encouraged states to seek to avoid blocking a majority where one exists. If a member state does not agree with a policy, it still does not have to implement it, and if it really objects, it can still block the Union from agreeing to the policy in the first place.

QMV can clearly be an effective tool to pass legislation (as its use in the area of the single market has shown), but it is only acceptable to member states under the conditions discussed earlier—when the gains of imposed common action seem greater than the risks. For all the claims of a commitment to strengthening the CFSP, this condition does not yet appear to enough states to have been met.

Integrating the WEU and the EU

The Amsterdam summit made minor progress toward enhancing the EU's defense capability by associating the Union more closely with the Western European Union (WEU). Going into the summit, France, Germany, Italy, Spain, Belgium, Luxembourg, and Greece—all traditional proponents of a greater defense role for the EU—put forth a proposal for a specific timetable for the gradual merger of the EU and WEU, but they were blocked by Great Britain.[25] Instead, all that could be agreed on was an unspecified commitment to "enhance cooperation" between the two organizations. Summit leaders also agreed that EU members that are not members of the WEU (this includes Austria, Denmark, Finland, Ireland, and Sweden) could participate in some WEU activities and that an EU-WEU merger could take place "should the European Council so decide" (article J.7, former J.4), a provision that makes merger possible without the need for a new IGC. The Amsterdam draft treaty also brings so-called Petersberg tasks—humanitarian and rescue tasks,

25. The merger proposal was first publicly outlined by French Foreign Minister Hervé de Charette and his Italian counterpart, Lamberto Dini, in "Innover pour Progresser," *Le Monde*, March 25, 1997.

peacekeeping tasks, and tasks of combat forces in crisis management—into the EU treaties for the first time and allows the EU to "avail itself" of the WEU, slightly stronger wording than the right to "request" WEU action stated in the Maastricht Treaty.[26]

These provisions further nudge the EU toward a defense role, but they fall well short of a merger with the WEU; indeed the draft treaty continues to treat defense as separate from foreign and security policy, and it preserves the right of any member state to see that this remains the case. Moreover, even moving closer to the WEU does not add much to the EU's capacity to use or threaten to use military force. Despite the recent attempts to strengthen its operational capabilities, the WEU still has no independent command structure, extremely limited intelligence-gathering capability, and a minimal capacity for force projection. NATO's June 1996 decision to make NATO assets potentially available for WEU-led missions could help, but it should not be forgotten that NATO actually has very limited assets of its own and that most of what it does have (an air defense system; some command, control, and communications capabilities; pipelines and bunkers; and eighteen AWACS) is not really appropriate for the types of missions the WEU might conceivably be asked to conduct. What the Europeans would really need in order to conduct autonomous operations are not NATO assets but *American* ones—long-range heavy transport aircraft, air-refueling capabilities, and satellite intelligence systems. Because the cost to Europe of developing its own such military capabilities would be tens of billions of dollars—unimaginable in the current context of tight budgets and serious social and economic problems—it seems safe to conclude that for the foreseeable future Europe will remain militarily dependent on the United States for all but small and nearby military missions.[27]

On the whole, then—and not surprisingly if one accepts the framework for analysis of the CFSP offered in this chapter—the out-

26. The Petersberg tasks were those accepted by the WEU at a WEU Council meeting held at the Petersberg castle outside Bonn on June 19, 1992. See Assembly of Western European Union, Sir Russell Johnson, rapporteur, *Western European Union: Information Report* (Brussels: Western European Union, March 1995), pp. 6–16.

27. For a more detailed assessment of European/WEU military capabilities and the implications of the new WEU-NATO arrangements, see Gordon (1997). For estimates of the costs of equipping a European intervention force or building satellite intelligence systems, see Berman and Carter (1993); and O'Hanlon (1997).

come of the Amsterdam IGC was extremely limited. The negotiations were plagued by some of the same divisions among member states—and an unwillingness to accept meaningful institutional integration—that had been present at Maastricht and before. Member states were in theory interested in "strengthening CFSP," but apparently they were not so keen as to be willing to make far-reaching institutional changes. In contrast to the ambitious proposals mooted in the run-up to the IGC and long supported by some of the Union's more integrationist member states, the changes made in Amsterdam were modest, and are unlikely significantly to affect the way the CFSP works.

Longer-Term Prospects: CFSP in the Coming Decades

If the conditions are not yet in place for a genuine integration of European foreign and security policies, will they ever be? Is the creation of an effective CFSP only a matter of time, or has foreign and security policy integration reached its limits? Going back to the theories with which this analysis began, is foreign and security policy just a "function" that is taking longer than some others to be pulled into the centrifuge of European integration, or is there something particular about it that makes it less susceptible to the forces and processes that have led to integration in so many other areas?

This chapter has argued that states only pool or delegate their sovereignty in particular functional areas if the perceived benefits of doing so outweigh the costs. In the area of foreign policy, because the gains of common action are not always obvious and do not accrue evenly to the members of the group, this condition is only likely to be met when national interests or government preferences have converged to the point where the potential costs and risks of binding common action are low. The most critical question about the future of foreign and security policy integration, then, is whether this is happening. If EU members' interests are more similar in the coming decades than they are today, integration will be more likely; if they are not, integration is less likely. This is not the only variable in the long-term development of the CFSP, but it is the most important one.

In favor of the view that European states' foreign and security interests will converge, it might be noted that they have been converging for the past forty years.[28] Some of the issues that most divided Europeans in the past—colonial relationships (and wars), memories of World War II, divergent economic philosophies, and different roles in the cold war—have lost significance, and even ancient cultural differences, while still strong, have become less strong through open communications, travel, and the very ideal of the European Union. More than thirty years of having a common commercial policy, growing monetary coordination, joint industrial projects, and the building of a single market have all made different European states' interests far more similar to each other than they were in the 1950s and 1960s.

A certain spillover process resulting from integration in other domains is also likely to lead to a relative convergence of European interests. Open EU internal borders stemming from the Schengen Agreement, for example, make all states susceptible to the same immigration worries and increase their stake in stabilizing all nearby regions, not just the regions near them. And monetary union, if it happens, will not only further harmonize European economic interests, but it will constrain states' ability to finance independent foreign policy adventures and perhaps contribute to the feeling of unity and commonality that a true CFSP requires.[29] All of these factors suggest that EU member states' interests will converge, and that the pressures for the CFSP will continue well into the future.

Whether they will result in sufficient convergence of interests to make these states willing to accept foreign and security policy integration, however, is another matter. Indeed there are three good reasons to believe they will not. The first reason is that the end of the cold war has taken away one of the most compelling forces behind the need for a common security policy. Without a common enemy and the simplicity of the two-bloc system of the cold war, security interests are potentially more differentiated than in the past. The division of Europe and the cold war harmonized EC foreign policy interests to an extent that is unlikely to be repeated any time in the future.

28. For a good recent argument to this effect, see Grant (1996, pp. 19–20).
29. For an argument that monetary union will increase pressures for more common foreign and security policy, see Jacquet (1996–97, p. 92).

The second reason that convergence of interests even in the long term will not be sufficient to provoke foreign policy integration is that the expected expansion of EU membership to as many as twenty-five to thirty countries will mean a significant expansion of the Union's geographical and cultural diversity. If a Community of six was unwilling to accept foreign policy integration during the cold war (when there was a common threat), a Community of twelve was unwilling to do so at Maastricht (when the French and German leaders were devoted to the idea of European unity and concerns about the future U.S. role in Europe were great), and a Union of fifteen was unwilling to do so at Amsterdam (in the wake of the Bosnian War), it is legitimate to ask why a Community whose membership will be more than twice as large is likely to accept integration sometime in the future. Indeed the European Union of the year 2020 will probably stretch from Portugal in the west to Estonia in the northeast, and from Sweden and Finland in the north to Bulgaria and Greece in the south. It will include a far greater diversity not only of material (economic and security) interests but also of foreign policy traditions, relationships, cultures, and attitudes toward the use of force and intervention. It is true that foreign policy traditions and cultures change with time and political evolution, and that interaction within the Union will help lead to more common thinking and attitudes toward international affairs. But it is also true that these things change extremely slowly, and the diversity in the "strategic cultures" even of current members of the EU (who, it might be noted, are currently unwilling to accept the integration of foreign policies) has hardly disappeared despite decades of interaction within the EC/EU.

It can be argued, of course, that the widening of the Union will *require* integration rather than prevent it because EU institutions will not be able to function with twenty-five separate states having veto power.[30] There is certainly something to this argument, and the use of QMV is likely to be extended incrementally into every domain in which the states will accept it, which they will do when the benefits of unity seem worth this concession. Where foreign and security

---

30. As Alain Lamassoure, former French minister for European Affairs, has put it, "doing things intergovernmentally with 30 members is like reinventing the CSCE or the League of Nations." *Agence Europe*, no. 6,451, March 30, 1995, p. 3.

policy is concerned, however, the question is whether widening to new and diverse states will provoke a willingness to integrate foreign policies to ensure the advantages of common action, or whether, on the contrary, it will provoke the opposite—large states insisting on maintaining their freedom of maneuver and refusing to submit to the will of a centralized institution or a majority that might not have the same interests as they. If there were an absolutely compelling need for integration—a new security threat in the absence of American protection, for example—integration would be a more likely response. Since there is not (even the performance of the EU in Bosnia, recognized as a failure, does not seem to have led to a willingness to integrate foreign policy at the current IGC), integration is unlikely.

Finally, the functionalist arguments for longer-term convergence—that forms of integration such as open borders and monetary union necessarily spread to other areas—can easily be exaggerated. Open borders, it is true, theoretically make all states equally susceptible to regional instabilities around Europe, but in fact states remain unequally susceptible to such problems because of geography, history, language, and culture. Schengen or no Schengen, refugees from central and eastern Europe will mostly go to Germany— the biggest, richest, and closest country to them—and refugees from North Africa will mostly go to France, where they might have family or other contacts and would understand the language. Similarly, monetary union might enhance the internal economic cohesion of the Union and prevent intra-EU exchange rate problems, but it is hard to see how and why it would lead to the harmonization of foreign interests. If economic cohesion were enhanced, it of course would only apply to those EU states participating in the monetary union—and for a very long time this will presumably not include all members—thus actually separating rather than harmonizing EU members' interests. European industrial collaboration also cuts both ways: the desire to sell Airbus aircraft to China may well help to unite the members of the Airbus consortium's foreign (and perhaps even security) policies toward that rising power, but it will not have the same effect on those EU states left out.

The interests of EU members, then, do not seem likely to converge to the point where the true integration of foreign and security policies becomes probable. The desire to preserve the notion of an

EU identity and more efficiently pursue those interests that are shared among Europeans will probably lead to even more interaction and discussion among member states, continued institutional tinkering, the spread of limited QMV to areas that do not involve the potential use of deadly force, and symbolic pronouncements about political solidarity. These things should not be underestimated, and any comparison of EU foreign policy solidarity today with ten, twenty, or thirty years ago is a reminder of how far cooperation has usefully come. But the end of the cold war, the widening of the Union, the continued differences in EU members' strategic culture, ambitions, values, and historical relationships, and the lack—even after forty years of integration—of a European identity sufficient to permit delegation of sovereignty to centralized institutions means that EU foreign policy cooperation will probably remain limited, fragmented, and intergovernmental in nature. Having eliminated wars and security competition among West European states is an enormous historical achievement; but eliminating distinctive national foreign and security policies and preferences will remain an elusive one. The United States' current status as the world's lone superpower may well be challenged in the twenty-first century but not by the European Union.

References

Abraham, Filip. 1994. "Regional Adjustment and Wage Flexibility in the EC." In *The Location of Economic Activity: New Theories and Evidence*, 445–76. London: CEPR.

Addison, John T., and W. Stanley Siebert. 1993. "The EC Social Charter: The Nature of the Beast." *National Westminster Bank Quarterly Review* (February): 13–28.

Alesina, Alberto, and Vittorio Grilli. 1992. "On the Feasibility of a One- or Multi-Speed European Monetary Union." Harvard University.

Arnold, R. Douglas. 1990. *The Logic of Congressional Action*. Yale University Press.

Baldassarri, Mario, ed. 1991. "Building the New Europe—I: Single Market and Monetary Unification in the EEC Countries." *Rivista di Politica Economica* 81 (May).

Bayoumi, Tamim, and Paul R. Masson. 1995. "Fiscal Flows in the United States and Canada: Lessons for Monetary Union in Europe." *European Economic Review* 39: 253–74.

Berenz, Claus. 1994."Hat die betriebliche Altersversorgung zukünftig noch eine Chance?" *Neue Zeitschrift für Arbeitsrecht*, 11 (9/10): 385–90 (part 1), 433–38 (part 2).

Berman, Morton B., and Gwendolen M. Carter. 1993. *The Independent European Force: Costs of Independence*. Santa Monica, Calif.: RAND.

Bieback, Karl-Jurgen. 1991. "Harmonisation of Social Policy in the European Community." *Les Cahiers de Droit* 32 (December): 913–35.

Bloom, Howard S., and H. Douglas Price. 1975. "Voter Response to Short-Run Economic Conditions: The Asymmetric Effect of Prosperity and Recession." *American Political Science Review* 69 (December): 1240–54.

Bonoli, Giuliano, and Bruno Palier. 1995. "Reclaiming Welfare: The Politics of French Social Protection Reform." Paper presented at the British Social Policy Association Annual Conference, Sheffield, July.

Burley, Anne-Marie, and Walter Mattli. 1993. "Europe before the Court: A Political Theory of Legal Integration." *International Organization* 47 (Winter): 41–77.

Cafruny, Alan, and Glenda Rosenthal, eds. 1993. *The State of the European Community: The Maastricht Debates.* Boulder: Lynne Rienner.

Calleo, David P., and Claudia Morgenstern, eds. 1990. *Recasting Europe's Economies: National Strategies in the 1980s.* University Press of America.

Cameron, David. 1992. "The 1992 Initiative: Causes and Consequences." In *Europolitics: Institutions and Policymaking in the "New" European Community,* edited by Alberta B. Sbragia, 23–74. Brookings.

Caporaso, James A. 1996. "The European Union and Forms of State: Westphalian, Regulatory or Post-Modern?" *Journal of Common Market Studies* 34 (1): 29–52.

Caporaso, James A., and John T. S. Keeler. 1993. "The European Union and Regional Integration Theory." Paper presented at the third biennial International Conference of the European Community Studies Association. Washington, D.C., May 27–29.

Cleveland, Harold van Buren. 1990. "Europe in the Economic Crisis of Our Time." In *Recasting Europe's Economies: National Strategies in the 1980s,* edited by David P. Calleo and Claudia Morgenstern, 157–99. University Press of America.

Club de Florence. 1996. *Europe: L'Impossible Status Quo.* Paris: Stock.

Cobham, David, ed. 1994. *European Monetary Upheavals.* Manchester University Press.

Coffey, Peter, and John R. Presley. 1971. *European Monetary Integration.* London: Macmillan.

Cohen, Benjamin. 1994. "Beyond EMU: The Problem of Sustainability." In *The Political Economy of European Monetary Unification,* edited by Barry Eichengreen and Jeffrey Frieden, 149–65. Boulder: Westview.

Commission of the European Communities. 1985. *Completing the Internal Market. White Paper from the Commission to the European Council.* Luxembourg: Office for Official Publications of the European Communities.

———. 1993. *Growth, Competitiveness, Employment: The Challenges and Ways Forward into the 21st Century.* Luxembourg: Office for Official Publications of the European Communities.

Conseil Européen. 1980. "Déclaration du 17e Conseil Européen sur le dialogue euro-arabe, et la situation au Proche-Orient." Venice, June 12–13.

Dalton, Russell J., and Richard C. Eichenberg. 1996. "Economic Perceptions and Citizen Support for European Integration." Manuscript.

Damrosch, Lori Fisler. 1993. *Enforcing Restraint: Collective Intervention in International Conflicts.* New York: Council on Foreign Relations.

Danthine, Jean-Pierre, and Jennifer Hunt. 1994. "Wage Bargaining Structure, Employment and Economic Integration." *Economic Journal* 104: (May): 528–41.

De la Dehesa, Guillermo, and others, eds. 1993. *The Monetary Future of Europe*. London: CEPR.

Délégation de l'Assemblée Nationale pour les Communautés Européennes (Pierre Lellouche, rapporteur). 1994. *L'Europe et sa sécurité: bilan et avenir de la politique étrangère et de sécurité commune de l'Union Européenne* (Paris: Assemblée Nationale, May 31.

Destler, I. M. 1991. "U.S. Trade Policy-Making in the Eighties." In *Politics and Economics in the Eighties*, edited by Alberto Alesina and Geoffrey Carliner, 251–84. University of Chicago Press.

DeSwaan, Abram. 1992. "Perspectives for Transnational Social Policy." *Government and Opposition*, 27 (Winter): 33–52.

———. 1994. "Perspectives for Transnational Social Policy in Europe: Social Transfers from West to East." In *Social Policy beyond Borders. The Social Question in International Perspective*, edited by Abram DeSwaan, 101–15. Amsterdam University Press.

Diebold, William Jr. 1959. *The Schuman Plan: A Study in Economic Cooperation, 1950–1959*. New York: Frederick A. Praeger for the Council on Foreign Relations.

Dittus, Peter, and Palle S. Anderson. 1995. "Sectoral and Employment Effects of the Opening Up of Eastern Europe." In *Western Europe in Transition*, edited by Patrick de Fontenay and others, 57–90. Rome: Banca d'Italia.

Dixit, Avinash K., and Barry J. Nalebuff. 1991. *Thinking Strategically*. W.W. Norton.

Doyle, Michael. 1996. "Liberalism and World Politics." *American Political Science Review* 80 (December): 1151–69.

Driffill, John, and Frederick van der Ploeg. 1995. "Trade Liberalization with Imperfect Competition in Goods and Labour Markets." *Scandinavian Journal of Economics* 97 (2): 223–43.

Due, Ole. 1992. "Article 5 du Traité CEE: Une disposition de caractère fédéral?" In *Collected Courses of the Academy of European Law*, vol. II book 1, 23–35. Dordrecht: Martinus Nijhoff.

Dyson, Kenneth. 1994. *Elusive Union: The Process of Economic and Monetary Union in Europe*. London: Longmans.

Dyson, Kenneth, and Kevin Featherstone. 1996. "Italy and EMU as a 'Vincolo Esterno': Empowering the Technocrats, Transforming the State." *South European Society and Politics* 1 (Autumn): 272–99.

Eichenberg, Richard C., and Russell J. Dalton. 1993. "Europeans and the European Community: The Dynamics of Public Support for European Integration." *International Organization* 47 (Autumn): 507–34.

Eichener, Volker. 1993. "Social Dumping or Innovative Regulation? Processes and Outcomes of European Decision Making in the Sector of

190   References

Health and Safety at Work Harmonization." Working Papers in Political and Social Sciences, SPS 92/28. Florence: European University Institute.

Eichengreen, Barry. 1992. "Should the Maastricht Treaty Be Saved?" *Princeton Studies in International Finance* 72: 32–37.

Eichengreen, Barry, and Jeffry Frieden, eds. 1994. *The Political Economy of European Monetary Unification*. Boulder: Westview.

Eichenhofer, Eberhard. 1992. "Die Rolle des Europaischen Gerichtshofes bei der Eintwicklung des Europaischen Sozialrechts." *Die Sozialgerichtsbarkeit* 39 (12): 573–80.

Emerson, Michael, and others. 1992. *One Market, One Money: An Evaluation of the Potential Benefits and Costs of Forming an Economic and Monetary Union*. Oxford University Press.

Esping-Andersen, Gosta. 1990. *The Three Worlds of Welfare Capitalism*. Princeton University Press.

———. 1996. *Welfare States in Transition: National Adaptations in Global Economies*. London: Sage.

European Commission. 1994. *European Economy*. Supplement A. July.

———. 1995. *Intergovernmental Conference 1996: Commission Report for the Reflection Group*. Brussels, May.

———. 1997. "List of Joint Actions Adopted by the Council since the Entry into Force of the Treaty on European Union (November 1993–September 1996)," and "List of Common Positions Adopted by the Council Since the Entry into Force of the Treaty on European Union (November 1993–September 1996)." *European Dialogue*. Brussels.

European Communities-Commission. 1993. *Growth, Competitiveness, Employment—The Challenges and Ways Forward into the 21st Century—White Paper*. Luxembourg: Office for Official Publications of the European Communities.

European Policy Centre. 1997. "The Treaty of Amsterdam." *Challenge Europe*. July 1.

Eurostat. 1996. *Social Portrait of Europe*. Luxembourg: Office for Official Publications of the European Communities.

Falkner, Gerda. 1993. "Die Sozialpolitik im Maastrichter Vertragsgebäude der Europäischen Gemeinschaft." *SWS-Rundschau* 33 (1): 23–43.

Feldstein, Martin. 1997. "EMU and International Conflict." *Foreign Affairs* 76 (November-December): 60–74.

Ferrera, Maurizio. Forthcoming. "The Uncertain Future of the Italian Welfare State." In *Southern European Politics and Society*.

Flora, Peter. 1989. "From Industrial to Postindustrial Welfare State?" *Annals of the Institute of Social Science*, special issue. University of Tokyo, Institute of Social Science.

Flora, Peter, and Arnold Heidenheimer. 1981. *The Development of Welfare States in Europe and North America*. Transaction Books.

Franklin, Mark, and others. 1996. *Choosing Europe*. University of Michigan Press.

Gatsios, Christos, and Paul Seabright. 1989. "Regulation in the European Community." *Oxford Review of Economic Policy* 5 (2): 37–60.

Ginsberg, Roy H. 1989. *Foreign Policy Actions of the European Community: The Politics of Scale*. Boulder: Lynne Rienner.

Giovannini, Alberto. 1993. "Economic and Monetary Union: What Happened? Exploring the Political Dimension of Optimum Currency Areas." In *The Monetary Future of Europe*, edited by Guillermo de la Dehesa and others. London: CEPR.

———. 1995. "A Report on the Politics of EMU in Italy." Columbia University.

Gnesotto, Nicole. 1996. "La défense européenne au carrefour de la Bosnie et de la CIG." *Politique étrangère* 61 (Spring): 113–24.

Golub, Jonathan. 1995. "State Power and Institutional Influence in European Integration: Lessons from the Packaging Waste Directive." Manuscript.

Gordon, Philip H. 1997. "The Western European Union and NATO's Europeanisation." In *NATO's Transformation: The Changing Shape of the Atlantic Alliance*, edited by Philip H. Gordon, 257–70. Lanham, Md.: Rowman and Littlefield.

Grant, Charles. 1996. *Strength in Numbers: Europe's Foreign and Defence Policy*. London: Centre for European Reform.

Gros, Daniel. 1996. *Toward Economic and Monetary Union: Problems and Prospects*. Brussels: Center for European Policy Studies.

Gros, Daniel, and Andrzej Gonciarz. n.d. "A Note on the Trade Potential of Central and Eastern Europe." Brussels: Centre for European Policy Studies.

Gros, Daniel, and Erik Jones. 1994. "Regional Stabilizers in the United States: Measurement Error and the Role of National Fiscal Policy." Working Document 83. Brussels: Center for European Policy Studies (January).

Gros, Daniel, and Erik Jones. 1996. "L'Europe dans une Economie globale: competition et adjustment." In "Union economique et monetaire et negotiations collectives," 43–52. Working Paper 14. Brussels: Observatoire social europeen (June).

Gros, Daniel, and Niels Thygesen. 1992. *European Monetary Integration: From the European Monetary System to European Monetary Union*. London: Longmans.

Haas, Ernst B. 1958. *The Uniting of Europe: Political, Social, and Economic Forces*. Stanford University Press.

Hagen, Kare. 1992. "The Social Dimension: A Quest for a European Welfare State." In *Social Policy in a Changing Europe*, edited by Zsuzsa Ferge and Jon Eivind Kolberg, 281–303. Boulder: Westview.

Haggard, Stephan, and Andrew Moravcsik. 1993. "The Political Economy of Financial Assistance to Eastern Europe, 1989–1991." In *After the Cold War: International Institutions and State Strategies in Europe, 1989–1991*, edited by Robert O. Keohane, Joseph S. Nye, and Stanley Hoffmann, 246–85. Harvard University Press.

Hall, Peter. 1986. *Governing the Economy: The Politics of State Intervention in Britain and France.* Cambridge: Polity.

———. 1994. "Central Bank Independence and Coordinated Wage Bargaining: Their Interaction in Germany and Europe." CES Working Paper Series 48. Cambridge.

Hefeker, Carsten. 1997. "Together or Separately: Is Wage Coordination Necessary in a Monetary Union?" *CEPS Review* 2 (Winter): 22–28.

Hibbs, Douglas A., and Henrik Jess Madsen. 1981. "Public Reactions to the Growth of Taxation and Government Expenditure." *World Politics:* 413–45.

Hill, Christopher. 1990. "European Foreign Policy: Power Bloc, Civilian Model, or Flop?" In *The Evolution of an International Actor: Western Europe's New Assertiveness,* edited by Reinhardt Rummel, 31–55. Boulder: Westview.

Hollis, Rosemary. 1997. "Europe and the Middle East: Power by Stealth?" *International Affairs* 73 (1): 15–29.

House of Lords, Select Committee on the European Communities. 1992. *Implementation and Enforcement of Environmental Legislation.* London: HMSO.

Hufbauer, Gary C., ed. 1990. *Europe 1992—An American Perspective.* Brookings.

Institut Français des Relations Internationales. 1996. "Quelle identité politique extérieure?" *Ramsès.* Paris: Dunod.

International Institute for Strategic Studies. 1996. "Europe and the Middle East Peace Process." *Strategic Comments* 2, no. 10 (December).

Italianer, Alexander. 1993. "Mastering Maastricht: EMU Issues and How They Were Settled." In *Economic and Monetary Union: Implications for National Policymakers,* edited by K. Gretschmann, 51–113. Maastricht: European Institute for Public Administration.

Italianer, Alexander, and Jean Pisani-Ferry. 1992. "Regional Stabilization Properties of Fiscal Arrangements: What Lessons for the European Communities." Brussels: Centre for European Policy Studies, paper presented for the CEPS conference on Economic and Social Cohesion (June 22–23).

Jacquet, Pierre. 1993. "The Politics of EMU: A Selective Overview." In *The Monetary Future of Europe,* edited by Guillermo de la Dehesa and others. London: CEPR.

Jacquet, Pierre. 1996–97. "European Integration at a Crossroads." *Survival* (Winter): 92.

Jones, Erik. 1994. "The European Monetary Trade-Off: Economic Adjustment in Small Countries." Working Document 85. Brussels: Centre for European Policy Studies (April).

Jones, Erik. 1998. "The Netherlands: Top of the Class." In *Joining Europe's Monetary Club: The Challenges for Smaller Countries*, edited by Erik Jones, Jeffrey Frieden, and Francisco Torres, 149–70. New York: St. Martin's.

Jones, Erik, Jeffry Freiden, and Francisco Torres, eds. (1998). *Joining Europe's Monetary Club: The Challenges for Smaller Countries*. New York: St. Martin's.

Jopp, Mathais. 1994. *The Strategic Implications of European Integration*. Adelphi Paper 290. London: IISS.

Kahneman, Daniel, and Amos Tversky. 1979. "Prospect Theory: An Analysis of Decision under Risk." *Econometrica* 47 (March): 263–91.

———. 1984. "Choices, Values, and Frames." *American Psychologist* 39 (April): 453–58.

Kaufer, Erich. 1990. "The Regulation of New Product Development in the Drug Industry." In *Deregulation or Re-regulation?* edited by Giandomenico Majone, 153–75. London: Pinter.

Kenen, Peter. 1969. "The Theory of Optimum Currency Areas: An Eclectic View." In *Monetary Problems of the International Economy*, edited by Robert A. Mundell and Alexander K. Swoboda, 41–60. University of Chicago Press.

Keohane, Robert O., and Stanley Hoffmann, eds. 1991. *The New European Community: Decisionmaking and Institutional Change*. Boulder: Westview.

Keohane, Robert O., Joseph S. Nye, and Stanley Hoffmann, eds. 1993. *After the Cold War: International Institutions and State Strategies in Europe, 1989–1991*. Harvard University Press.

Kernell, Samuel. 1977. "Presidential Popularity and Negative Voting: An Alternative Explanation of the Midterm Congressional Decline of the President's Party." *American Political Science Review* 71 (March): 44–66.

Kindleberger, Charles. 1970. *Power and Money*. New York: Basic Books.

Kirshner, Jonathan. 1995. *Currency and Coercion: The Political Economy of International Monetary Power*. Princeton University Press.

Klein, Rudolf, and others. 1996. "Globalization and the Welfare State." Unpublished manuscript.

Kosonen, Pekka. 1994. "The Impact of Economic Integration on National Welfare States in Europe." Paper presented at the Thirteenth World Congress of Sociology, Bielefeld, July.

Kramer, Heinz. 1993. "The EC's Response to the 'New Eastern Europe.'" *Journal of Common Market Studies* 31 (June): 222.

Lamers, Karl. 1996. "Facing the IGC in 1996." *Studia Diplomatica* 49 (1): 81–90.

Lange, Peter. 1992. "The Politics of the Social Dimension." In *Europolitics: Institutions and Policymaking in the "New" European Community*, edited by Alberta M. Sbragia, 225–56. Brookings.

———. 1993. "Maastricht and the Social Protocol: Why Did They Do It?" *Politics and Society* 21 (March): 5–36.

Lau, Richard R. 1985. "Two Explanations for Negativity Effects in Political Behavior." *American Journal of Political Science* 29 (February): 119–38.

Laudati, Laraine. 1996. "The European Commission as Regulator: The Uncertain Pursuit of the Competitive Market." In *Regulating Europe*, edited by Giandomenico Majone, 229–61. London: Routledge.

Layard, Richard, Stephen Nickell, and Richard Jackman. 1991. *Unemployment: Macroeconomic Performance, and the Labor Market*. Oxford University Press.

Leibfried, Stephan, and Paul Pierson, eds. 1995. *European Social Policy*. Brookings.

Ludlow, Peter. 1982. *The Making of the European Monetary System: A Case Study in the Politics of the European Community*. London: Butterworth Scientific.

McCarthy, Patrick. 1990. "France Faces Reality: Rigueur and the Germans." In *Recasting Europe's Economies: National Strategies in the 1980s*, edited by David P. Calleo and Claudia Morgenstern, 25–78.

McCarthy, Patrick. 1996. "Between European and Exclusion: The French Presidential Elections of 1995." Occasional Paper: European Studies Seminar Series, no. 1. Bologna: Johns Hopkins Bologna Center (January).

MacDougall, Donald. 1977. "The Role of Public Finance in the European Communities." Brussels: Commission of the European Communities.

McLennan, William. 1995. "Working Together as Partners in European Statistics." In *European Statistics in Perspective*, edited by P. Crescenzi, 24–48. Rome: ISTAT.

McNamara, Kathleen R. 1997. *The Currency of Ideas: Monetary Politics in the European Union*. Cornell University Press.

———. 1998. *The Currency of Ideas: Monetary Politics in the European Union*. Cornell University Press.

McNamara, Kathleen, and Erik Jones. 1996. "The Clash of Institutions: Germany in European Monetary Affairs." *German Politics and Society* 14 (3): 5–30.

Magnifico, Giovanni. 1973. *European Monetary Unification*. London: Macmillan.

Majone, Giandomenico. 1993. "The European Community: An Independent Fourth Branch of Government?" Lecture given on the occasion of the 10th Anniversary of the Zentrum für Europäische Rechtspolitik, University of Bremen. April.

———. 1994. "The Rise of the Regulatory State in Europe." *West European Politics* 17 (3): 77–101.

———. 1996. *Regulating Europe*. London: Routledge.

Marjolin, Robert. 1975. *Report of the Study Group, Economic and Monetary Union 1980*. Brussels, Commission of the European Community (March).

Marschall, Christin. 1994. "The European Community and the Arab World, 1972–1991: From Economics to Politics." *Harvard Middle Eastern and Islamic Review* 1 (2): 56–80.

Mazey, Sonia, and Jeremy Richardson. 1993. "Introduction: Transference of Power, Decision Rules, and Rules of the Game." In *Lobbying in the Euro-*

pean Community, edited by Sonia Mazey and Jeremy Richardson. Oxford University Press.

Meunier-Aitsahalia, Sophie, and George Ross. 1993. "Democratic Deficit or Democratic Surplus." *French Politics and Society* 11 (Winter): 57–69.

Michelmann, Hans J., and Panayotis Soldatos, eds. 1994. *European Integration: Theories and Approaches.* University Press of America.

Milgrom, Paul, and John Roberts. 1992. *Economics, Organization, and Management.* Prentice Hall.

Milner, Helen V. 1988. *Resisting Protectionism: Global Industry and the Politics of International Trade.* Princeton University Press.

Milward, Alan S. 1992. *The European Rescue of the Nation-State.* University of California Press.

Moe, Terry. 1987. "Interests, Institutions, and Positive Theory: The Politics of the NLRB." *Studies in Political Development* 2: 236–99.

Moravcsik, Andrew. 1991. "Negotiating the Single European Act: National Interests and Conventional Statecraft in the European Community." *International Organization* 45 (Winter): 19–56.

———. 1993. "Preferences and Power in the European Community: A Liberal Intergovernmentalist Approach." *Journal of Common Market Studies* 31 (4): 473–524.

———. 1994. "Why the European Community Strengthens the State: International Cooperation and Domestic Politics." Center for European Studies Working Paper Series 52. Harvard University.

———. 1995. "Explaining International Human Rights Regimes: Liberal Theory and Western Europe." *European Journal of International Relations* 1 (Summer): 157–89.

———. 1996. "Federalism and Peace: A Structured Liberal Perspective." *Zeitschrift für internationale Beziehungen* 2 (Spring).

———. 1998. *The Choice for Europe: Social Purpose and State Power from Messina to Maastricht.* Cornell University Press.

Morgan, Roger. 1993. "France and Germany as Partners in the European Community." In *France-Germany, 1983–1993: The Struggle to Cooperate,* edited by Patrick McCarthy, 93–112. New York: St. Martin's.

Mosley, Hugh G. 1990. "The Social Dimension of European Integration." *International Labour Review* 129 (2): 147–64.

Nicolaïdis, Kalypso. 1993. *Mutual Recognition among Nations: The European Community and Trade in Services.* Ph.D. dissertation, Harvard University, Political Economy and Government Program.

Nicoll, William. 1984. "The Luxembourg Compromise." *Journal of Common Market Studies* 23 (September): 35–43.

———. 1993. "Maastricht Revisited: A Critical Analysis of the Treaty on European Union." In *The State of the European Community,* edited by A.W. Cafruny and G. G. Rosenthal, vol. 2, 19–34. London: Longman.

Noll, Roger G. 1990. "Regulatory Policy in a Federalist System." Paper presented at the Conference on Regulatory Federalism. Florence: European University Institute.

North, Douglass C. 1990. *Institutions, Institutional Change, and Economic Performance.* Cambridge University Press.

Nugent, Neill. 1991. *The Government and Politics of the European Community.* Duke University Press.

Nutall, Simon J. 1992. *European Political Co-operation.* Oxford: Clarendon Press.

O'Hanlon, Michael. 1997. "Transforming NATO: The Role of European Forces." *Survival* (Autumn): 5–15.

Olson, Mancur. 1965. *The Logic of Collective Action: Public Goods and the Theory of Groups.* Harvard University Press.

O'Neal, Frances, and others. 1996. "The Liberal Peace: Interdependence, Democracy and International Conflict, 1950–1985." *Journal of Peace Research* 33 (February): 11–28.

Organization for Economic Cooperation and Development (1994). *The OECD Jobs Study: Evidence and Explanations.* Paris: OECD.

———. 1995. "Effects of Aging Populations on Government Budgets." *OECD Economic Outlook* 57 (June): 33–42.

Ostner, Ilona, and Jane Lewis. 1995. "Gender and the Evolution of European Social Policies." In *European Social Policy,* edited by Stephan Leibfried and Paul Pierson, 159–93. Brookings.

Oye, Kenneth A. 1992. *Economic Discrimination and Political Exchange: World Political Economy in the 1930s and the 1980s.* Princeton University Press.

Pelkmans, Jacques. 1984. *Market Integration in the European Community.* London: Nijhoff.

Petersen, Jørn Henrik. 1991. "Harmonization of Social Security in the EC Revisited." *Journal of Common Market Studies* 29 (5): 505–26.

Petersen, Jørn Henrik. 1993. "Europäischer Binnenmarkt, Wirtschafts- und Wahrungsunion und die Harmonisierung der Soziapolitik." *Deutsche Rentenversicherung* January/February: 15–49.

Peterson, Paul E., and Mark G. Rom. 1990. *Welfare Magnets: A New Case for a National Standard.* Brookings.

Pierson, Paul. 1994. *Dismantling the Welfare State? Reagan, Thatcher and the Politics of Retrenchment.* Cambridge University Press.

———. 1996a. "The New Politics of the Welfare State." *World Politics* 48 (2): 143–79.

———. 1996b. "The Path to European Integration: A Historical Institutionalist Analysis." *Comparative Political Studies,* April.

———. 1997. "The Politics of Pension Reform." In *Reform of Retirement Income Policy: International and Canadian Perspectives,* edited by Keith G. Banting and Robin Boadway, 273–93. Queen's University, School of Policy Studies.

Pisani-Ferry, Jean. 1996. "Variable Geometry in Europe." Paris.

Polanyi, Karl. 1944. *The Great Transformation.* New York: Rinehart.

Reder, Melvin, and Lloyd Ulman. 1993. "Unionism and Unification." In *Labor and an Integrated Europe,* edited by Lloyd Ulman, Barry Eichengreen, and William T. Dickens, 13–44. Brookings.

Regini, Marino, and Ida Regalia. Forthcoming. "Employers, Unions and the State: The Resurgence of Concertation in Italy?" In *Southern European Politics and Society*.

Rein, Martin, and Lee Rainwater, eds. 1986. *Public-Private Interplay in Social Protection: A Comparative Study*. Armonk, N.Y.: M.E. Sharpe.

Rhein, Eberhard. 1996. "Besser als ihr Ruf: die EU Aussenpolitik." *Internationale Politik* (Summer): 55.

Rhodes, Martin. 1995. "A Regulatory Conundrum: Industrial Relations and the Social Dimension." In *European Social Policy*, edited by Stephan Leibfried and Paul Pierson, 78–122.

Richez-Battesti, Nadine. 1996. "Union Economique et monetaire et Etat-providence: la subsidiarite en question." *Revue Etudes internationales* 27 (March): 109–28.

Robertson, David Brian. 1989. "The Bias of American Federalism: The Limits of Welfare State Development in the Progressive Era." *Journal of Policy History* 1 (3): 261–91.

Ross, George. 1995. *Jacques Delors and European Integration*. Oxford: Polity Press.

Ryba, Barbara-Christine. 1995. "La politique étrangère et de sécurité commune: Mode d'emploi et bilan d'une année d'application." *Revue du marché commun de l'Union européenne* 384 (January): 15–35.

Sala-I-Martin, Xavier, and Jeffrey Sachs. 1992. "Fiscal Federalism and Optimum Currency Areas: Evidence from the United States." London: Centre for Economic Policy Research, Discussion Paper 632 (March).

Sandholtz, Wayne. 1992. *High-Tech Europe: The Politics of International Cooperation*. University of California Press.

———. 1993. "Choosing Union: Monetary Politics and Maastricht." *International Organization* 47 (Winter): 1–40.

Sandholtz, Wayne, and John Zysman. 1989. "Recasting the European Bargain." *World Politics* 42 (April): 95–128.

Sauter, Wolf. 1995. *The Relationships between Industrial and Competition Policy under the Economic Constitution of the European Union*. Ph.D. dissertation, European University Institute, Law Department.

Sbragia, Alberta, ed. 1992. *Europolitics: Institutions and Policymaking in the "New" European Community*. Brookings.

Scharpf, Fritz W. 1994a. "Community Policy and Autonomy: Multilevel Policy-Making in the European Union." EUI Working Paper 94/1, Fiesole.

———. 1994b. "Mehrebenenpolitik im vollendeten Binnenmarkt." MPIFG Discussion Paper 94/4. Köln: Max-Planck-Institut für Gesellschaftsforschung.

Scherer, Frederic M. 1994. *Competition Policies for an Integrated World Economy*. Brookings.

Sheridan, Jerome. 1995. "The Deja-Vu of EMU: Considerations for Europe from Nineteenth Century America." Manuscript.

Silber, Laura, and Alan Little. 1995. *The Death of Yugoslavia.* London: Penguin Books.

Slaughter, Anne-Marie. 1997. "The Real New World Order." *Foreign Affairs* September–October: 183–97.

Soskice, David. 1991. "The Institutional Infrastructure for International Competitiveness: A Comparative Analysis of the UK and Germany." In *The Economics of the New Europe,* edited by Anthony B. Atkinson and Renato Brunetta, 45–66. Macmillan.

Spruyt, Hendrik. 1994. *The Sovereign State and Its Competitors: An Analysis of Systems Change.* Princeton University Press.

Stein, Kenneth. 1996. "Transatlantische Partnerschaft im Nahen Osten?" *Internationale Politik* (9): 33–39.

Steinberg, James B. 1993. *"An Ever Closer Union": European Integration and Its Implications for the Future of U.S.–European Relations.* Santa Monica, Calif.: RAND.

Steinberg, James B. 1993. "International Involvement in the Yugoslavia Conflict." In *Enforcing Restraint: Collective Intervention in International Conflicts,* edited by Lori Fisler Damrosch, 1–26. New York: Council on Foreign Relations.

Streeck, Wolfgang. 1989. "The Social Dimension of the European Economy." Paper prepared for the meeting of the Andrew Shonfield Association. Florence: EUI.

———. 1995. "From Market Making to State Building? Reflections on the Political Economy of European State Building." In *European Social Policy: Between Fragmentation and Integration,* edited by Stephan Leibfried and Paul Pierson, 389–431.

Streeck, Wolfgang, and Philippe Schmitter. 1991. "From National Corporatism to Transnational Pluralism: Organized Interests in the Single European Market." In *Social Institutions and Economic Performance: Studies of Industrial Relations in Advanced Capitalist Economies,* edited by Wolfgang Streeck, 197–231. London: Sage.

Tavlas, George S. 1993. "The New Theory of Optimum Currency Areas." *The World Economy* 16 (November): 663–85.

Thatcher, Margaret. 1995. *The Path to Power.* London: HarperCollins.

Torres, Francisco, ed. 1996. *Monetary Reform in Europe: An Analysis of the Issues and Proposals for the Intergovernmental Conference.* Lisbon: Universidade Catolica Editora.

Tsebelis, George. 1994. "The Power of the European Parliament as a Conditional Agenda-Setter." *American Political Science Review* 88: 128–42.

Tsoukalis, Loukas. 1977. *The Politics and Economics of European Monetary Integration.* London: Allen and Unwin.

———. 1993. *The New European Economy,* 2d ed. Oxford University Press.

———. 1996. "Economic and Monetary Union." In *Policy Making in the European Union*, edited by Helen Wallace and William Wallace, 279–300. Oxford University Press, 3d ed.

Tyrie, Andrew. 1991. "A Political Economy of Economic and Monetary Integration." In *Rivista di Politca Economica* 81 (May), edited by Mario Baldassarri, pp. 411–42.

Vaubel, Roland. 1994. "The Political Economy of Centralization and the European Community." *Public Choice* 81: 151–90.

Visser, Wessel, and Rein Wijnhoven. 1990. "Politics Do Matter, but Does Unemployment?" *European Journal of Political Research* 18: 71–96.

Vogel, David. 1995. *Trading Up*. Harvard University Press.

von Hagen, Jurgen. 1991. "Fiscal Arrangements in a Monetary Union: Evidence from the U.S." *Discussion Paper 58*. Bloomington, Indiana: Indiana Center for Global Business (March).

Weaver, R. Kent. 1986. "The Politics of Blame Avoidance." *Journal of Public Policy* 6 (October-December): 371–98.

Weiler, Joseph J. H. 1995a. "European Democracy and Its Critique." *West European Politics* 18 (July): 4–39.

———. 1995b. "The State 'über alles': Demos, Telos, and the German Maastricht Decision." In *Festschrift für Ulricht Everling*, edited by Ole Due, Marcus Lutter, and Jürgen Schwarze. Baden-Baden: Nomos.

———. 1996. "Legitimacy and Democracy of Union Governance: The 1996 Intergovernmental Agenda and Beyond." ARENA Working Paper 22. Oslo, November.

Wessels, Wolfgang. 1995. "How to Mix Transformation and Integration: Strategies, Options, Scenarios." In *Monitoring Association and Beyond: The European Union and the Visegrád States*, edited by Barbara Lippert and Heinrich Schneider, 401–03. Bonn: Europa Union Verlag.

———. 1996. "Verwaltung im europäischen Mehrebenensystem." In *Europäische Integration*, edited by Markus Jachtenfuchs and Beate Kohler-Koch, 165–92. Opladen: Leske+Budrich.

Wilensky, Harold J. 1976. *The "New Corporatism": Centralization and the Welfare State*. London: Sage.

Willis, F. Roy. 1965. *France, Germany, and the New Europe: 1945–1963*. Stanford University Press.

Wilson, James Q. 1973. *Political Organizations*. Basic Books.

Wooley, John. 1992. "Policy Credibility and European Monetary Institutions." In *Europolitics: Institutions and Policymaking in the "New" European Community*, edited by Alberta Sbragia, 157–90. Brookings.

Zaldivar, Carlos, and Andrés Ortega. 1992. "The Gulf Crisis and European Cooperation on Security Issues: Spanish Reactions and the European Framework." In *Western Europe and the Gulf*, edited by Nicole Gnesotto and John Roper, 127–40. Paris: Institute for Security Studies of Western European Union.

Zelikow, Philip. 1996. "The Masque of Institutions." *Survival* 38 (Spring): 9–10.

Zuleeg, Manfred. 1989. "Die Zahlung von Ausgleichszulagen über die binnengrenzen der Europäischen Gemeinschaft." *Deutsche Rentenversicherung* 10: 621–29.

About the Authors

Philip H. Gordon
Carol Deane Senior Fellow for U.S. Strategic Studies, International Institute for Strategic Studies, London, and Affiliate Professor of Economic and Political Science, INSEAD, Fountainebleau

Erik Jones
Lecturer, Department of Politics, University of Nottingham

Giandomenico Majone
Professor of Social Science, European University Institute, Florence

Andrew Moravcsik
Associate Professor of Government, Harvard University

Paul Pierson
Associate Professor of Government, Harvard University